AF148086

Progress in IS

Progress in IS encompasses the various areas of Information Systems in theory and practice, presenting cutting-edge advances in the field. It is aimed especially at researchers, doctoral students, and advanced practitioners. The series features both research monographs, edited volumes, and conference proceedings that make substantial contributions to our state of knowledge and handbooks and other edited volumes, in which a team of experts is organized by one or more leading authorities to write individual chapters on various aspects of the topic. Individual volumes in this series are supported by a minimum of two external reviews.

The Series is SCOPUS-indexed.

Robert Winter

Editor

Designing the Information Systems Artefact

Typology, Architecture, Abstraction, Collaborative Evolution and Design Patterns

 Springer

Editor
Robert Winter
Institute of Information Systems and Digital Business
University of St. Gallen
St.Gallen, Switzerland

ISSN 2196-8705   ISSN 2196-8713   (electronic)
Progress in IS
ISBN 978-3-031-98310-8   ISBN 978-3-031-98311-5   (eBook)
https://doi.org/10.1007/978-3-031-98311-5

© The Editor(s) (if applicable) and The Author(s), under exclusive license to Springer Nature
Switzerland AG 2025

This work is subject to copyright. All rights are solely and exclusively licensed by the Publisher, whether
the whole or part of the material is concerned, specifically the rights of translation, reprinting, reuse of
illustrations, recitation, broadcasting, reproduction on microfilms or in any other physical way, and
transmission or information storage and retrieval, electronic adaptation, computer software, or by similar
or dissimilar methodology now known or hereafter developed.
The use of general descriptive names, registered names, trademarks, service marks, etc. in this publication
does not imply, even in the absence of a specific statement, that such names are exempt from the relevant
protective laws and regulations and therefore free for general use.
The publisher, the authors and the editors are safe to assume that the advice and information in this book
are believed to be true and accurate at the date of publication. Neither the publisher nor the authors or the
editors give a warranty, expressed or implied, with respect to the material contained herein or for any
errors or omissions that may have been made. The publisher remains neutral with regard to jurisdictional
claims in published maps and institutional affiliations.

This Springer imprint is published by the registered company Springer Nature Switzerland AG
The registered company address is: Gewerbestrasse 11, 6330 Cham, Switzerland

If disposing of this product, please recycle the paper.

Preface

The artefact is at the core of Design Science Research for Information Systems (DSR). Early DSR was focused on developing IT-oriented artefacts (usually information systems) to address relevant design problems in organizations and administrations. Along with the growing adoption and maturity of DSR, artefacts became not only more complex, but also their character evolved by incorporating more and more business and adoption aspects, up to the level where artefacts are mainly of an organizational nature. Much of the extant methodological guidance for DSR, however, is still characterized by differentiating only a few very abstract artefact types (e.g., constructs, models, methods and instances), not referring to a common architectural foundation for what constitutes design knowledge contribution from a DSR project, not providing alignment concepts for the different aspirations and capabilities of researchers and practitioners in DSR projects, and not supporting systematic reuse of solution patterns for recurrent design problems.

Since the general perception of "research methods" is often reduced to process models and activity (and maybe role) specifications, existing methodological guidance for DSR often (i) focuses on the overall design process (e.g., Peffers et al.'s DSR Model, the Action Design Research approach, or the echelonized DSR approach), (ii) focuses on specific DSR activities (e.g., research design, requirements engineering or evaluation), or (iii) provides "anatomy" models to better understand the internal structure of important DSR outcomes (e.g., design theories or design principles). Although constituting the paramount object of designing, the Information Systems (IS) artefact is often treated only either on an extremely abstract level (by differentiating, e.g., constructs, models, methods and design knowledge) or on an extremely contextualized level (as a solution instance). While generalized DSR processes and activities seem to be more easily instantiated in a research project, the "intermediate levels" between highly abstract artefacts and concrete instances appear to be harder to conceptualize, resulting in less elaborate methodological guidance for design researchers and reflective IS design practitioners. Even if they deal with the DSR artefact, most contributions focus on a specific artefact type, forcing designers to prematurely limit their design options in the absence of type-agnostic guidance.

This book aims at consolidating methodological guidance around the IS artefact to address these challenges by

- proposing a more differentiated, ontologically and empirically justified DSR artefact typology,
- presenting an artefact-agnostic architecture model for DSR project knowledge contributions,
- conceptualizing DSR artefact abstraction in a type-agnostic way and proposing a set of generic, elementary transitions to navigate between abstraction levels,
- using the concept of managed evolution and insights from tension theory to propose a collaboration model for researchers and practitioners in DSR and
- identifying design patterns based on associating empirically grounded classes of functional requirements with generic solution approaches—and vice versa identifying types of functional problems where a certain artefact type could be usefully applied.

All contributions are linked by a contemporary understanding of DSR artefacts as complex compounds of IT, organizational and use components—ranging from algorithms to informal interventions in organizations, being based on descriptive knowledge or empirical justification (or preferably both) and being exemplified by contextualized instantiations that solve situated problems in organizations or administrations.

The book intends to support advanced (graduate) design researchers and reflective IS design practitioners by complementing existing, mostly process-oriented guidance with artefact-centric guidance. Instead of existing, largely intuitive and very abstract artefact typologies, an empirically grounded and validated, much more fine-grained typology is proposed. Instead of separating foundational statements, generic means-end statements and empirical effectivity evidence, a comprehensive architecture model is proposed that allows one to express and validate these three important facets of design knowledge contributions from DSR projects in an integrated form. Instead of conceptualizing only the extremes (design theory vs. contextualized solution) and leaving all other artefacts "somewhere in the middle" between abstract and instance levels, intermediate abstraction levels are discussed—and generalization/specialization operations are proposed—in an artefact type-agnostic form so that researchers and practitioners can better navigate the complex IS artefact universe. Instead of focusing on researchers and their objectives only, a "managed evolution" process model is presented that integrates researcher and practitioner ambitions. Finally, instead of treating every DSR project as a unique search in the problem and solution spaces, recurrent classes of functional requirements are identified and associated with common solution classes, resulting in a set of 30 IS design pattern candidates.

Based on 40 years of design-oriented research, teaching and practice of the editor, contributions from many others were needed to elaborate and justify the proposed analyses and methodological contributions. I am thankful to Alan Hevner not only for our teamwork on Chapter "Collaborative Evolution of the IS Artefact: Negotiating Research/Practice Tensions", but also for many inspirations, conversations and joint projects over the last two decades. Wiel Bruls is a perseverant and inspirational co-author not only of our multi-year DSR outcome classification effort (Chapter "Typology of IS Artefacts: Providing an Organizing Foundation for Design Science Research Outcomes"), but also of artefact-oriented publications in the domain of IT/business alignment. Since I worked closely together with Stephan Aier over two decades in many architecture- and design-related projects, I am happy that we joined forces to establish an "architectural" conceptualization of project design knowledge in DSR (Chapter "The Architecture of Project Design Knowledge in Design Science Research"). Together with Antonia Albani, I explored the fields of enterprise engineering and enterprise ontology a long time ago. I am happy that she was able to support me in conceptualizing abstraction and abstraction levels in DSR (Chapter "Abstraction and Abstraction Levels in Design Science Research"). Last not least, I am thankful to my two last PhD students, Benedict Lösser and Simon Michael Schmid, for planning and driving the analysis of a large number of DSR studies that provide a sound foundation for identifying DSR function-construction pattern candidates (Chapter "Function-Construction Patterns for Designing IS Artefacts")—of course from an artefact-centric perspective.

I also want to acknowledge the discussions and the feedback from more than 200 international PhD students of over 15 "Design Science" courses conducted on behalf of the German Academic Association for Business Research; students of many DSR classes conducted as (compulsory) components of University of St. Gallen's Doctoral Programme in Business Innovation; discussions at nearly every DESRIST conference since 2005; and my co-authors as well as practice collaborators in many design research or design science projects over all these years.

St. Gallen, Switzerland   Robert Winter
April 2025

Contents

Typology of IS Artefacts: Providing an Organizing Foundation for Design Science Research Outcomes

Wiel Bruls and Robert Winter

1 Introduction

As a problem-solving paradigm that complemented the then dominant behavioural research at business schools which focused on the macroscopic aspects of Information Systems (IS)—such as their contribution to productivity or impact on society (Orlikowski & Iacono, 2001), Design Science Research (DSR) in Information Systems gained momentum over the last decades. Rooted in engineering and the 'Sciences of the Artificial' (Simon, 1996), DSR puts the design of socio-technical systems into the centre (Benbasat & Zmud, 2003) and aims at building useful, projectable solutions to organizational problems that involve information technology (Baskerville & Pries-Heje, 2019).

Through the years in which the discipline matured, discussions on scope and type of contents have continued and influenced what are considered as valid outcomes. The initial subject matter scoping of the DSR discipline (March & Smith, 1995; Simon, 1996; Hevner et al., 2004) focused on the Information Technology (IT) component of problems and solutions. Many authors have argued since then for a more extended subject matter scope, including organizational and social components of the IS artefact, or less tangible entities such as strategies and interventions (Lee et al., 2013). The differentiation in type of contents that is an outcome of design (prescriptive knowledge gained from purposeful design actions) versus that of behavioural science (descriptive knowledge gained from interpreting observed behaviour) has been an important yet debated scope restriction (Gregor & Hevner, 2013; Baskerville et al., 2015; Prat et al., 2022). Where initially the focus was primarily on artefact design (Hevner et al., 2004), debates on the lack of the concept of

W. Bruls · R. Winter (✉)
Institute of Information Systems and Digital Business, University of St. Gallen,
St. Gallen, Switzerland
e-mail: Robert.Winter@unisg.ch

© The Author(s), under exclusive license to Springer Nature
Switzerland AG 2025

1

R. Winter (ed.), *Designing the Information Systems Artefact*, Progress in IS,
https://doi.org/10.1007/978-3-031-98311-5_1

theory in DSR and how to introduce this (Fischer & Gregor, 2011; Venable, 2013) have added design theory as an aspired outcome of DSR (Gregor & Hevner, 2013; Baskerville et al., 2018). Various authors have proposed conceptualizations that identify theory constituents, and that emphasize the role of the logic behind a design and the justificatory knowledge that derives from supporting kernel theories, possibly from external domains (Gregor & Jones, 2007; Baskerville & Pries-Heje, 2010; Gregor & Hevner, 2013; Venable, 2013; Gregor et al., 2020). This history of evolutions implies that the scope of the discipline and valid outcomes of design research have been subject to quite some debate, introducing new views that classifications of DSR outcomes need to support.

Existing classifications: A number of different classifications have been proposed over the years, which surface these evolving insights. The first classification from March and Smith (1995) which is still widely used focuses on a very limited number of design constituents such as models and methods. Later classifications broke this down into more detailed components from the design lifecycle such as requirements, principles, architectures, frameworks, and testable propositions (Vaishnavi & Kuechler, 2004; Gregor & Jones, 2007; Venable, 2013). The concept of theory was included containing design logic and justificatory knowledge (Vaishnavi & Kuechler, 2004; Gregor & Jones, 2007; Vaishnavi et al., 2019). A more extended classification of descriptive behavioural knowledge was proposed, including items such as measurements, classifications, catalogues, and patterns (Gregor & Hevner, 2013). Empirical-derived classifications have been proposed with additional constituents, including more primitive items such as guidelines, lessons, recommendations (Dwivedi et al., 2014) and aggregated items that stretch across artefact classes such as ontology, taxonomies, and frameworks (Mwilua et al., 2016).

These existing classifications are broad and generic enumerations with often implicit structure. As our analysis will show, they differ across authors, with overlapping yet different constituents, with different decompositions, different levels of granularity and scope, different definitions of key terms that show some drift over time (e.g. the term models initially defined as a set of statements, with later authors referring to these as principles) and only recently addressing standardization across research and practice (Gregor et al., 2020). We identify as root cause of these findings the lack of 'systematics' (Bailey, 1994) that can resolve the often implicit structure of and variations across current classifications: identifying the key differentiating dimensions that create clearly separated artefact types (Nickerson et al., 2013), with clear operational definitions and examples (Bailey, 1994).

Benefits: Being able to provide a consistent classification of DSR outcomes is an important organizing foundation for DSR as a research field with three key benefits. First, it allows design researchers to understand what the scope of their research can be, where it fits in, and how to identify related work. Second, it allows both researchers and practitioners to develop a common knowledge base that systematically provides artefact-related design guidance. Third, it helps to settle ongoing debates on terms and definitions. For example, when discussing how to integrate the concept of theory into DSR, Baiyere et al. (2015) suggest 'to re-articulate our definition of artifacts or use design theory as the way out?' (Baiyere et al., 2015). In discussing similar definitional problems and overload of terms, a call for a well-structured taxonomy comes from Deng and Ji (2018).

Objective: We aim to develop in this study a classification of DSR outcomes that can support the three benefits identified above, which are the operational benefits of a well systematized typology. However, in addition and more importantly, we put a particular focus on establishing the key differentiators that surface the most important innate artefact's design characteristics (e.g. process versus product, and models versus logic), as well as the foundational debates that aspire to disentangle foundational concepts by understanding, for example, how design, knowledge, and theory differentiate. By building on this analysis for identifying the organizing dimensions of the typology, we aim for an approach that not only allows to structure the outcomes, but also creates a crisp view on what is the discipline's core identity.

Taxonomies and typologies: To produce a well-structured DSR outcome typology, we will apply a combination of established taxonomy and typology concepts and development methods that have been carried over from the social sciences to IS research (Bailey, 1994; Nickerson et al., 2013). The role of taxonomies is well recognized in the IS literature. Glass and Vessey (1995) note that taxonomies provide an organizing structure to the IS body of knowledge. That is, taxonomies facilitate the study of relationships among concepts and, therefore, to hypothesize about these relationships. In a similar vein, McKnight et al. (2002) argue that taxonomies allow researchers to postulate on the relationships among IS concepts in that taxonomies *order* these otherwise *disorderly* concepts.

Although definitions differ across authors, typologies in general are more aimed at conceptual clarification, while taxonomies address much more detailed subject matter classifications.[1] As our intention is the first, we refer to the classification[2] of DSR outcomes we develop as a typology. Projecting generic outcome types into a context (Baskerville & Pries-Heje, 2019) such as, for example, the large enterprise domain, creates more detailed context-specific artefacts that can be organized in potentially highly detailed taxonomies. An example is the taxonomy of mobile applications that Nickerson et al. (2013) create to illustrate their method. Our focus in this study will be on the generic DSR outcome typology, therewith primarily addressing the DSR researcher. We will discuss how these can be contextualized and produce more detailed taxonomies that allow to organize more specific design guidance (Deng & Ji, 2018).

---

[1] An example to illustrate the difference is provided in the introduction to Bailey's work (1994) using the classification of nation states as example. A typology is developed by differentiating on two conceptual dimensions: political (with as values "democratic" versus "authoritarian") and economic (with as values "market" versus "controlled"), whereas a taxonomy is developed using 100 observed variables taken from U.N. Statistical Yearbooks, and establishing clusters.

[2] Note that we will use the term classification in a more generic sense without reference to the organizing approach or structure, for example to identify the existing classifications. For the organizing process we will use the terms classifying, or classifying process.

Structure of the chapter: First, we introduce the concepts behind typology and taxonomy development, and explain our research method that is rooted in both the DSR and the typology/taxonomy literature. In the analysis section, we consider existing classifications, identifying both weaknesses in their systematization and potential dimensions for our proposed typology, and reviewing key concepts that have been the topic of considerable debate in DSR. Next in the design section, we explain the iterations we performed to find the most differentiating dimensions, how the design is matured, and how our using it in teaching contributed to detailing and representation. We present the design of our final DSR outcome typology and summarize the rationale for our design choices. In the evaluation section, we evaluate the typology's structure against criteria developed for both artefact (Prat et al., 2015) as well as taxonomy soundness (Nickerson et al., 2013). We summarize the result of the mapping to the new typology of existing classifications, and of samples from recent practitioner conferences. In the discussion part, we discuss the extension to theorizing that our typology supports (from a single class to a family of classes), the process of contextualization that produces context-specific taxonomies, scope issues such as the types of contexts that can be projected to and the extent to which non-IT artefacts can be included, and the options for implementing a classification process. Finally, in the conclusion section, we summarize the critical aspects of our choices made, the elusiveness that one cannot escape when trying to cast scientific outputs into strictly delineated terminology, and we provide an outlook to further work.

Appendices: Supplementary material is provided in four appendices. Appendix 1 contains a glossary with definitions for each characteristic and indicator examples from the large enterprise context. Appendix 2 includes the mapping of existing classifications. Appendix 3 contains feedback on our proposal from our teaching practice. Appendix 4 presents the mapping of empirical samples that we acquired from DESRIST conferences.

2   Typologies and Taxonomies

Typologies and taxonomies serve as sorting schemes to systematically organize objects in a domain of interest, a fundamental problem in many research disciplines. Working in the field of the social and biological sciences, the development processes (i) for typologies that are aimed at conceptual clarification and are conceptually constructed top down, and (ii) taxonomies that are aimed at detailed subject matter classifications and are empirically constructed using grouping approaches on random, systematic, or convenience samples from practice, have been described by Bailey (1994). He proposes an operationalization phase that bridges between conceptual construction and empirical categorization by crisp definitions of types along with empirical examples. In addition, he describes a process for classification of samples into the taxonomy, which is straightforward for typologies of limited complexity—assessing characteristics of a sample and matching these to the characteristics of types in the typology. In case of many dimensions exact matches are difficult, and a reduction process is described which centres on identification of key types (e.g. ideal, constructed, or polar), and assessing the extent that an artefact's characteristics match those of the reduced type.

Working in the field of IS, Nickerson et al. (2013) review the different available definitions and note these are quite interchangeable. They continue to use the term taxonomy (for the classes) and taxonomy system (for the meta-data used for classifying). The method they propose starts with the definition of a meta-characteristic that sets the intent with which the classification will be used, and it ends with an ending condition that establishes when the taxonomy has been developed sufficiently (it is concise, robust, comprehensive, extendible, and explanatory). The method for construction rests on interleaved iterations of both conceptual and empirical approaches as Bailey (1994) defines them, in which both identify dimensions, either conceptually inspired or empirically inspired. This method has been frequently applied in IS research (e.g. Prat et al., 2015; Siering et al., 2017).

Technically, Nickerson et al. (2013) define a taxonomy T as a set of n dimensions, with each dimension consisting of at least two mutually exclusive and collectively exhaustive characteristics such that each object under consideration instantiates one and only one characteristic for each dimension (Nickerson et al., 2013).

3   Research Method

As our research finds itself at the intersection of DSR and the broader literature on taxonomies and typologies, we inherit from research methods from both areas. For the overall process, we lean on Peffers et al. (2007): identify the problem and motivation, define the objectives, analyse the problem space, design and develop our proposed artefact, evaluate and communicate. For the analysis and design steps, we mostly use taxonomy/typology development techniques, while for evaluation we use empirical data, plus criteria for both artefact (Prat et al., 2015) and taxonomy soundness (Nickerson et al., 2013). The process that we applied was strongly iterative—echelon-like[3] (Tuunanen et al., 2024), with initial iterations of designs, then intertwined steps of design and evaluation, and finally intertwined steps of communication and design.

Problem identification, motivation, and objectives are based on a high-level assessment of the structural underpinnings of established classifications from the literature, debate in the literature on definition of DSR's scope and key concepts, the needs for an organizing foundation of DSR research, and benefits expected from a well-structured classification.

---

[3] Echelons are independent organizational units of the research process.

Analysis is performed in two areas using dimensional and definitional analysis—that can produce the dimensions and characteristics values of the taxonomy system as Nickerson et al. (2013) define it. First, definitions of foundational concepts such as design, knowledge, and theory that have been debated in the DSR literature are analysed. Second, both a dimensional and definitional analysis is performed on an existing set of classifications from the literature. These are retrieved using relevant keyword searches[4] and selecting those that add new insights. This resulted in seven papers that propose conceptually constructed classifications and three with empirically constructed ones.

Design follows the conceptual top-down approach with feedback loops. It consisted of a number of preliminary iterations in which both authors contributed initial ideas. Analysis of key concepts and an initial assessment of existing classifications resulted in a considerable conceptual refinement of these initial ideas that produced full new typology parts. After a first mapping of existing classifications, smaller changes were made particular at the leaf node level, and after more detailed harmonizations of these, smaller definitional changes were made. Feedback from our teaching practice during communication clearly surfaced the need for a comprehensive scheme with well-recognizable terminology, which triggered another round of design with smaller changes at the leaf level that produced the final classification.

Communication: The developed classification was used in teaching to three focal groups of Ph.D. students that attended a DSR methodology course in subsequent years. Various combinations of existing classifications and our proposed typology were presented, and the authors requested to answer open questions and provide scores on closed questions.

Evaluation includes both empirical and analytical evaluations. The empirical evaluation step shares with Bailey (1994) and Nickerson et al. (2013) the use of empirical samples that are classified according to the DSR outcome typology. Empirical samples were obtained as convenience samples from DESRIST conferences (2020–2023).

4   Analysis

In this section, we analyse key concepts that underly the genesis and evolution of DSR, as well as assess the structure of existing classifications by performing both a dimensional and definitional analysis. Dimensional analysis identifies the dimensions that underly the selected classifications and reveals their implicit structure. This allows to both assess weaknesses in systematization and identify potential candidates for dimensions for the design of the newly proposed typology. Definitional analysis analyses definitions of detailed constituents of these classifications and

---

[4] Selecting from the Senior Scholars' Basket of Eight, plus ICIS, ECIS, and DESRIST conferences, using as keywords "DSR" OR "DESIGN" "Outcome" OR "Art*fact" "Classif*" OR "Typ*" OR "Pattern*".

clarifies overlap and shifting semantics. This allows both assessing weaknesses in current definitions and developing the rationale for selecting a well-defined set of constituents for the newly proposed typology.

4.1 Assessment of Key Concepts

Artefacts and design: Artefacts in DSR are manmade, purposeful objects that involve IT (March & Smith, 1995; Simon, 1996; Hevner et al., 2004), and require design that lays out their internal construction and their external behaviour (Simon, 1996; Weigand et al., 2021). The external characteristics of artefacts at their interface (the features derived from their material properties) create abilities (the affordances that an actor can put to use) (Gregor et al., 2020). DSR considers artefacts at the generic level: a class of solutions that address a certain set of requirements (Gregor & Hevner, 2013). Such generic designs may be organized again into broader classifications—identified as taxonomies, genera, or families (Pohl et al., 2005; Gregor & Hevner, 2013; Weigand et al., 2021). Designs materialize into artefacts by projecting them into an implementation space (Baskerville & Pries-Heje, 2019). Design constituents may be specified at several levels of decomposition (Gregor & Jones, 2007; Venable, 2013; Weigand et al., 2021).

Knowledge and theory differentiate from design as they are more abstract and cannot be materialized (Gregor & Hevner, 2013). Knowledge is returned by theories that are either prescriptive design oriented that produce Λ-knowledge, or descriptive behavioural oriented that produce Ω-knowledge (Drechsler & Hevner, 2018).[5] Theories for design focus on the logic behind the design and linkages with supporting theories that provide justificatory knowledge and may come from other scientific domains (Walls et al., 1992; Gregor & Hevner, 2013).[6] Descriptive theories from the broader IS may contribute at various abstraction level and return knowledge across single class designs (Gregor & Hevner, 2013), such as analytical and explanatory insights (Gregor, 2006).

4.2 Assessment of Existing Classifications

We split our assessments of existing classifications from related work into two sets. The first set (listed in Table 1) is comprised of classifications that have been developed conceptually top down. The second set (listed in Table 2) is comprised of

---

[5] This terminology is adopted from Mokyr (2002) who analyses the integration of workmanship knowledge and science-based knowledge at the start of the industrial revolution.

[6] For example, the theory of relational calculus that supports the design of relational databases (March & Smith, 1995), statistical theory that supports the field of data science (Gregor & Hevner, 2013), and the theory of interpersonal trust for online interactions (Gregor & Hevner, 2013).

Table 1 Conceptual classifications

Reference and characteristics	Proposed types of artefacts
A. (March & Smith, 1995) First simple enumeration developed when DSR was conceived.	• **Construct:** Conceptual vocabulary • **Models:** Propositions or statements of relationships between constructs • **Methods:** Steps to perform tasks • **Instantiation:** Realization of an artefact
B. (Vaishnavi & Kuechler, 2004; Vaishnavi et al., 2019) Developed for educational purposes.	• **Construct, Methods, Models, and Instantiation:** As in A. (March & Smith, 1995) • **Frameworks, Architectures, and Design Principles:** Conceptual guides, high-level structure and statements, respectively • **Design Theories:** Prescriptive set of statements on how to do something to achieve an objective (may include the other artefacts as well)
C. Identify the components of a design theory covering the full lifecycle	
C.1 (Walls et al., 1992)	• **Meta-requirements, meta-design, method, kernel product/process theories, and testable design product/process hypothesis**
C.2 (Gregor & Jones, 2007)	• **Purpose and scope, constructs, principles of form and function, artefact mutability, testable propositions, justificatory knowledge, principles of implementation, and expository instantiation**
C.3. (Venable, 2013)	• **General requirements** (general goals, functional requirements, constraints, or anti-goals) • **General design** (components, relationships, principles of form/function, and artefact mutability) • **Utility** (efficacy, effectiveness, and efficiency)
D. (Gregor & Hevner, 2013) Intended to differentiate knowledge contributions that DSR papers can make. Provides classifications of descriptive Ω-knowledge and prescriptive Λ-knowledge. Further develops the concept of a design theory, extending that with a maturity model.	**Λ-knowledge:** • **Constructs** (concepts, symbols), **Models** (representation, syntax) • **Methods** (Algorithms, techniques), **Instantiations** (systems, products/processes) • **Design Theories:** An abstract, coherent body of prescriptive knowledge that describes the principles [, ..], methods, and justificatory theory [..] used to develop an artefact or accomplish some end. **Ω-knowledge:** • **Phenomena** : Observations, classification, measurement, and cataloguing • **Sensemaking:** Natural laws, regularities, patterns, principles, and theories
E. (Drechsler & Hevner, 2018) Identifies modes of contributing to a knowledge base. Differentiates Λ-knowledge into materializable, model-based knowledge versus more abstract, statement-based knowledge.	• **Solution Design Entities:** As in A. (March & Smith, 1995). • **Solution Design Knowledge** such as technological rules, requirements, and principles.

Table 2 Empirical classifications

Reference and characteristics	Proposed types of artefacts
F. (Offermann et al., 2010) The first full bottom-up categorization developed by grouping artefact occurrences for DESRIST 2006–2009 papers into discrete types. Based on a total of 33 identified types, 8 abstract types are proposed. No attempt made to systematize.	**System Design:** Description of structure/ behaviour **Methods**: Activities to create/interact with a system. **Guideline:** Suggestion for support. **Requirements**: Statement of need **Language/Notation, Algorithm**: Reality/ executable description **Pattern**: Reusable elements **Metric**: Mathematical model to measure systems/method aspects
G. (Mwilua et al., 2016) Combines a conceptual and empirical approach, classifying artefact occurrences for two BI subject matter areas (using a broad search across the literature from 2004 to 2010, scoped down to 66 papers). Adds a number of aggregate artefacts across classes, which until now counted as Ω-knowledge (D. Gregor and Hevner).	**Construct**: Language, meta-model, concept. **Models**: System design, ontology, taxonomy, framework, architecture, requirement. **Methods**: Methodology, guideline, algorithm. Method fragment, metric. **Instantiation**: Implemented system.
H. (Dwivedi et al., 2014) Develops two empirical enumerations of knowledge types, one from papers (8) that theorize about knowledge, and one by grouping knowledge contributions from DESRIST 2011–2013 papers (24) into 9 types. The theorized list contains advanced theory types, while actual research produces more primitive insights.	**Knowledge contributions theorized in the literature**: Design theory, mode 2 knowledge, design proposition, technological rule, generative mechanism, mid-range theories, design principles, principles of form and function, nascent (level 2) and design (level 3) theories. **Knowledge contributions identified in DESRIST papers:** Guideline, lesson, proposition, hypothesis, design principle, design pattern, design requirement, design recommendation, generative mechanism

classifications that are grounded in empirical data and have been developed bottom up—at least partially.

Conceptual Classifications

These classifications mark specific steps in the evolution history of DSR, such as the first classification of design constituents (March & Smith, 1995), the introduction of design theory and the identification of its constituents (Walls et al., 1992; Gregor & Jones, 2007; Venable, 2013), a maturity view of design theories as well as the differentiation between Λ-knowledge and Ω-knowledge (Gregor & Hevner, 2013), and finally the differentiation between design knowledge and design models (Drechsler & Hevner, 2018).

The classification A. (March & Smith, 1995) was developed when DSR was conceived. It is a simple enumeration of four constituents (constructs, models, methods, and instantiations) that has been used and still is used by many when in need of an artefact definition. Of these four, *models* and *methods* are the core constituents that make up the design of an artefact. The first describes the contents of the design (the 'what'), the second the way it is created (the 'how'). This difference reflects an implicit *product/process* dimension. *Models* represent situations as both problem and solution statements, a difference that reflects a hidden *lifecycle* dimension through which a design evolves. The definitions of models identify them as *propositions* that consist of *design 'logic'*. *Constructs* describe the full design space that an artefact lives in, and *instantiations* are the result of materialization of the design in an implementation space.

The classification B. (Vaishnavi & Kuechler, 2004; Vaishnavi et al., 2019) is included in an online handbook for educational purposes. Building on A. (March & Smith, 1995), it introduces the notion of decomposition and aggregation. Models are decomposed into architectures and design principles, methods into frameworks. Design theory is defined as an aggregation of these design constituents. From a representation perspective, architectures are defined as *conceptual diagrams*, design principles as a *set of statements*.

The classifications C.1 (Walls et al., 1992), C.2 (Gregor & Jones, 2007), and C.3 (Venable, 2013) are concerned with defining the constituents of a design theory, such as requirements (C.1), principles (C.2), and relationship models (C.3), and kernel/justificatory theory (C.1/C.2). All three use a lifecycle view through which the design evolves, to identify constituents. For C.1 and C.2, it is an 'implicit' continuum. C.3 identifies three distinct groups: the problem, the solution space, and a utility relationship between these. This utility relationship corresponds to the evaluation phase that (Hevner et al., 2004) recommend. This simplifies the *lifecycle* into the three phases that we will propose as well. To define what exactly constitutes the theory contents, C.1 and C.2 build on the view of Dubin (1978) of theories in the natural and social sciences, where law-like relationship between units is mirrored in DSR in the design principles that reference models. Theories from external domains are included as justificatory knowledge (C.1 and C.2).

The classification D. (Gregor & Hevner, 2013) further refines what constitutes descriptive Λ-knowledge and prescriptive Ω-knowledge. For design focused Λ-knowledge they build on A. (March & Smith, 1995), adding MOF-like meta descriptions to constructs (concepts and symbols) and models (representation and syntax), and specializations to methods (techniques and algorithms) and instantiations (systems, products, and processes). Behavioural-focused Ω-knowledge is split into analytical knowledge of phenomena (with subtypes such as classifications, cataloguing, etc.) and explanatory knowledge of underlying relationships (with subtypes such as patterns, regularities, principles, etc.). In their definition of design theories, they emphasize the role of design logic held in principles, and of justificatory theories. They provide a maturity view of design theories that does emphasize the underlying logic as a core constituent—as it becomes increasingly generic at increasing levels of maturity.

The classification E. (Drechsler & Hevner, 2018) focuses on differentiating solution design knowledge (that contains 'statement'-like items such as *technological rules*, *requirements*, and *principles*) from solution design entities (such as *models* and *methods*). Solution design knowledge is more abstract and cannot be materialized, whereas solution design entities can. This differentiation combines both a 'materialization' dimension with a 'representation' dimension (statements versus models). We will apply a similar differentiation between statements and models, but solely based on the representation dimension, avoiding the term knowledge and the materialization criterion as differentiator, as we intend keeping that for knowledge that reaches across artefact classes.

Empirical Classifications

In Table 2, we summarize the classifications from the papers that are grounded at least partially in empirical data, by grouping and classifying outputs from existing research. All authors struggle to develop a structured classification out of this, even when using a top-down conceptual scheme to start with. The empirical classifications mostly cover artefacts that are design constituents, and all three papers create new types that they add to existing lists.

The classification F. (Offermann et al., 2010) provides an enumerated list of types derived bottom up by grouping artefacts from DESRIST research papers (from 2006 to 2009). The groupings of individual artefacts extracted from research papers abstract the context away. For example, the *methods* artefact covers business method, evaluation method, learning method, design method, etc., and the *statements* artefact covers actions, constraints, specifications, needs, definitions, etc. There is no attempt made to relate the resulting artefact types. However, the authors do observe the separation between structural and behavioural artefacts (referring to the model/method of A. (March & Smith, 1995)) and the design product/design process of Walls et al. (1992). The 'randomness' of the resulting list of eight abstracted types illustrates how difficult it is to perform typology development of the broad variety of DSR outcomes without a conceptual design. This may lead to superficial ad hoc classifications that miss the underlying structure. For example, *specifications*, *needs*, and *definitions* that in F. (Offermann et al., 2010) that are all abstracted to statements will end up in quite different parts of our proposed classification.

The classification G. (Mwilua et al., 2016) aims to provide a mapping template for artefacts described in Business Intelligence research papers. Noting its 'randomness', they first organize the list developed by F. (Offermann et al., 2010) as sub-types of classification A. (March & Smith, 1995). Next they use it to classify artefacts encountered in the down-select of 66 papers (from a broad search) and enrich the classification with additional types not yet accounted for. This effectively applies a single conceptual/empirical iteration of the method described by Nickerson et al. (2013). The types added include aggregated types that stretch across artefact classes (such as ontology, taxonomies, and frameworks) that were classified as descriptive Ω-knowledge in D. (Gregor & Hevner, 2013) but now are constructed outputs and count as design as well.

The classification H. (Dwivedi et al., 2014) aims to assess the extent to which actual research reported in DESRIST conferences produces knowledge types that have been theorized in the literature. Hence, they provide two classifications: one of the theorizing papers, and one of the artefacts extracted from DESRIST papers mapped to the first list, with new types added if needed. This also constitutes a single conceptual/empirical iteration as described by Nickerson et al. (2013). No attempt is made in structuring both lists, with the explicit comment that a cohesive structure is difficult to build across these classes. The terminology of the theorized list is adopted as is. New types added are mostly informal types such as lesson, guidelines, and hypothesis. The authors find that actual research produces more primitive outcomes than the methodological literature develops.

4.3   Dimensional Analysis

We summarize in Table 3 the various dimensions we identified in the assessment of existing concepts and classifications in the previous sections and discuss their potential for using them in the classification we plan to develop.

Class vs. Family/Genus: DSR is concerned with the design of classes of arte-facts (hence the use of the terms meta-requirements and generic requirements in C.1 and C.3).[7] Weigand et al. (2021) identify such artefact classes as an artefact 'universal' and make the presence of design products a mandatory condition for something to be called an artefact: a designed object. Structure across artefact classes has not been a large consideration in DSR. Classifications C.1 to C.3, for example, that identify the constituents of a design theory, use as scope a single artefact class. An organizing structure across artefacts is described by Weigand et al., using the term 'genus', considering them as variants that differentiate on their construction (using the example of a car engine, petrol versus a diesel engine). The conceptually developed classification D. (Gregor & Hevner, 2013) includes classifications and catalogues as output of descriptive research, whereas the empirically developed classification G. (Mwilua et al., 2016) includes similar aggregations like ontology, taxonomy, and framework but now as constructed outputs from design research. In the typology that we will propose, structure across classes will be an important extension that facilitates a broader view that can cover types of knowledge across classes, such as the aggregations mentioned.

Product vs. Process: The differentiation between product and process has been noted by most classifications listed in Tables 1 and 2.[8] Particularly in practitioner competencies, application of structured methods are key instruments of professional behaviour (with TOGAF, MSP, BiSL, etc., as examples). In addition, as

---

[7] Instances are considered as valid topics of DSR research, however, with the intent to achieve insights that then can be matured to describe a generic class (Gregor & Hevner, 2013).

[8] The classification C.2 (Gregor & Jones, 2007) is the exception; it wraps methods into the definition of design constituents, driven by the author's desire to simplify classification.

Table 3 Dimensions in existing classifications

No	Dimension	Description	Example
1	Class/Family or Genus	Differentiates the generic artefact class from a higher level organization across artefacts	An artefact type versus a taxonomy that classifies artefact types as in D. (Gregor & Hevner, 2013) and G. (Mwilua et al., 2016).
2	Design product/ design process	Differentiates the 'what' from the 'how to' of design constituents	Models versus methods in A. (March & Smith, 1995) and system design versus methods in F. (Offermann et al., 2010).
3	Design lifecycle	Differentiates design constituents by their placement in the lifecycle	The problem, solution, and evaluation context that differentiate design artefacts such as requirements, design models and principles, and testable propositions in classifications C.1–C.3
4	Design models versus design statements	Differentiates the representation of design constituents into relationship models versus logic-based expressions	A design model that depicts a component model, versus a set of design principles that contain the prescriptive logic across.
5	Design constituent/ knowledge constituent	Differentiates design that can be instantiated from knowledge that is more abstract	Design constituents (such as meta-requirements, meta-design and method) versus justificatory knowledge (such as kernel process/product theories) in C1. (Walls et al., 1992).
6	Knowledge abstraction level	Differentiates knowledge types according to an abstraction level.	Catalogues and classifications that are the result of analysis of external characteristics versus patterns and theories that are produced as underlying explanations of artefact behaviour as in D. (Gregor & Hevner, 2013).

Dwivedi et al. (2014) observe, a large proportion of outputs from DSR papers address methods as their sole deliverable. We will therefore include product versus process as a key differentiating dimension.

Lifecycle: Where identification of design sub-constituents has been performed ad hoc in some classifications such as B. Vaishnavi and Kuechler (2004/2019) (Vaishnavi & Kuechler, 2004; Vaishnavi et al., 2019), classifications C.1–C.3 use an 'implicit' lifecycle perspective to decompose into constituents. This stretches design from the context of the problem through the context of solution to the context of evaluation. The exact set of artefacts identified varies with each classification. We will apply the same differentiation and will harmonize the detailed constituents.

Design models vs design statements: Where the differentiation between models (diagrammatic representations of structure) and statements (logic-based propositions across this structure) in most cases is implicit, classification E. (Drechsler & Hevner, 2018) differentiates them explicitly into two separate constituents, using the criterion if the constituent is materializable. In their view models can be, while logic remains more abstract. We will propose the differentiation between models and statements as an important dimension for decomposing design contents, but base it on the difference in representation between statements and models only. Following Cross (2001), we argue that also design-related propositions are materializable, as they can be reengineered from implemented artefacts. For example, if a service integration layer is found which allows access to legacy systems, then design principles that prescribe this can be inferred from this presence.

Design constituent versus knowledge constituent: The previous paragraph has defined design constituents differentiating them into models and statements. Where the latter has been termed design knowledge in classification E. (Drechsler & Hevner, 2018), we prefer to reserve the term knowledge for non-materializable entities. This includes both justificatory knowledge provided by broader theories (possibly from non-IS domains) and artefact-related knowledge that stretches across artefact classes such as the taxonomies, classification, ontologies, and meta-models, from classifications D. (Gregor & Hevner, 2013) and H. (Dwivedi et al., 2014) to the extent that they are constructed outputs.

Knowledge abstraction level: The abstraction level of the type of theory that returns the knowledge is in this case the differentiator. Gregor (2006) describes a number of theory types (I for analysis, II for explanation, III for prediction, and IV for prediction and analysis) of which the first two correspond to the observational and sensemaking knowledge that classification D. (Gregor & Hevner, 2013) defines. We will use this dimension to decompose knowledge across artefacts, but with a more fine-grained division.

4.4 Definitional Analysis

Key concepts such as artefact, design, knowledge, and theory as reviewed in Sect. 4.1 constitute the theoretical core of DSR. They have been used by many authors, with different definitions and sometimes shifting semantics (see Table 4 for an example). Differentiating them through crisp definitions is a prerequisite for developing a well-structured outcome classification. We intend to strictly delineate these terms and integrate them into the key dimensions of the design of our proposed classification to achieve a largest degree of conceptual clarity as possible.

Artefacts are artificially constructed things. Most authors of classifications, such as E. (Drechsler & Hevner, 2018), refer back to Simon (1996) who characterizes an artefact by the fact that it consists of an internal environment with its construction and an interface to the external environment in which it is used. In a recent ontological analysis of artefacts, Weigand et al. (2021) centre it on the physical instantiation and propose that an artefact needs to be a design for something. When in need of a definition of artefact design, many authors refer to the simple enumeration that A. (March & Smith, 1995) compiled, which includes instantiations that materialize designs. As these definitions emphasize that artefact designs materialize into 'real' things, extension beyond the initial IT technology scope (Hevner et al., 2004) needs to be argued separately. For example—as we propose in one of our first design iterations of the outcome classification and as we use it in the contextualization of our

Table 4 Example of shifting semantics

The interplay between the terms models and principles that are constituents of a design, illustrates how definitions may evolve over time. Where a model was initially defined in March and Smith (1995) as a set of propositions or statements expressing relationships among constructs, over time this meaning carried over to the term principles, with models referring to semantic relationship diagrams. Gregor and Jones (2007), for example, in their enumeration of design contents limit themselves to the term 'Principles of Form and Function', the first construction and the second usage focused.[a] Examples reveal a statement-like representation, with a definition that refers to an architecture blueprint as well. Venable (2013) introduces component and relationships in addition to principles as constituents. Almost a decade later, Gregor et al. (2020) adopt the term 'Design principles', now limited to statement-like prescriptions, with the explicit intent to reach across research and practice

We will adopt the terms models and principles and differentiate them on their representation (diagrams versus logic).

[a] Weigand et al. (2021) use this same differentiation to identify two design products: a "make plan" and a "use plan"

typology into the large enterprise context—by including a separate 'tangibility' dimension that differentiates between operational, tactical, and strategic horizons to include business and IT strategies that are much less 'tangible' than business and IT operating models, and explaining how these become 'real'.

Designs guide construction of a single class of artefacts and consist of a set of constituents as initially defined in A. (March & Smith, 1995) and later detailed by follow on classifications, with a considerable spread in constituents. Common dimensions that are used include process/product and lifecycle. We will harmonize contents across these different classifications and propose a comprehensive set that meets our evaluation criteria.

The term *design theory* has been the subject of much debate. Except for early work from C2.1 (Walls et al., 1992) that introduced kernel theories from non-IS domains as supporting theories, it was initially absent. Fifteen years later, C2.2 (Gregor & Jones, 2007) build on Walls et al. (1992) with a refined list of constituents. Theory is defined as an aggregation across constituents with equal weight given to all the components identified. The classification D. (Gregor & Hevner, 2013) that aimed to reconcile the debate if theory should be an output of DSR, shifts the emphasis of design theory at higher levels of maturity towards the design logic held in principles as the key part,[9] together with linkages to justificatory theory. We will maintain the view of theory as an aggregation across design constituents ('primitives'), but will propose a broader scope, that extends it across classes or related artefacts that constitute broader families with additional theoretical insights at family level.

The term *knowledge* is perhaps most overloaded and difficult to pinpoint. The differentiation in D. (Gregor & Hevner, 2013) that has been most influential in DSR is that between prescriptive and descriptive knowledge as the boundary between

---

[9] We note a similar identification of models and principles in the field of enterprise architecture, that, however, does not prioritize one against the other (Lankhorst & Proper, 2012, pp. 41–42).

design and behavioural science. On a more detailed level, the materialization criterion that Gregor proposes to differentiate between design and knowledge is adopted by E. (Drechsler & Hevner, 2018) to differentiate between design constituents such as solution design entities and solution design knowledge. As already indicated in the dimensional analysis in the previous section, in both cases we will adopt different delineations, including knowledge across artefacts such as classification and patterns as potentially constructed items, and reserving the term knowledge for such insights across classes.

4.5 Summary of Findings

The analysis of existing classifications highlights the need for a conceptual approach as those compiled empirically struggle to develop the systematics for a well-designed classification. The conceptual classifications illustrate the progress of the DSR discipline over time by including new concepts as they emerge. The dimensional analysis reveals a number of implicit dimensions that together constitute a set of potential candidates. It also illustrates the differences across authors, with confusing overlaps in particularly concepts such as artefact, knowledge, and (design) theory that appear to be quite central, and unclear subtyping (method, model, system design, architecture, proposition, principles, algorithms, etc.). Overall, the lack of sufficient systematization appears to be the root cause. Definitions of classes are not consistent overall, with the same term with different meaning (e.g. the term knowledge indicating multiple abstractions), different terms used for similar components (e.g. 'design entities' and 'models', 'principles of form and function', and 'design principles'), and definitions drifting over time (e.g. the meaning of the terms 'models' and 'design theory")).

5 Conceptual Design

We first describe the conceptual iterations we performed, then present the proposed design, first of the top-level structure and then the detailing into leaf entries. We summarize the dimensions we proposed in what Nickerson et al. (2013) identify as the taxonomy system (that we will refer to as the definition system).

5.1 Conceptual Iterations

The conceptual design started with both authors contributing a number of different organizing dimensions. These preliminary contributions proposed three different dimensions for the top-level structure: a constituent dimension differentiating between a process view (the 'how') versus a product view (the 'what') of the design, a scope dimension indicating the 'tangibility' of the artefact subject matter, and a meta-level description dimension adding a layer with definitions.

The intent of the first was to explicitly capture the difference between the act of designing an artefact (the design process) and the design itself (the designed product). This was quickly carried over to our final design, because, as already explained in Sect. 4.3, it is a foundational difference that many authors of established classifications have recognized and that has been acknowledged as highly significant by many DSR authors (Bucher & Winter, 2008; Baskerville & Pries-Heje, 2010; Deng & Ji, 2018), because methods and models are produced by many DSR papers as separate outputs (Dwivedi et al., 2014), and because methods are a key instrument in practitioner competencies.

The intent of the second dimension was to explicitly capture a 'scope' extension of the original IT focus, which was proposed by Hevner et al. (2004). This can be achieved, for example, by scoping subject matter in terms of 'tangibility' using the difference between operational, tactical, and strategic horizons—including business and IT strategies that are much less 'tangible' than business and IT operating models. Extensions like these have been suggested (Lee et al., 2015) and reflect the scope of today's DSR practice beyond a purely technology focus. However, we realized that when selecting characteristics values for this dimension, this would tie the classification to a specific context, such as for example the choice of operational, tactical, and strategic ties the classification to the large enterprise context, with many more options for dimensions available. This conflicts with our intent to focus the DSR outcome typology on the generics of design at the level of DSR as a research discipline, not dependent on context. We therefore decided to include context-specific subject matter dimensions into more detailed taxonomies (see Sect. 8.2). It is conceptually clearer, and it better matches our objective of providing a standardized template that existing classifications that are also almost fully context agnostic[10] can map to.

The intent of the third dimension was to introduce a meta-level description of the artefact, with three options considered: (i) a MOF-like definitional level (*Meta Object Facility*. https://www.omg.org/spec/MOF/) defining the artefact (e.g. syntax, representation), (ii) a type of maturity/abstraction level, such as nascent or well developed, as in the maturity view of a design theory from Gregor and Hevner's (2013), or (iii) a qualification of how knowledge about artefacts was acquired based on the genre of inquiry, such as design, qualitative or quantitative research (Baskerville et al., 2015) and the resulting purpose of the knowledge, such as descriptive/explanatory 'Ω-knowledge' or prescriptive 'Λ-knowledge' (March & Smith, 1995; Hevner et al., 2004). However, when reviewing the detailed contents of existing classifications and the empirical samples, the role became apparent that knowledge and in particular knowledge that stretches across artefacts can play. This

---

[10] Particularly, empirical classifications are very context sensitive with respect to the specific artefacts they harvest from DSR papers, but almost fully abstract this away. E.g., a BI specific "taxonomy of data mining algorithms" is abstracted to a "taxonomy" (Dwivedi et al., 2014) and a large enterprise specific "business model" is abstracted to a "model" (Offermann et al., 2010).

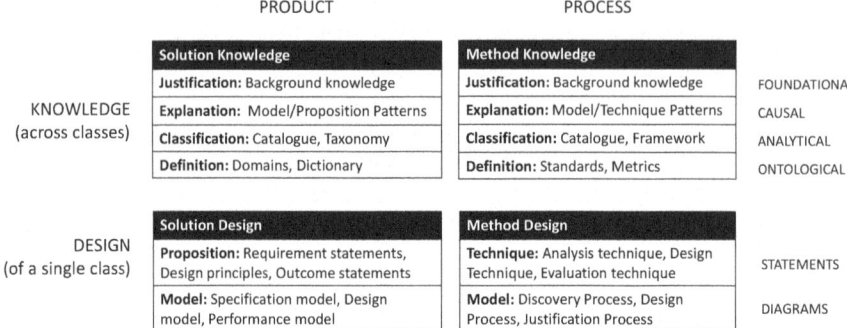

Fig. 1 DSR outcome typology

includes definitional and analytical knowledge such as ontologies and classifications, explanatory knowledge such as patterns and regularities, and justificatory knowledge with linkages to mid-range/substantive theories possibly from other domains. Given the potential of this type of knowledge to extend the scope of a design theory from a single class to families of classes, we decided to introduce this type of knowledge as a metalevel with several abstraction levels as a separate dimension.

5.2 Design of DSR Outcome Typology

Figure 1 graphically illustrates the structure of the DSR outcome typology that we propose (leaf entries are detailed in the next section).

The top-level structure differentiates on the horizontal dimension into product constituents (the what) versus process constituents (the how), and on the vertical dimension into design constituents (of a single class) versus knowledge constituents (across classes)—the first can be materialized, the second are more abstract. As explained already above, the first is carried over from existing classifications: it is mapped directly from the 'Product/Process' dimension from Table 3. The second emerges as a new candidate from the initial conceptual iterations and covers a considerable extension of existing classifications, as it introduces the differentiation between design of a single class versus knowledge across classes.

Design quadrants structure (the two bottom level quadrants in Fig. 1). Constituents in these quadrants have been the core topic of the existing conceptual classifications from Table 2. The mapping is straightforward: design constituents go into the lower left quadrant, method constituents into the lower right quadrant, using the design lifecycle to decompose. In addition to the decomposition by existing classifications into more detailed constituents from the lifecycle, we interleave a dimension that differentiates the logic that is held in *statements* ('prescriptive' propositions for product constituents, and 'actionable' instructions for process constituents) from the relationship descriptions that are held in *diagrams* ('semantic' models for product constituents and 'flow' models for process constituents). This difference has been noted consistently throughout the evolution of DSR, and is implicitly present in each classification from Table 1. It traces back to the first classification A. (March & Smith, 1995), who emphasize the propositions that express relationship among constructs as the key constituent of designs. The same emphasis is applied by Gregor and Jones (2007), who identify 'Principles of Form and Function' as key constituents of design theories, comparing these with the laws of interaction between units of a domain of interest in the natural and social sciences (Dubin, 1978). Drechsler and Hevner (2018) partition the contents of designs into the same two parts although worded differently: solution design entities and solution design knowledge (models and statements in our choice of terminology). Interleaving them as characteristics values on an explicit dimension allows our proposed classification to recognize these differences.[11]

Knowledge quadrants structure (the two top-level quadrants in Fig. 1). Constituents in these quadrants (such as classification, cataloguing, patterns, rules, as well as the linkages to external theories) have been categorized traditionally as Ω-knowledge (Gregor & Hevner, 2013). As our analysis of existing classifications (Mwilua et al., 2016) and empirical samples finds, they are also becoming outcomes of DSR as constructed items. Their inclusion in our proposed typology reflects therewith the increased focus on knowledge that has developed in DSR research. In addition, including this type of knowledge across artefact classes supports an extension in design theories from the design of a single class across families of artefact classes. In Sect. 8.1, we discuss how such an extension could work using simple examples (of operating models and bridges), and what the increased potential for understanding is that this more extended theorizing allows.

Where the classification D. (Gregor & Hevner, 2013) provides a rudimentary view on the decomposition of Ω-knowledge into two levels (observations and sensemaking), our increased focus on constructed knowledge as outputs leads us to a decomposition into four characteristics values with increasingly abstract knowledge: *Definition, Analysis, Explanation*, and *Justification*. The rationale for selecting them comes from two sources: the identification of different types of IS theories particularly those for analysing and explaining (Gregor, 2006), and the conception of kernel theories used to justify design theories (Walls et al., 1992). The *Definition* constituents cover the ontological view of the design space and identify items such as subject matter domains and dictionaries (of constructs, design constituents, and space dimensions). It incorporates the initial idea of a MOF-like layer that defines meta-level properties. The *Classification* constituents cover the analytical view of the design space and arrange solution constituents based on their characteristics into catalogues, taxonomies, and frameworks. Both are inspired on the Type I theory for analysis (Gregor, 2006) that defines and analyses phenomena, but now from a

---

[11] We also note a similar differentiation between models and principles in the field of enterprise architecture that, however, does not prioritize one against the other (Lankhorst & Proper, 2012, pp. 41–42).

Table 5 Definition system

Lvl	Dimension	Differentiating characteristic	Characteristic values	Table 4 reference
1	Vertical	Materialization	Design/knowledge	1. Class/family or genus 5. Design/knowledge
	Horizontal	Representation	Process/product	2. Design product/process
2	Bottom part (design)	Representation	Models/statements	4. Design models/statements
	Top part (knowledge)	Abstraction	Ontology/analysis/causal/foundational	6. Knowledge abstraction level
3	Bottom left (solution design)	Lifecycle	Lifecycle phases	3. Design lifecycle
	Bottom right (method design)			
	Top left (solution knowledge)	Various	Various	
	Top right (method knowledge)			

construction perspective. The *Explanation knowledge* constituents provide causal insights into solution and method patterns across classes of artefacts. They are inspired on the Type II theory for explaining (Gregor, 2006) that provides causal explanations of behaviour that tie back to underlying mechanisms. We also differentiate here between diagrams (solution model and method process patterns) and statements (solution propositions and method techniques) as well. The *Justification knowledge* constituents consist of foundational background theories that help to justify *Explanation* knowledge. These can be substantive theories or generic mechanisms that arise in the domain itself (Gregor, 2006), or external theories that can be translated into the specific subject matter domain (Walls et al., 1992).

Definition system: Table 5 summarizes the dimensions we propose—the 'taxonomy system' in the terminology of Nickerson et al. (2013), which we refer to as the definition system.

The proposed definition system constitutes the formal systematization of our classification, listing dimensions, characteristics, and characteristics values. In the last column in Table 5, we include a reference to the respective dimensions from existing classifications (Table 3).

5.3 Detailing Leaf Entries

Figure 2 graphically details the leaf items that we propose. Precise definitions and examples are provided through the glossary in Appendix 1.

Solution Knowledge	Decomposition
Justification: Background knowledge	Kernel theory (domain specific theories), Foundational theory (deep and far reaching theories)
Explanation: Causal knowledge	(Solution) Model Patterns (regularities), Proposition Patterns (regularities)
Classification: Analytical knowledge	Catalogue (sorted list of solutions), Taxonomy (nested categorizations)
Definition: Ontological knowledge	Domains (to partition the design space), Dictionary (to define constituents)

Method Knowledge	Decomposition
Justification: Background knowledge	Kernel theory (domain specific theories), Foundational theory (deep and far reaching theories)
Explanation: Causal knowledge	(Method) Model Patterns (regularities), Technique Patterns (regularities)
Classification: Analytical knowledge	Catalogue (sorted list of methods), Framework (method/design guides)
Definition: Ontological knowledge	Standards (for key components), Metrics (to quantify measures)

Solution Design	Decomposition
Proposition: Logic based statements	Requirement statements (what is needed), Design principles (what the design should look like), Outcome statements (what is (to be) achieved)
Model: Relationship based diagrams	Specification model (features and affordances), Design model (construction and use), Performance model (behavior and measures)

Method Design	Decomposition
Technique: Instruction statements	Analysis techniques (how to assess problems), Design techniques (how to create the design), Evaluation techniques (how to assess outcomes)
Model: Flow based diagrams	Discovery process (exploring the problem space), Design process (developing the design), Justification process (exploring the outcome space)

Fig. 2 DSR outcome typology—leaf items

Bottom quadrants: The bottom quadrants in Fig. 2 with product and process design constituents are decomposed using the design lifecycle as dimension. We divide into three phases that cover the analysis of the problem, the design of the solution, and evaluation of outcomes, with each phase contributing a single constituent. Many authors recognize a cycle like this although worded differently and not always explicit. For example, Hevner et al. (2004) describe the existence of a problem and solution space that are connected by models, and introduce the concept of a justification/evaluation phase that follows the design phase. Fischer and Gregor (2011) introduce the context of discovery and the context of justification as separate sources for the logic (inductive, deductive, and abductive) used to develop a theory, with their choice of terms emphasizing the research aspect. The above discussed conceptual classifications C.1 (Walls et al., 1992), C.2 (Gregor & Jones, 2007), and C.3 (Venable, 2013) implicitly share the design lifecycle dimension we propose. Venable's (2013) proposal is most explicit in partitioning constituents into three types (requirements, design, and utility) that can be produced as output from the same lifecycle phase.

- *Solution design quadrant*: The terms we selected for this quadrant have a *passive* connotation that corresponds with a product as output, and a *precise* connotation that corresponds with a clearly delineated result. Leaf types of propositions include *requirements* (summarizing what an artefact should be able to do), *design principles* (providing logic on what the internal artefact construction should look like), and *outcome* statements (summarizing the intended outcomes to be achieved from artefact behaviour). Leaf types of models include *specification models* (identifying the external characteristics of an artefact and the abilities these provide to an actor), *design* models (describing the organization of an artefact's constituents), and *performance* models (describing the behaviour of an artefact in use and measurement of its performance).

• *Method design quadrant*: The terms we selected for this quadrant have an *active* connotation that corresponds with a process as output, and a *loose* connotation that corresponds with an investigative approach—that fans out into the problem and justification space, differentiating it from routine designs. Leaf types of techniques include *analysis* techniques (specifying how to perform problem space activities, such as impact assessment, root cause analysis, etc.), *design* techniques (specifying how to perform design of construction models, such as componentization approaches, partitioning techniques, etc.), and *evaluation* techniques (specifying how to assess outcomes of artefact behaviour, such as measure determination, artefact validity, etc.). Leaf types of process include *discovery process* models that represent the flow through the various activities that explore the problem space, *design* processes through those that explore the design space, and justification processes through those that explore the *evaluation* space.

Top quadrants: For detailing the knowledge leaf items in the top quadrants from Fig. 2, no related work exists. Conceptual classifications from DSR ignored these or ranked them as Ω-knowledge with rudimentary detailing, and empirical classifications produce enumerated lists without explicit conceptual structure. As the type of knowledge at the four levels proposed differs considerably no common decomposition dimension exists, and we therefore apply a variety of approaches.

• *Solution knowledge quadrant*: Definitional knowledge differentiates space characteristics such as *domains* that are coherent subject matter partitions, and dimensions along which partitions are created, and constituent characteristics such as *dictionaries* that include MOF-level type descriptions such as definitions syntax and grammar rules. Classification knowledge differentiates based on the type of grouping logic: e.g. sorting on a simple characteristic producing *catalogues* of artefact classes in a domain, or more complex classifications that address internal construction and external behavioural differences producing *taxonomies*. Explanation knowledge differentiates along the same model/ statement dimension as design constituents do: *Solution patterns* are models that establish regularities in behaviour across classes of artefacts, which involve artefact interactions and can be traced back to construction relationships; *Operational rules* are statement-based logic that addresses the same regularities.[12] Justification knowledge differentiates on scope of applicability and 'deepness' of the knowledge: *Kernel theories* constitute domain-specific mid-range or substantive theories that justify mature designs (Walls et al., 1992; Gregor, 2006); *Foundational theories* constitute deep and far-reaching theories that provide foundational insights on which designs are grounded (Gregor, 2006).

---

[12] Note that both design principles and operational rules can be phrased as action statements: "'if you want to achieve Y in situation Z, then use the generic design X (or perform the action type X): Y = X(Z)" (van Aken et al., 2016, p. 4).

- The *method knowledge quadrant* applies similar differentiations as for the solution knowledge quadrant. Definitional knowledge differentiates on the qualitative versus quantitative dimension of meta-level information: *Standards* apply to inputs/outputs (e.g. XML) or key activities of methods (e.g. UML); *Metrics* apply to measures used to perform quantification (e.g. of performance). Classification knowledge differentiates based on the type of grouping logic *catalogues* as above (defining simple sorting lists of method classes in a domain) and *frameworks* (linking methods in a domain with solution design primitives). Explanation knowledge differentiates on models versus statements: *Method patterns* are process models that establish regularities in method execution for classes of problems, and *technique patterns* are instruction statements that establish regularities in techniques that solve classes of problems. Justification knowledge differentiates in the same way as for the solution knowledge quadrant, producing *kernel* and *foundational* theories but now for method knowledge.

Rationale: The decomposition into leaf items that we propose aims to provide a well systematized substrate for future DSR outcomes, and should as well be able to harmonize across the differences in constituents in existing classifications. The terms that we use for the leaf nodes in each quadrant are adopted from the existing classifications where clear consensus exists and they are broadly accepted by researchers and practitioners (such as requirements, principles, models, etc., in the bottom quadrants, and frameworks, catalogues, patterns, etc., in the top quadrants). In the other cases, we opted for terms (such as analysis, techniques, performance, evaluation, etc., in the bottom quadrants, and rules, instructions, etc., in the top quadrants) that are intuitive and represent the intent of each phase in an easy to comprehend way. As we will discuss in the Evaluation section, how leaf entries are named is important for how well they are recognized and accepted. An example of the considerations applied is included in Table 6.

The selected set is limited and to avoid overspecification and too much detailing, terms are 'broad' in the sense that they cover a large number of more specific terms. For example, a design model may cover a business model, a platform architecture, a component model, or a process model, and a specification model may refer to results from the analysis performed in the discovery process, such as an impact analysis or root cause analysis. And for example, a performance model covers the description of behaviour of an artefact as well as the assessment thereof.[13]

Summarizing dimensions: Table 7 summarizes the dimensions and their characteristics that create this detailed subtyping structure.

---

[13] It does differentiate from operational rules as these are linked to patterns across artefact classes, and are action oriented.

Table 6 Example of naming

Where the naming of items in the top-level decomposition (Table 1) aims at full semantic and definitional correctness, for naming leaf items (Table 2) recognizability and ease of use are key criteria, and therefore we propose short names.[a] We illustrate the considerations for selecting short names, by the alternatives we considered as short name for the fully qualified name 'Solution Knowledge Proposition Pattern'. These include 'Action rules', 'Behavioural rules', and 'Operational rules', the latter that we settled for.

Solution Patterns and Operational Rules from the Knowledge quadrants are equivalent in their differentiation to Design Models and Design Principles from the Design quadrants: both differentiate on representation (diagrams versus statements). The difference is that where Design Models and Design Principles focus on the *design* of an artefact class, Patterns and Rules focus on *behavioural* differences across artefact classes (that can be traced back to construction). Where the first are mostly created using design science research as genre of inquiry, the second can be created as well using action research, which immediately responds to observations of behaviour with changes to how artefact operate.

The terms 'action', 'behaviour', and 'operate' from above considerations create the three alternatives we considered: 'Action rules', 'Behavioural rules', and 'Operational rules'. Assessing these we dismissed the first two in favour of the third. The term 'action' we assessed as too much 'genre of inquiry' focused and labelling by purpose rather than by contents, the term 'behaviour' as underestimating the linkage with construction. The term 'operational' focuses on the artefacts in use, it has both an observational connotation but also one that covers change.[b] The term 'rule' as opposed to 'principle' as second part of the name carries the connotation of an actionable change.

[a] Compare this to the Linnaeus taxonomy in which fully qualified names are used in the academic discourse, and short names in common language
[b] 'Technological rules', the term that van Aken coined in the strategic management sciences to introduce research aiming to produce more practical recommendations, covers the same contents, but we do not consider the term as differentiating, as DSR in IS involves technology always

Table 7 Definition system for leaf types

Dimension	Subtype	Characteristic type	Characteristic value
Top right quadrant (Method knowledge)	Justification	Scope/deepness	Kernel/foundational
	Explanation	Models/statements	Method/technique
	Classification	Grouping logic	Sorted list/matrix
	Definition	Qualitative/quantitative	Standards/metrics
Top left quadrant (solution knowledge)	Justification	Scope/deepness	Kernel/foundational
	Explanation	Models/statements	Solution/rules
	Classification	Grouping logic	Sorted list/hierarchical list
	Definition	Space/unit	Partitioning/meta typing
Bottom left quadrant (solution design)	Proposition, models	Lifecycle phase	Discovery, creation, justification
Bottom right quadrant (method design)	Technique, models		

6 Demonstration

We demonstrate the application of the typology by classifying the outputs from a research project (Bruls et al., 2021) with a scope large enough to deliver constituents that can provide examples for every leaf entry from Fig. 2. The mapping is summarized in Fig. 3.

The project's objective was to develop an integrated approach to modelling the adaptability of the business and operating model of large enterprises, covering the full spectrum of changes—from routine adaptability managed within the configurability of individual operating model components, through transitional adaptability adding new business model and operating model components, to foundational adaptability producing full new business model and operating model partitions. The approach centred on a partitioned and componentized model of the operating environment with two techniques to cover the broad range of adaptability: partitioning and componentization to allow major extensions, and configuration within specified bandwidths to allow routine configurability using a feature-based configuration language. The theoretical background is set for the first in established architectural partitioning and componentization techniques, and for the second in the theory of Product Line Engineering (Blecker & Friedrich, 2006) that centres on families of products that vary in their features (e.g. a car with different types of engines and colour) and was ported from mass customization in manufacturing industries to IS (Pohl et al., 2005; Hallsteinsen et al., 2006). A number of analysis techniques are required to analyse the impact of the different types of changes, and to design the adaptability at the various layers. For example, to assess the impact of both (disruptive) trends, innovations and routine changes on the business model and operating model, to model the required partitioning and componentization using best

Solution Knowledge		Method Knowledge	
Justification:	Kernel theory – PLE ported to IS, business model theory, metadata-based adjustments of generic domain models Foundational theory – Mass customization using Product Line Engineering (PLE)	Justification:	Kernel theory - Common Variability Analysis, Component based design Foundational theory – modular design in manufacturing industries, civil engineering (e.g. building design)
Explanation:	Model Patterns – outside inside landscape partitioning pattern, metadata integration pattern Proposition Patterns – optimum bandwidth proposition patterns for various constellations (enterprise/ecosystem, strict/loose)	Explanation:	Model Patterns – trend impact, partitioning and componentization pattern Technique Patterns – orthogonal/hierarchical feature combination pattern
		Classification:	Catalogue – list of techniques, Framework – change paths impact guide (type of change versus impact on stack), process guide (type of phase versus activity/model)
Classification:	Catalogue – list of features, list of transformation options, list of trends Taxonomy – industry specific versions of componentization		
Definition:	Domains – industry sectors Dictionary – model/method constituents, definitions, Common Variability Language, Feature combination language	Definition:	Standards –OWL definitions (OMG), Common Variability Language (OMG) Metrics – configuration time, configuration/customization ratio

Solution Design		Method Design	
Proposition:	Requirement statements: limited side effects of trend impact on operating model, optimum bandwidths for configuration of components, integration of technology specific metadata Design principles: build on existing methods, simple enough, designed adaptability Outcome statements: a full set of change paths, that support foundational changes by new landscape partitions, transitional changes by new components, and routine changes by configuration bandwidths of existing components	Technique:	Analysis techniques innovation impact assessment, trend impact assessment, commonality and variability analysis, adjustment analysis Design techniques business model entity design techniques, architectural partitioning and componentization techniques, optimum bandwidth design techniques, family & feature design techniques, configuration center integration techniques Evaluation techniques grounding in the literature, empirical, internal consistency
Model:	Specification model business model change cases, operating model trend impact map, commonality & variability model (CV model) Design model business model entity design model with change cases applied, landscape map with partitions and components, and impact applied, feature map supporting CV model), configuration center design Performance model adaptable industry solutions that cover a full set of change paths, with separately available components, and integrated configuration across	Model:	Discovery process assessing utility of solution paradigms from the literature, identifying anti-pattern cases from practice that identify problems and suggest solutions, exploring similar concepts in other engineering industries, Design process analysis and engineering in three phases (strategy, architecture and design steps)) Justification process feedback from applying in development of an industry solution, insights from joint academic/practice research project, expository instantiation

Fig. 3 Mapping of DSR study outcomes to typology

practices from other industries such as in physical building construction and design of production machinery (Engel & Reich, 2015), to model the commonality and variability of components using a standards based language (Haugen et al., 2008), and to design a feature language for configuration selecting between hierarchical and orthogonal approaches (Budiardjo & Zamzami, 2014). Included in the research was knowledge across classes that identified, for example, solution patterns such as componentized versions of operating models for different industries, and different approaches to integration of meta-data, as well as method patterns, such as impact analysis approaches for different types of changes. Figure 3 summarizes the outcomes mapped to the typology proposed in the study at hand.

7   Evaluation

We evaluate our proposed typology fourfold: by mapping related work, by mapping artefacts from a selected set of empirical examples, by analytical evaluation, and by feedback from a focal group. The first evaluation maps existing classifications that are conceptually derived (Table 1) and empirically constructed (Table 2). Being able to cover those conceptually derived implies that we are complete in our conceptual coverage of the DSR research field, as we can map and hence support the differentiations that previous authors considered. Being able to cover those empirically derived implies casting a wide net across an empirical base of research papers that these authors selected as samples—as these underly the abstractions included in the classification from Table 2. The second evaluation intends to test our proposed outcome typology with a set of empirical examples; it allows to assess the extent to which the ending condition at the leaf level (Nickerson et al., 2013) is achieved. Examples come from papers from recent DESRIST conferences. The third analytical evaluation assesses our proposed typology against criteria developed for both artefact (Prat et al., 2015) and taxonomy soundness (Nickerson et al., 2013). The final and fourth evaluation draws insights from the feedback from our teaching practice with audiences of PhD students, attending a course on artefact design.

7.1   Mapping of Related Work

Detailed mappings of existing classifications from Tables 1 and 2 to our proposed outcome typology are included in Appendix 2. Mappings of conceptual classifications from Table 1 mostly address a limited but coherent part of the new typology's quadrants (matching their conceptual viewpoint), while those of empirical classifications from Table 2 display a larger amount of scatter, as they are constructed bottom up. Both the method part and the knowledge part are more sparsely populated, apparently reflecting a reduced researcher interest (Winter et al., 2009). The harmonization is straightforward, as it is mostly in semantics and detailing. Where the existing classifications contain more detail, it requires abstracting these away.

The fact that we use broad leaf type definitions in our proposed typology, and abstract away from details of existing classifications in our proposal, plays to the question of an ending condition—when is sufficient detail provided? We expect details not to be encountered as separate outcome types of DSR research (e.g. representation is studied as part of a broader definition of characteristics), and hence they should not surface in an outcome typology. Their inclusion would make the typology more complex without justifying the additional complexity by significant knowledge organization or knowledge creation support. We further test the design and ending condition in the second evaluation described next.

7.2 Analytical Evaluation

Prat et al. (2015) identify evaluation criteria for an artefact that relate to both the artefact's structure (fidelity to modelled phenomenon, simplicity, completeness, and consistency) and fit to the target audience's environment (usefulness and ease of use). Nickerson et al. (2013) identify as an ending condition for a taxonomy that it should be concise, robust, comprehensive, extendible, and explanatory. We evaluate as follows against these criteria:

- Artefact structure: As we follow the major concepts that have emerged in DSR (artefact, knowledge, and theory), we claim fidelity to modelled phenomenon, simplicity is provided by the fact that we limit ourselves to decomposition in a minimum number of dimensions (2) and a reasonable number of characteristics on each dimension (from 2 to 4), completeness is provided by the fact that the characteristics cover the full dimension, and consistency by the fact that they are mutually exclusive.
- Artefact fit to the target audience: Usefulness and ease of use are established by evaluation with a focal group of inexperienced researchers.
- Taxonomy ending condition: Conciseness and comprehensiveness are provided by the limited number of dimensions and characteristics, robustness by the selection of key terms and generic characteristics that are foundational concepts not easily overridden or exchanged, extensibility is provided through standard operations such as specializing, abstracting, and subtyping, and explanatory power through the choice for highly differentiating concepts.

7.3 Feedback from Our Teaching Practice

Three groups of Ph.D. students who attended a DSR methodology course in subsequent years served as focal groups to communicate our research and receive feedback. The details of the communication and feedback process are described in

Appendix 3. Students list as benefits of an outcome classification those that we identified (developing a common language, understanding where your research fits in, and a foundation for knowledge building). They observe the lack of clear definitions of and differentiation between concepts of existing classifications, and see the value of the new proposed typology, but at the same time struggle with its complexity too. They see its role in later stages of research design development and for experienced researchers, but prefer simpler guidance in early stages. Overall, our learnings from the courses were that crisp differentiation and definitions were a prerequisite, and that using simple and especially well-recognizable terms greatly added to the understanding.

Based on these three rounds of feedback, we performed several iterations during our research to further strengthen the understandability and comprehensiveness. As an example, we reduced the number of leaf types in the design quadrants to three across the lifecycle and further simplified the terminology used to denote the knowledge abstraction levels in our final iteration.

For our follow-on research, we conclude that for these less experienced researchers there will remain a gap to be bridged (with simplified version and examples). As we see the current structure of the typology as required for guiding mature designs and supporting foundational discussions, further reduction of the complexity is not something we aspire.

7.4   Classifying a Sample of Empirical Artefacts

Appendix 4 contains the results of classifying a sample of empirical artefacts harvested from recent DESRIST conference papers. The examples from DESRIST served as the testing ground of the finalized typology using samples of real research. The examples were selected with sufficient diversity to test the full scope. It did not result in any further changes of the typology, but provided input to the discussion on how to scope (see Sect. 8.3), as the research papers contained a wide variety of cases, some of them with limited IT contents.

8   Discussion

In this section, we discuss the extension to theorizing that our typology supports (from a single class to a family or genera of classes), how contextualization might work, scope issues such as the types of contexts that can be projected to, the extent to which non-IT artefacts can be included, and the options for implementing a classification process.

8.1   Extending the Concept of Theory

Like the theories defined in C.1 (Walls et al., 1992), C.2 (Gregor & Jones, 2007), and C.3 (Venable, 2013), a theory that is defined on top of the proposed typology can be constructed as an aggregation of any of the constituents in the bottom design part of Fig. 1 (the scope that C.1–C.3 cover), plus in our extension any of the constituents from the knowledge quadrants of Fig. 1 which reach across classes. Adding such knowledge across classes as DSR outcomes now allows us to extend the scope of a design theory from a single class to reach across classes of artefacts. The new scope that we propose addresses families (Pohl et al., 2005) or genera (Weigand et al., 2021) of artefacts that share a common abstraction as ancestor but vary in patterns of usage and construction. This extension has the advantage of adding insights into the suitability of specific classes for specific circumstances, their differentiating characteristics, and the theories behind these, etc.

We illustrate this approach with two examples, the first from civil engineering concerned with the design of different types of bridges for supporting the traffic flow across obstacles (Xanthakos, 1995), and the second from IS engineering concerned with the design of different types of operating models for supporting the production processes across the large enterprise (Campbell et al., 2017). Table 8 provides an overview that includes examples for both the knowledge part of our typology across classes (the design space that defines relevant constructs, the different family members that can be identified, their construction/usage patterns, and the justification theories) and the design part of our typology per class (the models and logic behind them).

Table 8   Examples of design theory constituents

Design theory constituent	Operating models	Bridges
Justification knowledge	Availability and throughput calculation theory Transactional, process, and batch integrity theory	Load bearing and stress calculation theory Traffic optimization theory
Explanation knowledge	Construction patterns (dedicated, layered, componentized, and platform) Control patterns (straight through, pipelines, and planned)	Construction patterns (tower based, span based, and arch based) Control patterns (free flow, traffic lights, and opening windows)
Classification knowledge	*Transactional*, *process*, and *batch* types	*Suspension*, *beam*, and *arch* types
Definitions	Production flow context (flow intensity, enterprise landscape properties, and external relationships)	Traffic flow context (traffic intensity, landscape properties, and environmental conditions)
Design models	Construction blueprints	Construction blueprints
Design statements	Design insights	Design insights

Bridges have a large spread in usage patterns, small or large distances that need to be covered, with extensive or limited traffic and resistant to different environmental conditions, such as weather extremes, earthquakes, and flooding. A *'Theory and Design of Bridges'* (Xanthakos, 1995) will cover different construction patterns such as *suspension* bridges, *beam* bridges, and *arch* bridges, focusing on the construction differences such as the load bearing mechanisms (the suspension cords, the reinforced beam material, or the arch shape of the pillars) and on control differences such as traffic regulation mechanisms (free flow with entry and exits ramps, traffic lights, and opening windows). Justification knowledge produced by load and stress calculation and traffic optimization theories will support the design. In addition, construction blueprints and design logic are available per type. Insights at the level of the family will allow to assess which class fits which context best. For example, suspension bridges are suitable to bridge long distances and can cope with large traffic streams, but are very expensive and sensitive to extreme climate conditions, whereas beam bridges are less expensive but block more of the underlying space due to their pillars, and arch bridges aesthetics match ancient city centres.

Similar to bridges, operating models have a large spread in usage patterns, with different volumes and timing of throughputs, and specific environmental requirements with respect to adaptability, integrity, and trust. A 'Theory and design of operating models' that could be developed across these classes will cover different patterns such as *real time*, *process driven*, or *batch processing,* focusing on construction differences such as load handling (transactions, queues, and batches) and control (straight through, pipelines, and planned). Justification knowledge produced by availability and throughput calculation theory and transactional, process, and batch integrity theory will support the design. Other theories are more specific for a domain and may come from both IS and non-IS domains. Examples are the theory of two-phase commit protocols that supports transactional integrity across production steps for providing integrity, blockchain-based ledgers to support ecosystem-based transaction processing for providing trust, and product line engineering-based configuration approaches to support families of products with predefined variability for providing flexibility (Bruls et al., 2021). In addition, in the same way as in the 'bridges' example, construction blueprints and design insights are available per type, that by comparing allow to assess which class fits which context best. For example, *real-time transactional* operating models are suitable to support atomic transactions (e.g. a money transfer, an online flight check-in) and can cope with large volumes and real-time processing needs, but are sensitive to single point of failure disruptions that impact customer experience severely. *Sequential process-driven* operating models are suited to support more complex products with a more extended online or physical logistics component (a mortgage request, a building permit, online purchase of physical contents), but need to offer a larger configuration space with potentially extensive options. *Planned batch processing* operating models are suited to support mass production processes that require carefully timed and executed steps (producing a batch of steel, or chemicals, running a vaccination campaign), but need resources to be dimensioned towards peak moments, with potentially large ramp on and off times.

Table 9 Exemplary taxonomy system for large enterprise context

Dimension	Characteristics
Alignment	Strategic, operational
Domains	Production, governance, transformation, innovation, culture
Sector	Finance, government, manufacturing, etc.
Platform	Business layer, operating layer, technology layer
Level of analysis	Ecosystem, enterprise, business unit, workgroup

8.2 Context-Specific Taxonomies

As indicated in Sect. 5.1, we decided to position the DSR outcome typology at the generic level of DSR as research discipline, and introduce more detailed context-specific taxonomies to classify outputs in specific subject matter domains. We use the term 'contextualizing' to denote such a 'projection' (Baskerville & Pries-Heje, 2019) of a generic artefact into a specific context and interleave these type of taxonomies between the generic outcome typology and the real physical instantiation of an artefact. Taxonomies that are created by such projection are at par with classifications such as the Linnaeus classification system (Linnaeus, 1756) used to classify biological organisms, which describes the diversity of artefact 'species' in a certain context.[14]

As was the case with developing the DSR outcome typology, developing contextualized taxonomies requires identifying dimensions and characteristics that can be used for taxonomy structuration.

As an example, Table 9 includes a taxonomy for the large enterprise context, with a number of exemplary dimensions and characteristics. The alignment dimension differentiates strategic versus operational artefacts (Henderson & Venkatraman, 1993), the industry dimension differentiates different sectors (Bruls et al., 2021), the domain dimension differentiates competencies that a large enterprise incorporates (Bruls et al., forthcoming), the platform dimension differentiates the layers in the Business-to-IT stack (Bruls et al., 2021), and the level of analysis dimension differentiates the various levels of organizational units, from headquarters down to workgroup (Blalock, 1979).

Obviously within the scope of Table 9, considerable detailing may be performed to produce, for example, a taxonomy of digitization strategies and corresponding digital platforms, a taxonomy of eCommerce processes at workgroup level, or a taxonomy of governance approaches of logistics platforms at ecosystem level. The

---

[14] As Bailey (1994, p. 8) summarizes in his introduction to classification techniques: "Systematics is defined by Simpson (1961, p. 7) as the scientific study of the kinds and diversity of organisms and of any and all relationships among them".

differentiation can be refined to considerable detail to describe all the possible situated options, as in the example that Nickerson et al. (2013) create for mobile applications. See Mueller et al. (2022) for a list of taxonomies that addresses specific subject matter areas.

8.3   Scope of Subject Matter

Contextualizing raises the question of a valid scope at two levels of the subject matter that may be addressed. One is the extent to which non-IT artefacts can be included, and the second which types of contexts can be projected to with our proposed outcome typology. The first question addresses the scope extension that has been occurring in DSR from the original focus on IT artefacts (Hevner et al., 2004) to extend beyond the IT and even the IS view. Extensions like these have been suggested (Lee et al., 2015) and the scope of today's DSR practice has certainly developed far beyond the original IT boundaries. Certainly that should be justified in view of the landslide shift that occurred in the relation between business and IT in the large enterprise, and the transformation that occurred in other areas such as social interactions, and more recently artificial intelligence. Issues arise, however, when we include what we identified in our first conceptual iteration as intangible artefacts, such as for example business and IT strategies in the large enterprise context. To define an artefact, we rely on a view of a designed thing with an internal and external environment (Simon, 1996), emphasizing materialization as a key property (Weigand et al., 2021). A strategy can be represented through a model—such as for example the business model (Osterwalder et al., 2005) that was used in the leaf type example to assess impact of future trends. This model consists of layers that interrelate strategic concepts such as value propositions and customer product portfolio with operational concepts such as production processes and resources. Considering this full model as a black box, however, with external affordances that show up at the outside, is quite a stretch. Materialization of strategic intents will only take place in the future after changes to the operating model. At the same time, it is difficult to see how such an adaptability analysis method could be developed without including the strategic level. It may require loosening the materialization criterion, for example to allow for indirect materialization (in the future, as the result of a strategic intent).

When extending the scope to include less tangible entities such as strategies, the question that then surfaces is how much IT should be involved, to claim such a topic as DSR. And in a similar vein, the amount of IT is probably very limited when we consider examples that address operational artefacts at the level of the business layer such as in case 7 from Appendix 4 that investigates guidelines for sustainable business model innovation, and in case 17 from Appendix 4 that assesses adoption of innovation policies in government. This scoping discussion has a parallel with an earlier debate on scoping of IT artefacts (Alter, 2015), whether to include, for example, the social aspects of artefact usage as part of its scope, and possibly treat these as separate artefacts. At the opposite side of the spectrum, the integration of the concept of action rules in the field of the management sciences has been floated by the introduction of 'technological' rules that steer the interventions that are required in strategic management (van Aken, 2004). A number of the cases in the empirical examples from Appendix 4 squarely fall within this category. These scoping discussions will require further debate.

The second scope discussion pertains to the type of contexts our proposed typology can be projected into. From the example of civil engineering included to illustrate the benefits of theorizing across a family, it is clear that parallels exist with such a very different context. Certainly the large enterprise context and software engineering that traditionally have been the subject matter of a lot of DSR studies are in scope. Other contexts of current interest in the IS research community are business ecosystems, human interaction, and using artificial and autonomous intelligence. See also Iivari (2007) for an early view on application usages beyond the classical IS which included a number of what then seemed like exotic categories such as gaming, art, or pets. As the definitions for the outcome typology are generic, we see no reason why it could not play to these. It will eventually be restricted by the applicability of the core constituents such as relationship-based *models* and logic-based *statements*, and the structure of supporting knowledge—to the domain of interest.

8.4   Classifying Outcomes

Researchers and practitioners require a structured approach to classify the outcomes of their research or projects according to the typology. Methods for classifying objects according to a typology (and taxonomy) have been documented extensively (Bailey, 1994). The process needs to match the differentiating characteristics of an artefact to those of the typology. In its simplest form, this implies identifying the dimensions that an artefact incorporates and the definition of the characteristic values on each, and matching these to those of the outcome typology. In case of an exact match this is straightforward However, as the mapping of existing classifications illustrates, there may be differences in the level of decomposition (e.g., prescription, recommendation, lesson, and guideline guidance are possible decompositions of design principles), in the naming (principles of form and function and design principles), and the semantics (is a model a set of propositions or an architecture blueprint?) even if the dimensions match. This requires some form of abstraction of detailed types, and translation of names and definitions. The examples of these mappings in both Appendix 2 and Appendix 4 illustrate that this is done without problem, as the complexity of the typology is limited.

If dimensions would be found to differ, then the mapping becomes more difficult. Particularly in the domain of the social sciences where Baily performed his research, a typology can have a very large number of dimensions. Some form of reduction is then required to limit the number of types that need to be named and that matter. They centre on identification of key types (e.g. ideal, constructed, or polar), and assessing the extent that an artefact's characteristics match to those of the reduced type. We do not see that need on the level of the typology, it may come back when creating more detailed taxonomies in specific contexts, e.g. the taxonomy of mobile applications that Nickerson et al. (2013) use as an example to illustrate their method.

Complexities do arise if a research study covers multiple outcomes or if the artefacts produced are not in a pure form. In such cases, a preliminary phase is required that splits the outcome of a study and then classifies the resulting outcomes. Artefacts that are not in a pure form are difficult to deal with. This often is the case in large and complex methods that underpin practitioner competencies. For example, process and product aspects may be combined in the same description documents. In such cases, for the overarching artefact, the term framework comes closest to a categorization. Clearly defined constituents then can be mapped more appropriately.

9 Conclusion

We have proposed a DSR outcome typology that focuses on outcomes of DSR as a research discipline across diverse contexts, while also considering design practice in more specific areas of subject matter by introducing the concept of contextualized taxonomies. We use highly differentiating, foundational concepts as choice for the dimensions that create the underlying systematization. Three of these stand out: Firstly, our use of the terms artefact design, knowledge, and theory is intended to follow up on the suggestion to reduce the 'overload' on the term artefact (Baiyere et al., 2015) by separating designs of artefact classes from knowledge across families of classes, and using the term design theory as the envelope that creates coherent bundles of both design and knowledge 'primitives' now with an extended scope that runs across a family. Other differentiations that matter are those between models and statements or between process and product. Both differentiations are running as broken threads through the evolution of DSR since its inception, mostly implicit, and with confusing alterations. In the choice of our leaf level items and terms we have aspired to create a simple as possible harmonization and standardization template We intended to organize this template as logically as possible and to upgrade a terminology that often was proposed decades ago, to what is used in today's research and practice. This lays the groundwork for a harmonized language that can integrate across research and practice.

Secondly, we have delineated the terms we use sharply to achieve definitional clarity. This puts a spotlight on the core of what the DSR discipline is concerned with. We do inherit from previous authors in defining them but are strict in applying them to only one of the types. Where this provides the rigour that we have aspired to achieve, it also creates risks with respect to gaining acceptance for such common terms that have been used previously so broadly. For example, our definition of the term knowledge follows the common definition that it cannot be materialized but reserves this term for insights across classes of artefacts (such as taxonomies, patterns). This strictly delineated definition implies that we do not count as knowledge the propositional statements that are part of a class design, and that increasingly have been positioned as part of the core of mature design theory. We refer to these as statements (referring to the syntax), or as design logic (referring to the semantics). We derive from Cross (2001) who identifies three sources of design knowledge: humans that create designs, processes used to perform design, and existing artefacts themselves, that the presence of design principles can be derived by observing the material properties of an instantiated artefact. As it will be difficult to fully give up on the usage of the term knowledge for propositional statements (and it might not be fully justified as well to fully do so), we suggest referring to this type of logic by qualifying it as *'embodied'* (design) knowledge. Using the term embodiment of knowledge may seem at crossroads with our observation that knowledge remains abstract and cannot be materialized. Embodiment, however, does not per se imply materialization, and it reflects quite well the instantiation as a source of 'embodied' knowledge.

Another example where terminology may not be settled that crisply is the emphasis on materialization as a key aspect of an artefact. This line of thought follows initial authors in the field such as Simon (1996) who emphasized artefacts as constructed things, adding to this a focus on an inner and outer environment, with external affordances that are different from internal construction relationships. A too strict definition along the lines of materialization and inner versus outer environment is not without problems, however. This surfaces when trying to decide the scope of contextualization, such as into the large enterprise context. Less tangible artefacts such as strategies and cultural, social, and innovation aspects might not pass the materialization test. As discussed before, this should remain a topic for future debate.

An area where we have been less strict is the differentiation of Ω-knowledge and Λ-knowledge, which brings its own acceptance risks, as it is so deeply rooted in the tradition of DSR as discipline. We have proposed to include most of the knowledge items across artefact classes that have until now been classified as Ω-knowledge such as dictionaries, taxonomies, frameworks, patterns, etc., on the ground that they can be both observed and constructed. This equivalence has led us to drop the genre of inquiry (Baskerville et al., 2015) as a differentiator in the typology. For defining a research project, the choice for either a qualitative or design research approach results in very different setups. For the outcome, however, if both genres can produce the same type, the genre of inquiry should not be a primary differentiator when designing the DSR typology.

Thirdly, we have evaluated our proposal through criteria from both IS (for taxonomy development) and from DSR (for artefact development). Our mappings of existing classifications and empirical samples confirm that what we propose can cover today's outputs. Feedback from our focal group of PhD students confirms that the proposed structure has utility potential, but due to its abstract nature, requires clear explanations and examples for these less experienced researchers.

Future research will need to clarify the completeness of the typology, the correctness of the choice of dimensions and characteristics, and the understandability of the terminology. In addition, more detailing of contextual taxonomies is an important topic to bridge research into practice. This requires digging into large populations of artefacts to assess them and iterate with the results. The example dimensions that have been identified in Table 10 require confirmation and other candidates may be added. Taxonomy development benefits from linkages with practitioner competencies to harvest such populations. Such integration is also required to ensure shared terminology and understanding and requires some form of governance to be established, similar to, e.g., the role that SWEBOK plays in the software engineering community (Bourque & Fairley, 2014). Preferably agreement and consensus should be reached on key typology terms, such as context, artefact, knowledge, and theory (see previous section), and the adoption of terms for the constituents in the various quadrants. This will require DSR authors as well as practitioners to voice their opinions and engage in debates.

Where we have touched on the representations of artefacts, for example the difference between models and propositions, we would welcome a more systematic view on how artefacts, knowledge, and theories are structured both from a semantic and syntactic perspective. The parallel that has been considered by authors defining the nature of design theories, with those in the natural and social sciences, where law-like relationship between units (Dubin, 1978) is mirrored in DSR in the principles that reference models (Gregor, 2006) is a superficial one. As the extent to which our outcome typology supports other contexts than IS, ES, and SE will likely depend on the extent that these 'law like' principles will support relationships in these other domains, further foundational research in this area would be useful. Interesting here, to understand these relationships better, is the area where DSR can connect with other research paradigms. As an example, consider how Niehaves and Ortbach (2016) explain the relationship between the internal construction and outcome with a structure that leans on structured equation modelling, which differs considerably from the logic-based representation of principles.

An increased understanding of the processes that contextualize and project designs would be required. This not only applies to the operations themselves, such as detailed by Prat et al. (2022), but also to the roles and responsibilities with respect to how knowledge is gained at the foundational level, is enriched when it is applied to an area of practice, and flows into practitioner competencies. For example, requirements and design principles are both important constituents in research and practice, but with different intent and detailing. We have emphasized in our use of terms the discovery aspect that differentiates the development of artefact designs in research from those in practice. From their role in discovery, requirements and design principles in research are more aimed at scoping and delineation of the problem space and design space, and as a consequence much less detailed, and often defined 'after the fact' (Maedche et al., 2019). In the example that we used to illustrate leaf entry detailing in Sect. 6, a very limited number of requirements and design principles were used, and indeed developed only after the discovery process.

Looking towards the future, we may expect a considerable larger array of environments and research methods that will need to be addressed. Where initially the focus of design researchers was on information rich systems, this has broadened with every new application of information technology such as in social online communities, and it will further develop in areas such as robotics and artificial or hybrid intelligence. Every new research area brings its own view of next-generation artefacts knowledge and theories. Understanding DSR outcomes is a relevant topic, therefore, that warrants the continued attention of the scientific and practitioner community.

Appendix 1. Glossary with Indicator Examples

Table 10 includes the results of the operationalization following (Bailey, 1994). It lists definitions and indicator examples selected from the large enterprise context from several sources:

- Practitioner methods such as enterprise architecture, program management
- Examples from the typology demonstration in Sect. 6
- Inline examples in the paper at hand
- Examples from the DSR and broader IS literature on research methods

Table 10 Definitions and indicator examples

Design meta-types	Definition	Examples
SOLUTION DESIGN		
SOLUTION DESIGN	The product view (the 'what') of design. It covers the total of the design lifecycle (including requirement, design, and evaluation) of a single class of artefacts. **Note:** We cover under this definition less tangible artefacts such as strategies and plans that express intent/control on (future) artefacts.	• A 'strategic profile', a 'business strategy', a 'tactical intervention', a 'business model', a 'target operating model', a 'transformation roadmap', a 'balanced scorecard', an 'innovation portfolio', an 'organizational maturity model', an 'operating model', a 'technology model', a 'platform', etc.

(continued)

Table 10 (continued)

Design meta-types	Definition	Examples
PROPOSITION, Requirements	Assertions of the demands on the artefact (as established from the context of discovery)	• 'The operating model should support straight through operations of standard transactions' • 'The governance model should support delegation of rights through self-service' • 'The technology platform should support fault resilient operations' • 'The governance model should support modes of control that match different degrees of enforcement ability in ecosystems' • 'The "digitization strategy" should support dual mode business set up, fully digital and hybrid'
PROPOSITION, Design Principles	Assertions of the (prescriptive) guidelines on the construction of the artefact that bridge from requirements to specification (as established from the context of design)	• 'Designed adaptability', 'Simple enough', 'Build on existing methods' (see Sect. 6).
PROPOSITION, Outcome Statements	Assertions and/or measures of external behaviour and related outcomes of the artefact in use (as established from the context of justification)	• 'The new production model improves time to market and at the same time lower costs' • 'The "digitization strategy" enables us becoming a digital frontrunner'
MODELS, Specification model	A structured specification of artefact characteristics (features and affordances) at the external interface in relation to their context of use.	• The features that a 'Digital Twin' provides, and how these combine to provide affordances to the needs of specific use cases • The key characteristics of a transformation roadmap, and how these support the needs of specific change cases
MODELS, Design model	A relationship model that describes the fundamental organization of an artefact's constituents.	• A 'reference architecture' that describes the component blueprints for a specific solution area: such as for Digital Twins, eCommerce, Cognitive Solutions, etc. • A 'business canvas model' that specifies the essential elements of a business and their relationships, such as values propositions, customers, resources, etc. • An 'organizational model' that describes the organizational units and their relationships • A 'business process model' of logistics processes that covers the needs of the different types of partner groups in the ecosystem.

(continued)

Table 10 (continued)

Design meta-types	Definition	Examples
MODELS, Performance	A structured description and/or assessment of the result of artefact behaviour	• A 'use case' model for selected outcomes • A 'capability' model that traces the linkage between goal, capability, and resource • A 'course of action' model that traces the linkage between outcome, course of action, capability, and behaviour • A 'balanced scorecard' that monitors key performance indicators against strategic thresholds
METHOD DESIGN		
METHOD DESIGN	The process view (the 'how') of the total of the design lifecycle of a single class of information systems.	• 'Enterprise architecture' method, 'Business model canvas' method, and 'Structured Business Reporting' method
TECHNIQUE, Analysis	Assessment techniques specify how to perform specific types of analysis, such as problem analysis, change analysis, and intent analysis	• A 'problem analysis' technique in design phase that analyses how issues contribute to problems • An 'impact analysis' technique in discovery phase that assesses the impact of trends on the operating model • A 'change analysis' technique in design phase that analyses the consequences of specific changes • An 'intent analysis' technique in justification phase that analyses the purpose of specific actions and intended outcomes
TECHNIQUE, Design	Design techniques specify how to perform design for a specific type of model	• 'Operating model partitioning adopts perspectives that produce coherent and well isolated parts'
TECHNIQUE, Evaluation	Evaluation techniques specify how to perform evaluation of specific artefact affordances	• 'Evaluation can be performed by observations/testing in cases/experiments or analytical/descriptive reasoning' (Venable et al., 2016)
MODEL, Discovery Process	The ordered set of tasks that need to be executed to assess the context of discovery	• Scan the environment for new developments and assess their usefulness in a specific context • Perform root cause analysis of existing classification, and extract the list of dimensions
MODEL, Design Process	The ordered set of tasks that need to be executed to design an artefact	• Peffers et al. (2007) identify six process steps for a design theory: (1) problem identification and motivation, (2) definition of the objectives for a solution, (3) design and development, (4) demonstration, (5) evaluation, and (6) communication.

(continued)

Table 10 (continued)

Design meta-types	Definition	Examples
MODEL, Evaluation Process	The ordered set of tasks that need to be executed to evaluate an artefact's design and use in a specific context	• Analyse constituents included in balanced score card in a specific context • Assess optimizations, adjust design, start next evaluation cycle.
SOLUTION KNOWLEDGE		
SOLUTION KNOWLEDGE	The knowledge view that applies to a family of artefact solution classes and that stretches across four abstraction levels	• See separate items
DEFINITION, Dictionary	Definitions of terminology and concepts that provide the language to describe the context	• Stakeholders, responsibilities, rights, etc., are concepts used in the governance domain of the enterprise context • Context of discovery, creation, and justification demarcates phases in the artefact's lifecycle
DEFINITION, Subject Matter Domain	Coherent areas from the design space populated with webs of related constructs, that artefacts can be scoped to	• Production, governance, transformation, innovation, and culture domains are coherent areas of the large enterprise design space.
CLASSIFICATION, Catalogue, Taxonomy,	Sequential or hierarchical categorization of solution models based on analysis (Gregor, 2006) of key dimensions	• A catalogue of governance models, organized on type of enforcement
EXPLANATION, Solution (Model) Patterns	Types of solutions that relate (Gregor, 2006) specific constructions and their features with specific behaviour in specific context.	• Design patterns for integrating legacy systems, primed on the integration mechanism (services based, replication based, master data based, etc.) • eCommerce patterns, primed on role in the value chains (advisor, distributor, marketplace, web seller, etc.).
EXPLANATION, Operational Rules	Rules that connect artefact features and affordances with outcomes, aimed at specific patterns of behaviour	• A set of interventions that have been developed to invoke when specific unwanted patterns of interactions occur.
JUSTIFICATION, Foundational Theories	'Deep' theories that underly causal mechanisms that predict (Gregor, 2006) how the artefact behaviour will be	• The Technology Acceptance model that explains which factors determine the adoption 'friendliness' of a solution.
JUSTIFICATION, Kernel Theories	'Applied' IS theories that can be derived top down from foundational theories, or abstracted from explanatory theories that underpin mature designs, or come from other disciplines	• 'A theory of interpersonal trust, which belongs as a reference theory to the social sciences..' that explains how '. . trust is engendered in online communications' (Gregor, 2009).

(continued)

Table 10 (continued)

Design meta-types	Definition	Examples
METHOD KNOWLEDGE		
METHOD KNOWLEDGE	The knowledge view that applies to a family of artefact method classes and that stretches across four abstraction levels	• See separate items
DEFINITION, Standards	Definitions of standards that prescribe the exact syntax and semantics of specific key areas of methods	• Standards for modelling such as UML • Industry-specific standards for defining message exchanges
DEFINITION, Metrics	The parameters used to quantify outcome, behaviour, etc.	• Measures for business performance in a 'Balanced Scorecard' method
CLASSIFICATION, Catalogue	A container of method constituents that are sorted based upon simple characteristics (name, type of method operation supported, etc.)	• A catalogue of method fragments that are building blocks for situated method construction (Brinkkemper et al., 1999).
CLASSIFICATION, Framework	An orderly process-driven multidimensional collection of a diversity of method constituents (tasks and inputs/outputs)	• TOGAF framework that creates an orderly collection of both method tasks and associated deliverables, with the architectural process leading the ordering
EXPLANATION, Method (Process) Patterns	Types of contextualized approaches to solving a similar class of problems	• A situated approach to business IT alignment that Saat et al. (2011) propose. They intend to preconfigure artefacts based upon alignment focus, such as business demand-driven, IT infrastructure-driven, innovation-driven, or compliance-driven.
EXPLANATION, (Method) Technique Patterns	Types of contextualized techniques that solve a similar class of problems	• Techniques identified by Langley (1999) to analyse process data applied to IS by Barquet et al. (2017): how to collect and evaluate them and how to describe them across cycles.
JUSTIFICATION, Foundational Theories	Definition as for Solution knowledge	• Hermeneutics (Gregory & Muntermann, 2014) as a foundational theory that assesses the role of logic in reasoning versus the role of rules of thumb and the heuristic search process.
JUSTIFICATION, Kernel Theories	Definition as for solution knowledge	• Types of logic developed in the philosophy of science (inductive, deductive, and abductive) that are used to develop the different approaches to artefact related theorizing (Fischer & Gregor, 2011).

Appendix 2. Mapping of Related Work

This Appendix contains the results of the mapping of existing classifications from Tables 1 and 2 to our typology proposal. Figure 4 depicts the results visually.

The black circles represent the mappings of the conceptual classifications from Table 2 as identified in Table 10, and the grey circles represent the mappings of empirical classifications from Table 3 as identified in Table 11.[15]

Mapping of conceptually derived classifications: The classifications from this category address a coherent part of the typology's quadrants that matches the conceptual viewpoints they adopted. The early classifications (A. (March & Smith, 1995), B. (Vaishnavi & Kuechler, 2004; Vaishanavi et al., 2019), and C.1 (Walls et al., 1992), C.2 (Gregor & Jones, 2007), and C.3 (Venable, 2013)) focus on the design and hence mostly map to the solution Design quadrant, with some excursions into the definitional part of the knowledge quadrant. Classification D. (Gregor & Hevner, 2013) includes a detailing of Ω-knowledge that we include as knowledge across classes in our proposed classification and hence these also extend into the knowledge quadrants. Classification E. (Drechsler & Hevner, 2018) focuses on differentiating solution design knowledge (that contains propositional knowledge about design) from solution design entities (that contain models), with as a result its mappings showing up mostly in the proposition and model parts of the Solution Design quadrant.

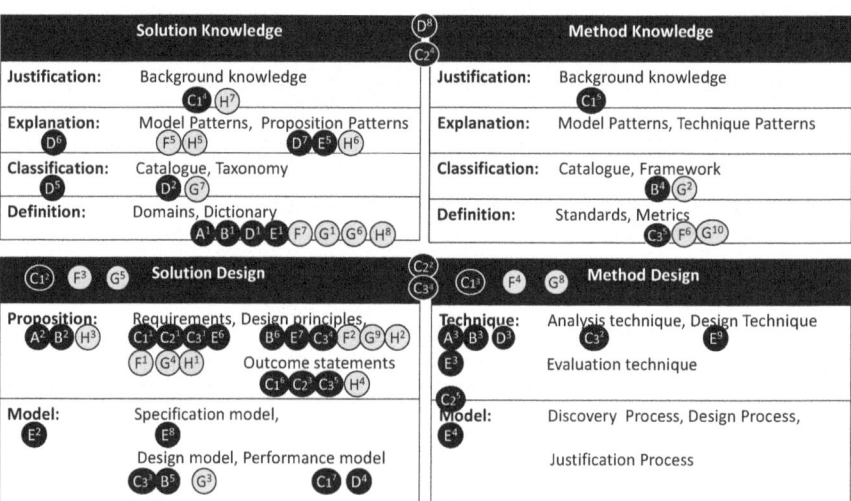

Fig. 4 Mapping existing classifications to the DSR outcome typology

---

[15] The letter symbols refer to the classification, with the letter-suffix combination referencing the constituent labels identified in Tables 9 and 10.

Mapping of empirically derived classifications: The empirically derived classifications from this category display a larger scatter, as they generate the structure bottom up. Those that focus on artefacts from DESRIST (F. (Offermann et al., 2010); G. (Mwilua et al., 2016)) produce quite basic artefacts[16] that map across the Solution Design quadrants, with only some extending into the Knowledge quadrants. H. (Dwivedi et al., 2014) addresses a broader set of papers selected from multiple sources, and with a narrower BI subject matter focus; these contribute more mappings to the Solution quadrant (taxonomy, ontology, etc.). Obviously the knowledge contributions that H. (Dwivedi et al., 2014) extract from the theorizing literature, map to the higher levels of the Solution knowledge quadrants, as they address a broader view of theory composition (e.g. mid-range theory, generative mechanism, etc.).

Overall most of the mappings of both categories are to the Design quadrants, with the method quadrants more sparsely populated than the design quadrants and with less detail. For the classifications from Table 2, this can be partly explained by the fact that some do not use this as a differentiating dimension, e.g. C.2 (Gregor & Jones, 2007). For the empirical ones, this appears to suggest that, if this large difference in population is not due to other sources such as for example classification bias, that researchers tend to focus on the design of the artefact rather than the method to develop it.

Harmonization: To be able to precisely map leaf items, harmonization of the individual items is required with those in the proposed classification. Difference arises partly because of different levels in the structure, decomposition, and semantics. It requires abstracting details away where terms are more specific, but also adjusting the naming and potentially the definition of terms where they address the same level and differently named contents and definitions. As an example of the first, *recommendation, lesson*, and *guideline* from H. (Dwivedi et al., 2014) are all abstracted to *design principles* (with specific attributes such as 'recommendation', instructive', 'guiding', 'or 'prescriptive'), *representation* and *syntax* that are detailed attributes of *models* from D. (Gregor & Hevner, 2013) are mapped as meta-information to the *dictionary*, and *efficacy, effectiveness*, and *efficiency* from C.3 (Venable, 2013) are mapped to parameters that may be referenced in *outcome* statements, with corresponding *metrics* specified in the Method knowledge quadrant.

Tables 9 and 10 include the mapping of the classifications in Tables 11 and 12 to the typology from Fig. 2. The suffix number attached to each type is used to cross reference it in the visualization of the mapping in Fig. 3 in the mainline text (Sect. 7.1).

---

[16] Perhaps due to the fact that DESRIST paper are conference papers of limited length.

Table 11 Mapping of conceptual artefact classifications

Classification	Mapping
A. (March & Smith, 1995) This influential yet simple four part enumeration addresses two major artefact types that differentiate the what from the how (dimension 2, Table 5). **Constructs**[A1] become part of the Dictionary leaf type (in the Definitional layer). **Models**[A2] and **Methods**[A3] map to the Solution Design and Method quadrants, following the differentiation between process and product (dimension 2, Table 5). Models (defined as sets of principles) map to Propositions, following the differentiation between models and statements (dimension 4, Table 5), Methods that are defined as 'a set of steps (an algorithm or guideline) used to perform a task' (March & Smith, 1995, p. 257), we interpret to cover the technique and hence we map them to the technique subtype of the Solution method quadrant. **Instantiations** are part of an implementation space. We interleave a process of contextualization.	
B. (Vaishnavi & Kuechler, 2004; Vaishnavi et al., 2019) This handbook version adds a number of subtypes that mostly map to design subtypes and introduces the concept of a Design theory that maps to an extended form. **Construct**[B1], **Models**[B2], **Methods**[B3], **Instantiation:** Adopt the definitions of A. (March & Smith, 1995) and hence map as above. **Frameworks**[B4] (defined as 'real or conceptual guides to serve as support or guide'), **Architectures**[B5] (defined as 'high level structures of systems'), and **Principles**[B6] (defined as 'core principles and concepts to guide design') are constituents of designs and methods and map to the same subtypes in these two bottom quadrants, following the differentiation between phases in the lifecycle (dimension 3, Table 5). **Design theories** map to the same aggregated type, but now extended to include knowledge constituents.	
C.1 (Walls et al., 1992) **C.2** (Gregor & Jones, 2007) **C.3** (Venable, 2013) Design constituents from these three classifications C.1–C.3 of a design theory map to corresponding (sub) types from the design quadrants, based on their place in the lifecycle (dimension 3, Table 5). And theory constituents from these classifications map to the justification layer of the knowledge quadrants, following the differentiation between design and knowledge (dimension 5, Table 5) and between knowledge abstraction levels (dimension 6, Table 5). The harmonization applied: C.1 **Meta-requirements**[C1.1] ('describe goals'), **Meta-design**[C1.2] ('describes a class of artefacts'), and **Design Method**[C1.3] ('description of procedures') map as requirement, solution design, and solution method (as no differentiating details are provided). **Kernel product**[C1.4] or **process**[C1.5] theories map to the justification layer of the knowledge quadrants. **Testable product**[C1.6] ('the meta-design satisfies the meta-requirements.') or **process**[C1.7] hypothesis ('the design method results in an artifact which is consistent with the meta-design') maps to outcome statements, and performance model. C.2 **Purpose and Scope**[C2.1] ('meta-requirements or goals') map to requirements. **Principles of Form** and **Function**[C2.2] (are defined both as principles and abstract blueprint or architecture) map to solution design and method. **Artefact mutability** we did not define as a separate subtype, but included as design principles or behavioural statements that focus on mutability—when defined as propositions, or as (parts of) design or specification models—when defined as models.[a] **Testable Propositions**[C2.3] map to outcome statements. **Justificatory Knowledge**[C2.4] maps to the justification layer of both knowledge quadrants shown in the middle. **Principles of Implementation**[C2.5] ('processes for implementing') map to the method design quadrant either as models or techniques depending on the representation (shown in between). See for **Constructs** and **Expository Instantiation** under A. (March & Smith, 1995). C.3 The three categories map to their place in the design lifecycle: **General Requirements:** Constituents of this category all map to subtypes from the context of the problem. **Desired Goals** and **Functional Requirements**[C3.1] map to requirements, and **Constraints or antigoals**[C3.2] map to specific types of analysis techniques. **General Design:** Constituents of this category all map to subtypes from the context of solution. **Components** and **Relationships**[C3.3] are included as constituents of models, **Principles of Form/Function**[C3.4] and **Artefact mutability** map as described above for the C.2 Gregor and Jones. **Utility:** Constituents of this category all map to subtypes from the context of evaluation: **Efficacy, Effectiveness,** and **Efficiency**[C3.5] map to parameters that may be referenced in outcome statements, with corresponding metrics specified in the method knowledge quadrant.	

(continued)

Table 11 (continued)

Classification	Mapping

D. (Gregor & Hevner, 2013)

Both Λ-knowledge and Ω-knowledge are subtyped and then further detailed with fine-grained values. Constituents of Λ-knowledge map to the lower design quadrants and constituents of Ω-knowledge map to the upper knowledge quadrants, following the differentiation between design and knowledge (dimension 5, Table 5). The subtyping of Ω-knowledge differentiates according to the knowledge abstraction levels (dimension 6, Table 5). The fine-grained values do not produce new leaf types but are included as attributes. The harmonization applied:

Λ-knowledge:
- **Constructs** see A. (March & Smith, 1995). The detailing into **Concepts and Symbols[D1]** can be part of the meta information in the Dictionary.
- **Model** may either be mapped to model or statement or both dependent on its specific definition (diagrams, propositions/instructions, or both); its detailing into **Representation and Syntax[D2]** may be included as meta-level information in the catalogue leaf type (in the classification layer).
- The term **Methods** and its detailing into **Techniques[D3]** are mapped with the same sub(typing) and name to the design method quadrant. See for the subtyping into **Algorithm** the description in Table 21 (under the F. Offermann et al. classification).
- For **Instantiations** see A. (March & Smith, 1995).

Design theories map to the same definition we use as aggregates of constituents, but with an extended scope of design and knowledge types.

Ω-knowledge:

Phenomena subtypes map partly to the design quadrants and partly to the knowledge quadrants:
- **Observations and Measurement[D4]** map to performance statements, both subtypes in the evaluation part of the design lifecycle (dimension 3, Table 5).
- **Classification** and **Cataloguing[D5]** map with the same name and meaning to the classification level of the knowledge quadrant.

Sensemaking subtypes map to the explanation and justification levels of the knowledge quadrants:
- **Regularities** and **Patterns[D6]** map to proposition and model patterns.
- **Principles[D7]** map to design principles (when addressing construction) or regularities (when addressing behaviour).
- **Natural Laws and Theories[D8]** provide justification knowledge.

E. (Drechsler & Hevner, 2018)

Solution Design Entities and **Solution Design knowledge** largely map to the models and statements subtypes of the bottom level design quadrants, following the differentiation between models and statements (dimension 4, Table 5).

The harmonization applied:

Solution Design Entities:
- **Meta-artefacts (Constructs[E1], Models[E2], Methods[E3])** see A. (March & Smith, 1995); except for **Models** that are typed as 'entities' that are differentiated against 'knowledge' (that largely consists of propositional logic), and we hence map to the term models.
- **Artefact instances (Systems, Products,** and **Processes)** are all instantiations (see A. (March & Smith, 1995)) with some specific subtyping that is not further defined but matches an enterprise level context.
- **Implementation, Instantiation,** and **Intervention** are contextualization and instantiation processes, largely out of scope for this paper.
- **Artefact Evolution** processes are comparable to the artefact mutability subtype in C.2 (Gregor & Jones, 2007) (see over there for our harmonization).
- **Solution Design processes and Design Systems[E4]** are methods to perform the design and as such map to our method models in the solution method quadrant.

Solution Design Knowledge:
- **Knowledge for Action**: The subtype **Technological Rules[E5]** are event and action focused and map to proposition patterns in the knowledge quadrant
- **Knowledge for Entity Realization**: The subtypes **Requirements[E6]** and **Principles[E7]** map to statements of the same subtype in the design quadrant, differentiating on their place in the design lifecycle (dimension 3, Table 5). The subtype **Features[E8]** can be included as detail of the specification subtype.
- **Knowledge for Solution Design Processes and Systems:** The subtypes in this category are largely out of scope.: **Design Techniques[E9]** map to method techniques, subtype design, with the same meaning, **Engagement method** is part of the contextualization and implementation processes, largely out of scope for this paper. **Research method** is a meta-level process at the level of DSR as a science, e.g., covering the research process (Peffers et al., 2007), evaluation criteria (Prat et al., 2015), etc., out of scope for this paper.

[a] See the detailed example in Sect. 6 that is fully dedicated to the mutability of solutions

Table 12 Mapping of empirical artefact classifications

Classification	Mapping
F. (Offermann et al., 2010)	

The enumeration of artefact types harvested from DESRIST paper is little differentiated and scattered across the classification we propose, with some contextual naming bias.

Requirement[F1] **and Guideline**[F2], **System Design**[F3], and **Method**[F4] are design constituents that map to constituents from the design quadrants, differentiating between product and process (dimension 2, Table 5), and phases in the lifecycle (dimension 3, Table 5). **System Design** is a term that we consider to be specific for a Large Enterprise context and may be obtained after projecting a (set of) models and/or proposition(s). **Requirement** and **Method** map with the same name as subtype of the solution design quadrant and as the overall type of the solution method quadrant. **Guideline** maps as design principle (optional rather than prescriptive). **Patterns**[F5] and **Metric**[F6] are knowledge constituents that map accordingly to the subtypes with the same names in the knowledge quadrant. **Language/Notation**[F7] are knowledge constituents that can be included as grammar and syntax rules in the Dictionary type. **Algorithm** is a term that we consider to be specific for a Software Engineering context and may be obtained after projecting a (set of) technique(s) and/or proposition(s).

G. (Mwilua et al., 2016)

Classifying the set of artefact types harvested from BI papers under the design focused classification of A. (March & Smith, 1995) adds a large number of subtypes most of which map to the design quadrants, plus some that map to the lower abstraction levels of the knowledge quadrants.

Construct: **Language, Meta-model, Concept**[G1]. All are definitions of the design space and can be included as details in the Dictionary, as concepts, grammar, and syntax rules (language), and space dimensions (meta-model).

Models: **Framework**[G2], **Architecture**[G3], **Requirement**[G4] are mapped as subtypes to the design quadrants (Design model, Requirement) or the knowledge quadrants (Framework). See for **System Design**[G5] above under F. Offermann et al. **Ontology**[G6] can be included as details in the dictionary (as concepts, grammar, and syntax rules). **Taxonomy**[G7] maps to the same subtype in the classification layer of the knowledge quadrant

Method: **Methodology**[G8], **Guideline**[G9], **Algorithm, Method Fragment, Metric**[G10]. For **Guideline, Algorithm,** and **Metric,** see F. Offermann et al. **Method Fragment** is defined as a method component that can be reused across context. We refer to these as subtypes.

Methodology actually refers to the method and is introduced to avoid confusion between the category and the subcategory. Our subtyping avoids this term duplication of terms.

Instantiation: **Implemented system, Example**. See A. (March & Smith, 1995).

Note: The definitions of meta-model and ontology that Mwilua et al. (2016, pp. 110–111) use are similar: they both reference concepts of a design space and semantic rules for specifying or combining them. The artefacts that they are applied to are the data integration design space (ontology) and a multi-dimensional data warehouse design space (meta-model), and these emphasize different aspects.

(continued)

Table 12 (continued)

Classification	Mapping
H. (Dwivedi et al., 2016)	

This undifferentiated enumeration of knowledge contributions harvested from DESRIST papers mostly map them to the design quadrants (differentiated across their place in the design lifecycle), while those from theorizing papers extend well into the knowledge quadrants, across all levels. The DESRIST papers return a number of informal design-oriented subtypes that are mapped as further refinements of more mature subtypes.

Knowledge contributions identified in DESRIST papers: Design Requirement[H1] maps to requirements, **Recommendation, Guideline, Lesson**, and **Design principle**[H2] map to design principle (with specific attributes such as 'recommendation', 'guiding', 'instructive', or 'prescriptive'), **Proposition**[H3] maps to proposition, **Hypothesis**[H4] maps to outcome statements, **Design Patterns**[H5] map to patterns, **Generative Mechanisms**[H6] (van Aken, 2004) are the descriptive observation of a pattern that can be turned into a technological rule (see under E. (Drechsler & Hevner, 2018)).

Knowledge contributions theorized in the literature: **Design Theory** maps to design theory, applied **Mode 2 Knowledge**[H7] can be understood as substantive knowledge from a domain and maps to justification knowledge, **Design Proposition**[H3] maps to proposition, for technological rule and generative mechanism see above, mid-range theories map to justification knowledge, **Design Principle** and **Principles of Form and Function**[H2] (and map to Design Principles see the discussion under C.2 (Gregor & Jones, 2007)), **Nascent** (level 2) and **Design** (level 3) theories categorize theories based on a maturity level, which may be recorded as an attribute of a theory in the Dictionary[H8].

Appendix 3. Feedback from Our Teaching Practice

Feedback on the current problems with existing classifications and the value of the proposed typology was obtained from three focal groups of Ph.D. students who attended a DSR methodology course in subsequent years. In the two-week course, run by one of the authors, PhD students were instructed on DSR methodology and had to develop a DSR research design in four iterations. In the first group, at the start of our research, students were presented with two existing classifications A. (March & Smith, 1995) and B. (Vaishnavi & Kuechler, 2004; Vaishnavi et al., 2019), in the second group halfway through our research with B. (Vaishnavi & Kuechler, 2004; Vaishnavi et al., 2019) and our proposed typology, and in the third group with five existing classifications A. (March & Smith, 1995), B. (Vaishnavi & Kuechler, 2004; Vaishnavi et al., 2019), F. (Offermann et al., 2010), D. (Gregor & Hevner, 2013), H. (Dwivedi et al., 2014), and E. (Drechsler & Hevner, 2018), and our proposed typology. Students were asked to rate each classification on criteria used in our analytical evaluation (comprehensiveness, explanatoryness, usefulness, and usability) and to provide feedback on open questions such as what they missed, usefulness of certain aspects, and the expected benefits.

Feedback from the first group confirmed the lack of an explicit systematization. While the B. (Vaishnavi & Kuechler, 2004; Vaishnavi et al., 2019) classification with more technical artefacts such as architectures, frameworks, and principles, was better understood (the overall rating went from 4.4 to 6.6 on a scale of 10) than the highly generic one from A. (March & Smith, 1995) that includes constructs, models, methods, instantiations, students still struggled considerably with conceptual definitions and differentiation. Assessments for improvements centred on (i) complete and consistent categorizations and definitions, (ii) clear differentiation such as between method and model and the newly added technical artefacts, and between instantiation, theory, and artefacts, as well as (iii) support for extensions with non-IT aspects such as business models and business process model, and with a richer set of artefacts such as pattern, algorithms, taxonomy, etc. The first two suggested improvements address the lack of systematization that we identified as root cause of the weaknesses in current classifications. The third addresses the extension with non-IT aspects that we cover in the Discussion section.

Three benefits from a consistent set of definitions and classifications were consistently mentioned: 1) a common language to describe, scope, and find artefacts, 2) an overview of types and their application that allows to understand the place where your research fits, and 3) a foundation for developing and publishing generalized knowledge.

These benefits correspond with our objectives for this paper (as formulated in the Introduction section).

Feedback from the second group (17 participants from three European countries) that compared the B. (Vaishnavi & Kuechler, 2004; Vaishnavi et al., 2019) classification versus our proposed typology, confirmed the potential value of the proposed typology, but with additional guidance required. Students rated B. (Vaishnavi & Kuechler, 2004; Vaishnavi et al., 2019) classification higher than our proposed typology (4.2 versus 3.6 on a scale of 6), but with unstructured comments on our proposed typology illustrating the potential, e.g. including statements such as 'provides better guidance, but needs more explanation' (2 respondents), 'complexity is justified if there is more context included', 'references to literature / background needed' (2 respondents), 'examples need to be provided', 'too complex for beginners'. When asked to identify the user group that would benefit most, comments on B. (Vaishnavi & Kuechler, 2004; Vaishnavi et al., 2019) included: 'for beginners (easy, overview)' (2 respondents), and on or proposed typology 'only for experienced researchers' (3 respondents).

Feedback from the third group that consisted of four groups of two students that were presented with five existing ones and our proposed typology, was diverse with average scores ranging from 2.5 for H. (Dwivedi et al., 2014), to 3.7 for our proposed typology. Feedback indicated that also here students struggled with the complexity of our proposed typology (e.g. 'lacks clarity in its category, some could be dropped').

We interpret these results as an indication of the fact that students see limitations of existing classifications. They recognize the value of our more elaborate typology in later stages of research design development and for experienced researchers, while they prefer simpler guidance in early stages even if only limited guidance is provided. Not surprising for a group of rather inexperienced researchers, they demanded not only a typology as guidance, but also references and examples.

Appendix 4. Classifying Empirical Data

To validate the coverage that our proposed outcome typology offers, empirical data have been obtained from DESRIST conferences. A convenience sample of artefacts from DESRIST conference is included in Table 13. We selected papers that

Table 13 Classifying empirical artefacts from DESRIST conferences

	Example	Description	DSR outcome type	Contextualization
1	**Machine learning system for predicting decisions of wound treatments**	Feature labelling of wounds, identifying treatment decision rules, validation of prediction accuracy based on expert/novice scoring of samples	**Analysis, Feature Specification, Operational Rules, Performance model**	BS, Healthcare sector
2	**Innovation policy adoption in developing country**	Innovation policy retrieval, design of website for policy access, evaluation of UAT based adoption factors using survey with SEM quantification	**Specification, Design, Performance model, Kernel theory**	BS, Public sector
3	**Public transport support for intellectually disabled (ID) users**	Exploration of problem context using multiple techniques (with end user involvement using photovoice to record ID user comments on pictures taken), extraction of requirements, testing of prototype in simulated transport environment	**Analysis Techniques, Requirement, Specification, Design, Evaluation**	BS/IS, Public sector
4	**Patterns with interdisciplinary design knowledge for smart personal assistants**	Use of kernel theories on cognitive overload for derivation of requirements and design principles to encode interdisciplinary knowledge (on software engineering and privacy regulations). Design of encoding patterns. Performing a field study on practitioners with and without access to encoded patterns.	**Kernel theory, Requirements, Design principles, Solution Patterns, Evaluation**	SE
5	**Multi interest profiling of users based on twitter messages**	Establishing of algorithms that from the tweet contents generate the multi interest profiles. Evaluating based on a sample from an actual population.	**Design, Evaluation**	Social Media, IS,

(continued)

Table 13 (continued)

	Example	Description	DSR outcome type	Contextualization
6	**A framework for classifying design principles**	Establishing of a number of subject matter dimensions that design principles can be perceived from.	**Typology**	Research Method: specializing design principles
7	**A method for developing design principles**	Establishing a number of process dimensions that development of design principles can be perceived from.	**Typology**	Research Method: specializing design principles
8	**A typology of sharing business models**	Top-down conceptual derivation of a typology of sharing business models using four dimensions	**Typology**	Ecosystems, BS
9	**Generation of design principles as a knowledge conversion process**	Use of kernel theory on knowledge conversion to provide a template for a four-step process with specific techniques for generation of design principles. Evaluation using three cases.	**Kernel theory, Design process, Design Techniques, Justification**	Research Method: specializing process for design principles
10	**Development of knowledge contribution diagrams to identify DSR outputs**	Based on previous debates on the composition of complex artefacts, analyses potential dimensions, and proposes a typology for classifying a proposed set of atomic outcomes of DSR projects	**Discovery, Analysis , Typology**	Research Method: specializing the DSR outcome typology
11	**Method for developing strategic mobility agenda for cities**	Using as input established mobility projects, a method is designed, prototyped, and evaluated that allows translation of strategy into choices for solutions	**Analysis, Design process, Evaluate**	BS, Government, Innovation
12	**Design requirement for governing sharing networks**	After analysis of the current literature, a model is proposed that centres on trust as the determining factor, and from there requirements are derived for governance of sharing networks	**Analysis. Model, Design Principles**	Ecosystems, BS

(continued)

Table 13 (continued)

	Example	Description	DSR outcome type	Contextualization
13	**Development of an Information Systems Ontology**	Using automated extracted keywords, and from existing classification schemes, a top-down ontology is developed, and evaluated with a sample of recent author-defined keywords	**Analysis, Design process, Ontology, Evaluation**	IS
14	**AI-supported customer service employees**	Starting with kernel theories that emphasize service employee needs (self-determination, cognitive load), design principles and features are derived for integrating an AI advisory function. Evaluation is performed using a prototype during actual SE interactions.	**Kernel theory, Design principles, Features, Web site design, Evaluation**	BS/IS, customer service
15	**A block chain enabled secure and smart healthcare system**	Main objectives are derived from the context (fairness, privacy, data security), with falsifiable propositions. A design is proposed that improves on deficiencies of existing implementations, using smart contracts between parties, and communication protocols across the blockchain. Quantitative results of a prototype are collected.	**Requirements statements, Outcome statements, Design, Performance model**	IS, Healthcare sector

(continued)

Table 13 (continued)

	Example	Description	DSR outcome type	Contextualization
16	**A conceptual framework for interoperable healthcare systems**	Performs analysis of weaknesses, identifies and literature based identification of governance constituents in the literature. Designs a layered framework (system, process, and mechanism) and evaluates this with expert interviews.	**Analysis, Framework Design, Evaluation**	IS/SE, Healthcare sector, Governance
17	**Design principles for National Innovation Agencies (NIA) in social market economies**	Analyses the need for government sponsored innovation, reviews four existing NIAs, and establishes a framework with design principles for sponsoring that respect the role of the market economy. Evaluates with expert interviews.	**Analysis, Framework, Design principles, Evaluation**	BS, Government, Innovation
18	**Neuro-Adaptive Interface System to Evaluate Product Recommendations in the Context of E-Commerce**	Reviews the literature on the impact of cognitive overload on the efficiency of product recommendations. Develops requirements for a neuroadaptive solution that detects load and adapts recommendations. Performs formative testing with a first user group. Summarizes results in a design theory.	**Literature based analysis, Requirements, Solution design, Evaluation, Design theory**	IS, eCommerce

DESRIST 2020: Hofmann, S., Müller, O., Rossi, M. (eds) Designing for Digital Transformation. Co-Creating Services with Citizens and Industry. Lecture Notes in Computer Science(), vol 12388. Springer, Cham

[1] Mombini, H. *et al.* (2020). Design of a Machine Learning System for Prediction of Chronic Wound Management Decisions. https://doi.org/10.1007/978-3-030-64823-7_2

[2] Senshaw, D., Twinomurinzi, H. (2020). Designing for Digital Government Innovation in Resource Constrained Countries: The Case of Woredas in Ethiopia. https://doi.org/10.1007/978-3-030-64823-7_5

[3] Wass, S., Hansen, L.A., Safari, C. (2020). Designing Transport Supporting Services Together with Users with Intellectual Disabilities. https://doi.org/10.1007/978-3-030-64823-7_6

(continued)

Table 13 (continued)

[4] Dickhaut, E., Janson, A., Leimeister, J.M. (2020). Codifying Interdisciplinary Design Knowledge Through Patterns – The Case of Smart Personal Assistants. https://doi.org/10.1007/978-3-030-64823-7_12

[5] Wandabwa, H., Naeem, M.A., Mirza, F., Pears, R., Nguyen, A. (2020). Multi-interest User Profiling in Short Text Microblogs. https://doi.org/10.1007/978-3-030-64823-7_15

[6] Hansen, M.R.P., Haj-Bolouri, A. (2020). Design Principles Exposition: A Framework for Problematizing Knowledge and Practice in DSR. https://doi.org/10.1007/978-3-030-64823-7_16

[7] Möller, F., Guggenberger, T.M., Otto, B. (2020). Towards a Method for Design Principle Development in Information Systems. https://doi.org/10.1007/978-3-030-64823-7_20

[8] Pouri, M.J., Hilty, L.M. (2020). A Typology of Digital Sharing Business Models: A Design Science Research Approach. https://doi.org/10.1007/978-3-030-64823-7_27

DESRIST 2021: Chandra Kruse, L., Seidel, S., Hausvik, G.I. (eds) The Next Wave of Sociotechnical Design. Lecture Notes in Computer Science(), vol 12807. Springer, Cham

[9] Wass, S., Hansen, L.A., Moe, C.E. (2021). Generation of Design Principles as Knowledge Conversion - Elucidating Dynamics. In: https://doi.org/10.1007/978-3-030-82405-1_17

[10] Schwartz, D.G., Yahav, I. (2021). Knowledge Contribution Diagrams for Design Science Research: A Novel Graphical Technique. https://doi.org/10.1007/978-3-030-82405-1_19

[11] Athanasopoulou, A., Valkenburg, R., den Ouden, E., Turetken, O. (2021). Supporting the Development of Strategic Mobility Agendas for Cities: The Pathway Method. https://doi.org/10.1007/978-3-030-82405-1_10

[12] Jagals, M., Karger, E., Ahlemann, F. (2021). Is Trust Shapeable? Design Requirements for Governing Sharing Networks. https://doi.org/10.1007/978-3-030-82405-1_28

DESRIST 2022. Drechsler, A., Gerber, A., Hevner, A. (eds) The Transdisciplinary Reach of Design Science Research. Lecture Notes in Computer Science, vol 13229. Springer, Cham

[13] Mueller, R.M., Huettemann, S., Larsen, K.R., Yan, S., Handler, A. (2022). Toward an Information Systems Ontology. https://doi.org/10.1007/978-3-031-06516-3_5

[14] Poser, M., Wiethof, C., Banerjee, D., Shankar Subramanian, V., Paucar, R., Bittner, E.A.C. (2022). Let's Team Up with AI! Toward a Hybrid Intelligence System for Online Customer Service. https://doi.org/10.1007/978-3-031-06516-3_11

[15] Das, D., Muthaiah, A., Ruj, S. (2022). Blockchain-Enabled Secure and Smart Healthcare System. https://doi.org/10.1007/978-3-031-06516-3_8

DESRIST 2023. Gerber, A., Baskerville, R. (eds) Design Science Research for a New Society: Society 5.0. Lecture Notes in Computer Science, vol 13873. Springer, Cham

[16] Matshaba, L., Nxozi, M., Herselman, M. (2023). Guiding the Development of Interoperable Health Information Systems: A Conceptual IT Governance Framework. https://doi.org/10.1007/978-3-031-32808-4_9

[17] Lehmann, D.M., Salenius, V.M. (2023). Design Principles for National Innovation Agencies in Social Market Economies https://doi.org/10.1007/978-3-031-32808-4_13

[18] Tadson, B. *et al.* (2023). Neuro-Adaptive Interface System to Evaluate Product Recommendations in the Context of E-Commerce. https://doi.org/10.1007/978-3-031-32808-4_4

contributed interesting cases with a good spread across the typology, and differentiating in characteristics, addressing theory driven versus experience driven analysis of requirements and design principles, business focus versus IS focus, focus on the full lifecycle versus parts such as discovery only, various uses of emerging technologies, different sectors of business and different operational domains, etc. We note that a considerable number of artefacts have been labelled as Research Method; they are not contextualized but are specializations at the level of our generic typology. The large number is not surprising as DESRIST is the 'home' of the community of researchers, who in addition to artefact design spent quite some time on the foundation of DSR as research discipline.

References

Alter, S. (2015). Work system theory as a platform: Response to a research perspective article by Niederman and March. *Journal of the Association for Information Systems, 16*(6), 485–514.

Bailey, K. D. (1994). *Typologies and taxonomies - An introduction to classification techniques.* Sage Publications.

Baiyere, A., Hevner, A. R., Gregor, S., Rossi, M., & Baskerville, R. L. (2015). Artifact and/or theory? Publishing Design Science Research in IS. In *Thirty Sixth International Conference on Information Systems (ICIS 2015).* Fort Worth, Tx.

Barquet, A. P., et al. (2017). Knowledge Accumulation in Design-Oriented Research - Developing and Communicating Knowledge Contributions. Designing the Digital Transformation, Proc. DESRIST 2017. A. Maedche, J. Vom Brocke and A. Hevner. Cham, Springer Nature.

Baskerville, R., Baiyere, A., Gregor, S., Hevner, A. R., & Rossi, M. (2018). Design science research contributions: Finding a balance between artifact and theory. *Journal of the Association for Information Systems, 19*(5), 358–376.

Baskerville, R., & Pries-Heje, J. (2019). Projectability in design science research. *Journal of Information Technology Theory and Application, 20*(1, Article 3).

Baskerville, R. L., Kaul, M., & Storey, V. C. (2015). Genres of inquiry in design-science research: Justification and evaluation of knowledge production. *MIS Quarterly, 39*(3), 541–564.

Baskerville, R. L., & Pries-Heje, J. (2010). Explanatory design theory. *Business & Information Systems Engineering, 2*(5), 271–282.

Benbasat, I., & Zmud, R. W. (2003). The identity crisis within the IS discipline - Defining and communicating the discipline's core properties. *MIS Quarterly, 27*(2), 183–194.

Blalock, H. M. (1979). *Social statistics.* McGraw-Hill.

Blecker, T., & Friedrich, G. (2006). *Mass customization: Challenges and solutions.* Springer.

Bourque, P., & Fairley, R. E. (2014). *Guide to the software engineering body of knowledge.* Version 3.0. from www.swebok.org

Brinkkemper, S., et al. (1999). "Meta-Modelling Based Assembly Techniques for Situational Method Engineering." *Information Systems 24*(3), 209–228.

Bruls, W., Winter, R., Foorthuis, R., van Steenbergen, M., Lankhorst, M., Mommers, B., & Brinkkemper, S. (forthcoming). Business-IT alignment – Where should we go: A view from practice. *EMISA Journal.*

Bruls, W. A. G., Edward, G., Lankhorst, M. M., Winter, R., & Slaets, H. (2021). Industry solution adaptability - An integrated solution model and an integrated analysis and engineering method addressing change in large and complex enterprises. *Enterprise Modelling and Information Systems Architectures – An International Journal, 16*(5), 1–41.

Bucher, T., & Winter, R. (2008). Dissemination and importance of the "method" artifact in the context of design research for information systems. In *Third International Conference on Design Science Research in Information Systems and Technology (DESRIST 2008), Atlanta, GA.* Georgia State University.

Budiardjo, E., & Zamzami, E. (2014). Feature modeling and variability modeling syntactic notation comparison and mapping. *Journal of Computer and Communications, 2*(2), 101–108.

Campbell, A., Gutierrez, M., & Lancelott, M. (2017). *Operating model canvas.* Van Haren.

Cross, N. (2001). Designerly ways of knowing: Design discipline versus design science. *Design Issues, 17*(3), 49–55.

Deng, Q., & Ji, S. (2018). A review of design science research in information systems: Concept, process, outcome, and evaluation. *Pacific Asia Journal of the Association for Information Systems, 10*(1).

Drechsler, A., & Hevner, A. R. (2018). Utilizing, producing, and contributing design knowledge in DSR projects. In S. Chatterjee, K. Dutta, & R. P. Sundarraj (Eds.), *Designing for a digital and globalized world* (pp. 82–97). Springer.

Dubin, R. (1978). *Theory building.* Free Press.

Dwivedi, N., Purao, S., & Straub, D. W. (2014). Knowledge contributions in design science research: A meta-analysis. In M. C. Tremblay, D. VanderMeer, M. Rothenberger, A. Gupta,

& V. Yoon (Eds.), *Advancing the impact of design science: Moving from theory to practice. DESRIST 2014* (pp. 115–131). Springer.

Engel, A., & Reich, Y. (2015). Advancing architecture options theory: Six industrial case studies. *Systems Engineering, 18*(4), 396–414.

Fischer, C., & Gregor, S. (2011). Forms of reasoning in the design science research process. In *Sixth International Conference on Design Science Research in Information Systems and Technology, DESRIST 2011, Milwaukee, Wisconsin.* Springer.

Glass, R. L., & Vessey, I. (1995). Contemporary application - Domain taxonomies. *IEEE Software, 12*(4), 63–76.

Gregor, S. (2006). The nature of theory in information systems. *MIS Quarterly, 30*(3), 611–642.

Gregor, S., Chandra Kruse, L., & Seidel, S. (2020). The anatomy of a design principle. *Journal of the Association for Information Systems, 21*(6), 1622–1652.

Gregor, S., & Hevner, A. R. (2013). Positioning and presenting design science research for maximum impact. *MIS Quarterly, 37*(2), 337–355.

Gregor, S., & Jones, D. (2007). The anatomy of a design theory. *Journal of the Association for Information Systems, 8*(5), 312–335.

Gregory, R. W. and J. Muntermann (2014). "Heuristic Theorizing: Proactively Generating Design Theories." *Information Systems Research 25*(3), 639–653.

Hallsteinsen, S., Stav, E., Solberg, A., & Floch, J. (2006). Using product line techniques to build adaptive systems. In *Software Product Line Conference, International (SPLC)* (pp. 141–150).

Haugen, Ø., Møller-Pedersen, B., Oldevik, J., Olsen, G., & Svendsen, A. (2008). Adding standardized variability to domain specific languages. In *12th International Software Product Line Conference* (pp. 139–148). Limerick.

Henderson, J. C., & Venkatraman, N. (1993). Strategic alignment: Leveraging information technology for transforming organizations. *IBM Systems Journal, 32*(1), 4–16.

Hevner, A. R., March, S. T., Park, J., & Ram, S. (2004). Design science in information systems research. *MIS Quarterly, 28*(1), 75–105.

Iivari, J. (2007). A paradigmatic analysis of information systems as a design science. *Scandinavian Journal of Information Systems, 19*(2).

Langley, A. (1999). "Strategies for Theorizing from Process Data." *Academy Of Management Review 24*(4), 691–710.

Lankhorst, M. M., & Proper, H. A. (2012). Agile architecture. In M. M. Lankhorst (Ed.), *Agile Service Development* (pp. 41–57). Springer.

Lee, A. S., Thomas, M. A., & Baskerville, R. (2015). Going back to basics in design science: From the information technology artifact to the information systems artifact. *Information Systems Journal, 25*(1), 5–21.

Lee, A. S., Thomas, M. A., & Baskerville, R. L. (2013). *Going back to basics in design: From the IT artifact to the IS artifact. AMCIS 2013.* AIS.

Linnaeus, C. (1756). *Systema Naturae.* Theodor Haak.

Maedche, A., Gregor, S., Morana, S., & Feine, J. (2019). Conceptualization of the problem space in design science research. In B. Tulu, S. Djamasbi, & G. Leroy (Eds.), *Extending the boundaries of design science theory and practice* (pp. 18–31). Springer.

March, S. T., & Smith, G. F. (1995). Design and natural science research on information technology. *Decision Support Systems, 15*(4), 251–266.

McKnight, D. H., Choudhury, V., & Kacmar, C. (2002). Developing and validating trust measures for e-Commerce: An integrative typology. *Information Systems Research, 13*(3), 334–359.

Mokyr, J. (2002). *The Gifts of Athena: Historical origins of the knowledge economy.* Princeton University Press.

Mueller, R. M., Huettemann, S., Larsen, K. R., Yan, S., & Handler, A. (2022). Toward an information systems ontology. In A. Drechsler, A. Gerber, & A. Hevner (Eds.), *The Transdisciplinary Reach of Design Science Research. DESRIST 2022* (pp. 55–67). Springer.

Mwilua, O. S., Comyn-Wattiau, I., & Prat, N. (2016). Design science research contribution to business intelligence in the cloud — A systematic literature review. *Future Generation Computer Systems, 63*, 108–122.

Nickerson, R. C., Varshney, U., & Muntermann, J. (2013). A method for taxonomy development and its application in information systems. *European Journal of Information Systems, 22*(3), 336–359.

Niehaves, B., & Ortbach, K. (2016). The inner and the outer model in explanatory design theory: The case of designing electronic feedback systems. *European Journal of Information Systems, 25*, 303–316.

Offermann, P., Blom, S., Schönherr, M., & Bub, U. (2010). Artifact types in information systems design science – A literature review. In R. Winter, J. L. Zhao, S. Aier, & St. (Eds.), *5th International Conference on Design Science Research in Information Systems and Technology (DESRIST 2010)*. Springer.

Orlikowski, W. J., & Iacono, C. S. (2001). Research commentary: Desperately seeking the "IT" in IT research—A call to theorizing the IT artifact. *Information Systems Research, 12*(2), 121–134.

Osterwalder, A., Pigneur, Y., & Tucci, C. L. (2005). Clarifying business models: Origins, present, and future of the concept. *Communications of the AIS, 16*(1), 1–25.

Peffers, K., Tuunanen, T., Rothenberger, M. A., & Chatterjee, S. (2007). A design science research methodology for information systems research. *Journal of Management Information Systems, 24*(3), 45–77.

Pohl, K., Böckle, G., & Linden, F. (2005). *Software product line engineering*. Springer.

Prat, N., Akoka, J., Comyn-Wattiau, I., & Storey, V. C. (2022). A granular view of knowledge development in design science research. In A. Drechsler, A. Gerber, & A. Hevner (Eds.), *The transdisciplinary reach of design science research. DESRIST 2022* (pp. 363–375). Springer.

Prat, N., Comyn-Wattiau, I., & Akoka, J. (2015). A taxonomy of evaluation methods for information systems artifacts. *Journal of Management Information Systems, 32*(3), 229–267.

Saat, J., et al. (2011). Analysis of IT/Business Alignment Situations as a Precondition for the Design and Engineering of Situated IT/Business Alignment Solutions. 44th Hawaii International Conference on System Sciences (HICSS-44), Kauai, HI.

Siering, M., Clapham, B., Engel, O., & Gomber, P. (2017). A taxonomy of financial market manipulations: Establishing trust and market integrity in the financialized economy through automated fraud detection. *Journal of Information Technology, 32*(3), 251–269.

Simon, H. A. (1996). *The sciences of the artificial*. MIT Press.

Simpson, G. G. (1961). *Principles of animal taxonomy*. Columbia University Press.

Tuunanen, T., Winter, R., & Vom Brocke, J. (2024). Dealing with complexity in design science research - A methodology using design Echelons. *MIS Quarterly, 48*(2), 427–458.

Vaishnavi, V. K., Kuechler, W. Jr., & Petter, S. (2019). *Design science research in information systems*. Retrieved May 28, 2021, from http://www.desrist.org/desrist/content/design-science-research-in-information-systems.pdf

Vaishnavi, V. K., & Kuechler, W. (2004). *Design research in information systems*. Retrieved October 06, 2009, from www.isworld.org/Researchdesign/drisISworld.htm

van Aken, J. E. (2004). Management research based on the paradigm of the design sciences: The quest for field-tested and grounded technological rules. *Journal of Management Studies, 41*(2), 219–246.

van Aken, J., et al. (2016). "Conducting and publishing design science research - Inaugural essay of the design science department of the Journal of Operations Management." Journal of Operations Management 47–48: 1–8.

Venable, J. R. (2013). Rethinking design theory in information systems. In J. V. Brocke, R. Hekkala, S. Ram, & M. Rossi (Eds.), *Design science at the intersection of physical and virtual design* (pp. 136–149). Springer.

Venable, J., Pries-Heje, J. & Baskerville, R. (2016) FEDS: a Framework for Evaluation in Design Science Research European Journal of Information Systems 25(1), 77–89 https://doi.org/10.1057/ejis.2014.36

Walls, J. G., Widmeyer, G. R., & El Sawy, O. A. (1992). Building an information system design theory for vigilant EIS. *Information Systems Research, 3*(1), 36–59.

Weigand, H., Johannesson, P., & Andersson, B. (2021). An artifact ontology for design science research. *Data & Knowledge Engineering, 133*.

Winter, R., Gericke, A., & Bucher, T. (2009). Method versus Model – Two sides of the same coin? In A. Albani, J. Barijs, & J. L. G. Dietz (Eds.), *Advances in Enterprise Engineering III* (pp. 1–15). Springer.

Xanthakos, P. P. (1995). *Theory and design of bridges*. Wiley & Son.

The Architecture of Project Design Knowledge in Design Science Research

Robert Winter and Stephan Aier

1 Introduction

Design Science Research (DSR) in Information Systems (IS) contributes to the design knowledge base. This base of prescriptive knowledge can be separated into solution design knowledge and solution entities (Drechsler & Hevner, 2018). DSR projects contribute to the knowledge base by adding project design knowledge (PDK), i.e. valid utility statements linking the solution space to the problem space (Drechsler & Hevner, 2018). PDK is created in different forms: On the one hand, solution entities such as IS system instances, methods, processes, and constructs (Drechsler & Hevner, 2018; Hevner et al., 2004) are suggested as useful solutions for relevant IS problems or problem classes. On the other hand, solution design knowledge such as technological rules, design principles, and design techniques are suggesting how to create solution entities (Drechsler & Hevner, 2018).

While all PDK is linking the solution space to the problem space, existing meta models for PDK are usually tailored for a specific artefact type. Examples of such proposals are the "anatomy" models for design theories (Gregor & Jones, 2007) and design principles (Gregor et al., 2020), or component models for technological rules (Denyer et al., 2008) and methods (Braun et al., 2005). However, the determination of the most effective artefact type should not be the first step of a DSR project but rather be based on a decent understanding of the problem, an analysis of informing descriptive and prescriptive knowledge, and the assessment of promising solution alternatives. For analysing the problem space and investigating promising solution

R. Winter (✉)
Institute of Information Systems and Digital Business, University of St. Gallen,
St. Gallen, Switzerland
e-mail: Robert.Winter@unisg.ch

S. Aier
Institute for Computer Science in Vorarlberg, University of St. Gallen, St. Gallen, Switzerland

© The Author(s), under exclusive license to Springer Nature
Switzerland AG 2025
R. Winter (ed.), *Designing the Information Systems Artefact*, Progress in IS,
https://doi.org/10.1007/978-3-031-98311-5_2

alternatives before deciding for a specific type of artefact, artefact type agnostic design support is needed. More concretely, researchers should be supported by guidance on which components and relations are essential and what fundamental guidelines are relevant for developing, validating, and evolving designs before deciding on the artefact type that is best suited to represent their design proposal.

Existing *output-centric* conceptualizations (e.g. in the form of utility theories in Venable, 2006) provide only limited support because they are intentionally abstract so that they cannot directly guide DSR endeavours. On the other hand, *process-centric* conceptualizations (e.g. Sein et al., 2011) are focusing on activities and abstract both from the sometimes complex structure of PDK and from the fact that PDK may take different intermediate forms along the design process (Tuunanen et al., 2024).

Therefore, our intended contribution is to propose a conceptualization of PDK that provides a foundation (1) for understanding the variety of relevant PDK components related to complex artefacts, (2) for understanding the relations between these components, and (3) for guiding the creation, evolution, and publication of PDK, which is embodied in its components and their relations.

The complexity of designed artefacts and/or of design processes is a well-known issue in all design-oriented disciplines. To support designers in dealing with complexity, *architectural* abstractions have been proposed as early as in Vitruvius' ten books on architecture (Gleiniger et al., 2012). In the context of software-intensive systems, *architecture* is defined as a combination of (1) an abstract structural model of a system's fundamental components (and their relationships to each other and to the environment) and (2) the respective principles for the system's design and evolution over time (Ieee, 2000). We extend this understanding to complex designed artefacts in the context of DSR and define *project design knowledge architecture (PDKA)* as

- An abstract structural model of fundamental PDK components
- Together with the relationships between these components and to the environment, as well as
- Guidelines for designing and evolving a particular PDKA

An architecture (in our case, a PDK architecture) always entails the need for abstractions and thus for parsimoniousness. While we aim at completeness and consistency of our DKA model design on a given level of abstraction, we do not intent to unify all the available (and useful) concepts discussed in DSR literature. Instead, we design our PDKA model in a way that it is not only internally consistent, but that it is also informed by extant discourses of artefact-agnostic conceptualizations in DSR. Next to the objective of parsimoniousness, we designed PDKA as a useful artefact having two essential use cases in mind: On the level of a *complete* PDKA, it informs IS design by providing specific guidance on how to fulfil quality and coherency requirements for complex IS artefacts; on the level of a PDKA *component*, it informs IS design by providing criteria on how components should be designed to fit the overall design.

We contribute beyond existing *anatomy* or *process* conceptualizations in DSR by not only proposing an extended set of fundamental DSR components, but also by specifying the relations between and within these components—on an abstract level as well as through an illustrative exemplar. In addition, we discuss what requirements need to be met for claiming a PDK contribution both on the level of a PDKA *component* and on the level of a *complete* PDKA.

The proposed PDKA model is intended to create utility for design researchers in IS by

- Providing a checklist with components and relations that are relevant even before choosing a specific artefact type to construct
- Providing support for navigating through complex PDK creation activities (design stages) and thus support partitioning and iterations of DSR initiatives and
- Defining coherency conditions between concepts and between relations that need to be addressed to avoid *knowledge gaps* (Avdiji & Winter, 2019).

Consequently, the PDKA model to be developed in this chapter should (i) ensure that design statement, empirical justification, and theoretical justification are covered (Goldkuhl, 2004), (ii) clarify the semantics of relationships among these components, and (iii) support mechanisms to check and improve consistency of these components.

As the proposed PDKA model is an artefact by itself, this chapter is generally structured following the DSR process model by Peffers et al. (2007). After motivating the problem and defining the objectives of the solution in the Introduction, Sect. 2 summarizes extant discourses that inform our problem understanding and design vision. Section 3 presents the *project design knowledge architecture*. In Sects. 4 and 5, we present an illustrative demonstration and evaluative evidence, which we gained from interviews with authors of well-published DK contributions. The evaluation results show, in how far the objectives and thus the utility claims of the proposed PDKA model are assessed by our targeted audience, that is by design science researchers. Finally, we discuss our main findings, their limitations, and their implications for further DSR methodology research in Sect. 6.

2   Research Background

In this section, we discuss related work and how it informs our problem understanding and our conceptualization of PDKA. Specifically, we analyse (i) which PDKA components are suggested and why, (ii) which relations among PDKA components are suggested and why, (iii) which explicit PDKA guidelines are suggested and why, and (iv) how the respective study informs our proposal.

2.1 Design-Related Knowledge

Gregor and Hevner (2013) differentiate Ω knowledge, which represents descriptive knowledge, and Λ knowledge, which represents (prescriptive) design knowledge. Ω knowledge informs design and can be used to justify Λ knowledge.

They further mention different levels of abstraction, completeness, and maturity of design knowledge (DK)—but without differentiating these sub-characteristics in their model. On the lowest level, DK is instantiated/situated (e.g. by concrete software solutions or implemented processes). On medium levels, DK can be projected to a wider range of problems, is more complete or more mature (such as represented by methods, technological rules, or design principles). On the highest level of abstraction, completeness, and/or maturity, DK is designated as well-developed design theory.

In addition to having a different character and a different level of abstraction, completeness, and/or maturity, the DK contribution varies: Known solutions may be applied to known problems (routine design) or to new problems (exaptation); New solutions may be applied to known problems (improvement) or to new problems (invention). Design is considered to constitute a knowledge contribution in case of exaptation, improvement, and invention. Routine design, however, does not create knowledge, but applies existing knowledge.

Viewed from a PDKA conceptualization perspective, from Gregor and Hevner (2013) follows (see Fig. 1[1]):

- DK exists on different levels of abstraction, completeness, and maturity
- DK is informed/justified by descriptive knowledge (and also may contribute to descriptive knowledge)

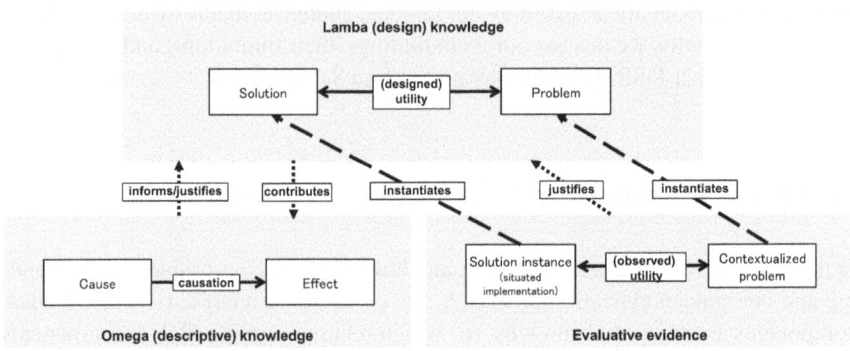

Fig. 1 How Gregor and Hevner (2013) inform PDKA model design

---

[1] In Fig. 1 and all subsequent Figures, grey boxes depict levels (usually statements), white boxes depict concepts, solid lines depict intra-level relationships, broken lines depict between-level instantiation relationships, and dotted lines depict other between-level relationships. Directed and mutually directed relationships are depicted by arrows.

- DK can be instantiated to create specific (new) problem solutions to specific design problems, and such instantiations justify DK claims

Some years later, Drechsler and Hevner (2018) expand the Gregor/Hevner model by (i) differentiating between abstract solution knowledge (e.g. technological rules, design principles) and reusable solution entities (e.g. methods, references models) and by (ii) putting project-level DSR concepts in the centre of knowledge creation. In their models, descriptive knowledge does not directly inform DK, instead it informs project-level design from which abstract solution knowledge or reusable solution entities can be derived.

Viewed from a PDKA conceptualization perspective, from Drechsler and Hevner (2018) follows (see Fig. 2):

- Descriptive knowledge is closer related to project-level design knowledge than to (abstract) DK
- Generative knowledge (that needs to be applied/instantiated, designated as "Solution Design Knowledge") is differentiated from more directly reusable knowledge (that could be directly reused or adapted, designated as "Solution Design Entities")

Referring to Venable's (2006) understanding of design and Drechsler and Hevner's analysis of DK (2018), vom Brocke et al. (2020) suggest three dimensions to characterize DK:

- Projectability: How broad is the class of problems (in the problem space) to which a design proposal can be applied?
- Fitness: How complete is the specification of a solution (in the solution space) that is used for the design (for problem-solving)?
- Confidence: How much evaluative evidence is provided for the design proposal's utility claim. E.g., what types of evaluation of the design have been performed, what level of rigour has been achieved when applying these evaluation methods, and how convincing were the evaluation results?

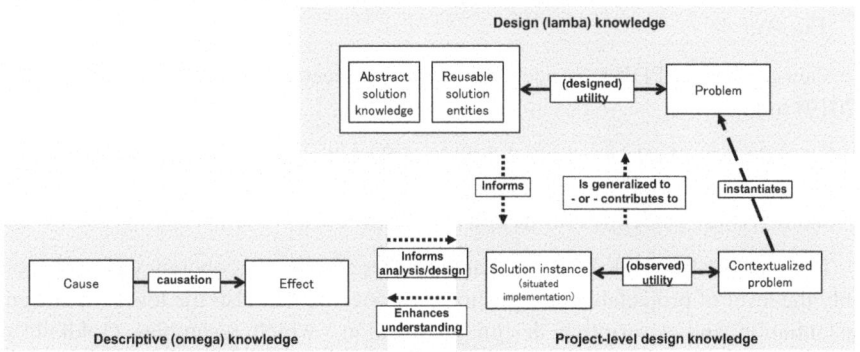

Fig. 2 How Drechsler and Hevner (2018) inform PDKA model design

They add an additional form of DK contribution that honours accumulating evaluative evidence: "Every DSR project has a starting point that is grounded on existing DK, i.e., on one or more relationships between specific solution spaces and specific problem spaces. The DSR project then creates new DK by linking the same problems to a different (or changed) solution space, the same solution to a different (or changed) problem space, or by conducting a different evaluation of DK that corresponds to the same problem and solution space" (vom Brocke, Winter et al. 2020)

Viewed from a PDKA conceptualization perspective, from vom Brocke, Winter et al. (2020) follows:

- PDK is situated, may be incomplete, and may be associated with limited evaluative evidence
- The relationship between fully developed DK and design instantiations is complex (can be described referring to three dimensions)
- A DK contribution can be made by increasing evaluative evidence, by enhancing projectability, or by enhancing completeness

Avdiji and Winter (2019) aim at identifying potential knowledge gaps when addressing complex DSR problems. They differentiate between the "domains" of descriptive theory, design solutions and design problems, thereby creating a DK model that comprises six base concepts and seven direct relations:

- DK components are cause-effect statements ("descriptive theory"), means-ends statements ("design theory"), and design feature-design requirements statements (for actual problem/solution instances).
- Direct relationships exist

    (a) Intra-level: Causes create effects, means achieve ends, and design features fulfil design requirements.
    (b) Between-levels: Causes inform means, effects correspond to ends, means are instantiated to design features, and ends are instantiated to design requirements.

- Indirect relationships exist (i) between cause-effect statements and means-ends statements, and (ii) between means-ends statements and design instantiations (Fig. 3).

Viewed from a PDKA conceptualization perspective, from Avdiji and Winter (2019) follows:

- Several types of relationships should be differentiated
- DK components and various relations form a reference for analysing consistency and deriving "guidelines for design and evolution".

To conceptualize PDK in a way that considers all relevant coherency aspects, not only the level of projectable design should be covered, but also the levels of design instantiation and descriptive design justification—which resembles Goldkuhl's (2004) idea of "multi-grounding" by combining empirical and theoretical justification.

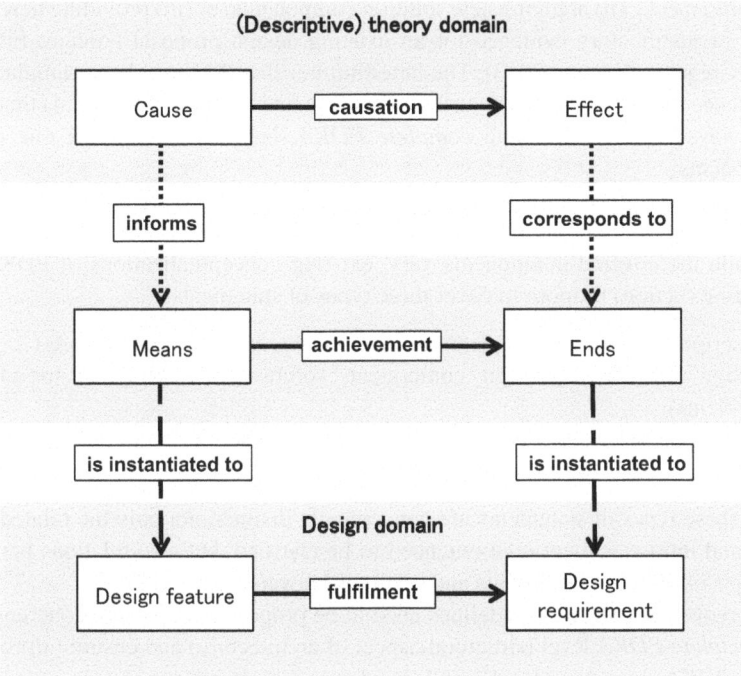

Fig. 3 How Avdiji and Winter (2019) inform PDKA model design

2.2 Objectives for Designing a Project Design Knowledge Architecture Model

From our discussion of the methodological problem and the targeted use cases in Sect. 1 as well as from discussing related work in the preceding section, we derive several foundational assumptions and objectives for designing a PDKA model.

Design means to solve relevant problems with innovative artefacts. Consequently, a relationship between goal/requirement/problem aspect/desired effect on the one side and solution artefact capability/intervention/action on the other side (Venable, 2006) needs to be represented.

With growing complexity and maturity of designed artefacts, architectural representations need to be used not only for structured analysis and communication, but also for design guidance and quality management. Consequently, not only fundamental concepts and relations/statements/interactions (for managing coherency) need to be represented, but also dynamic aspects (for managing evolution).

To make a knowledge contribution, essential PDK properties are projectability (size of problem class addressed), completeness (of deployed solution), and confidence (into the goodness of the proposed problem-solution linkage) (vom Brocke, Winter et al. 2020). This, its innovativeness can result from (i) addressing new problem aspects, (ii) applying new solution components, or (iii) providing new evaluative or justificatory evidence for an existing design proposal (Aier & Fischer, 2011; Gregor & Hevner, 2013). The latter implies that PDK can be accumulated in a sequence of self-contained contributions (Tuunanen, Winter et al. 2024) that may not always refer to the same *complete PDKA*, but can result from one of its components.

PDK needs to be grounded both regarding existing (descriptive and design) knowledge as well as empirical evidence of its effectiveness (Goldkuhl, 2004).

While the covered components vary, existing conceptualizations of PDK (see preceding section) propose to cover three types of statements:

- Descriptive statements (explanatory component, causes explain effects)
- Design statements (design component, solutions are designed to address problems)
- Observational statements (evaluative component, implemented design features fulfil contextualized solution requirements)

As these types of statements are conceptually distinct, not only the related concepts and intra-statement relations need to be clarified, but also relations between concepts of different statements and relations between statements.

Moreover, appropriate guidelines need to be proposed that ensure coherency on the *complete PDKA* level (structural aspect of architecture) and ensure fit/progress on the *PDKA component* level (evolutional aspect of architecture).

- Related work on conceptualizing DK has different aims:
- Supporting analysis and presentation of DK ("anatomy", e.g. Gregor & Jones, 2007, Gregor, Chandra Kruse et al. 2020)
- Supporting the development process of DK (e.g. Peffers, Tuunanen et al. 2007)
- Supporting consistency when developing DK (e.g. Avdiji & Winter, 2019)
- Supporting justification and evaluation when developing DK ("grounding", e.g. Goldkuhl, 2004)
- Supporting DK accumulation and evolution (e.g. across projects, cf. vom Brocke, Winter et al. 2020)

Our objective is, by means of the proposed PDKA artefact, to provide

- On the *complete PDKA* level: Guidance on how to fulfil quality and coherency requirements for complex IS artefacts
- On the *PDKA component* level: Guidance on how components need to be designed to fit the overall design

"Guidance" is provided by (i) a checklist of concepts and relations that need to be covered, (ii) supporting navigation in complex PDK models, and (iii) coherency conditions between concepts (within statements and between statements) as well as between statements that need to be addressed.

To be more concrete, referring to the common understanding of architecture as "fundamental components", "their relations/dependencies", and "guidelines for their construction" (Ieee, 2000), our design objective is to propose (i) a consistent conceptual structure model of PDK covering all three types of statements (see above), (ii) characterizations of relations within statements, between statements, and between concepts in different statements, as well as (iii) elaborating implied recommendations for constructing, validating, and cumulating PDK.

3 Design: Architecture Model for Project Design Knowledge

Based on the discussions in Sect. 2.1, several design/validation iterations resulted in the PDKA candidate artefact illustrated in Fig. 4. As a foundation for the meta model presented in Fig. 5, Fig. 4 illustrates candidate concepts not yet on the meta-model level, but also sketches their internal structure. For that reason, we use circles instead of boxes in Fig. 4.

Concepts: *Explanatory statements* represent causes that explain effects (m:n relationship). Only effect-related causes and problem-related effects are relevant. *Design statements* represent solution components that address problem dimensions (m:n relationship). On an aggregate level, projectable solutions address general problems. *Observational statements* represent (situated) design features that fulfil (contextualized) requirements (m:n relationship). On an aggregate level, features of situated solution instances fulfil requirements of contextualized problems.

Relationships: Explanatory statements justify (*ground*) design statements (m:n relationship). Design statements contribute to explanatory statements (e.g. by creating innovative artefacts whose behaviour can be studied). Observational statements justify (*ground*) design statements (m:n relationship). Design statements provide the foundation for observational statements as situated solutions (that instantiate a

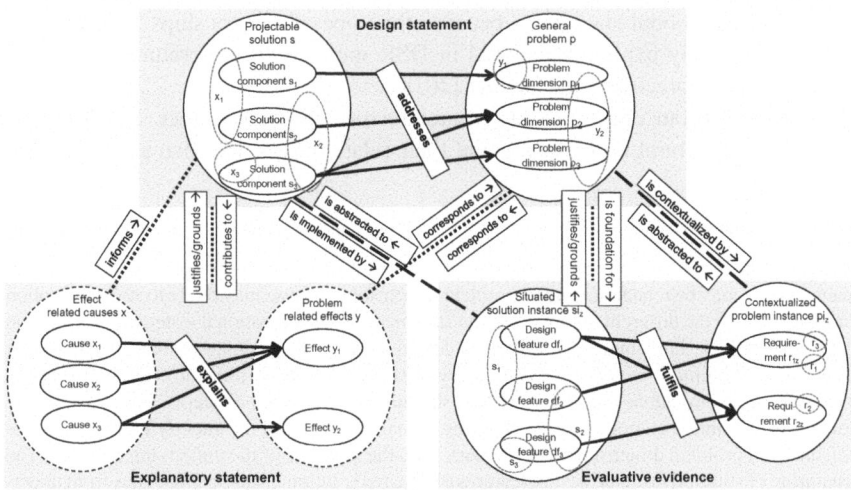

Fig. 4 PDKA candidate concepts, statements, and relations

projectable solution) constitute design hypotheses for contextualized problems (that instantiate the general problem).

It should be noted that, the structure of solution components will usually be different from the structure of causes, the structure of problem dimension will usually be different from the structure of effects, the structure of design features will usually be different from the structure of solution components, and the structure of requirements will usually be different from the structure of problem dimensions.[2]

Direct relationships between concepts from different statements represent that

- Solution component specification should be *informed by* causes
- Problem dimension specification should *correspond to* effects (and vice versa)
- Causes should *be facilitated by* solution components
- Design features should *implement* solution components (in case of deductive design)
- Problem requirements should *contextualize* problem dimensions and
- Design features and requirements should *be abstracted to* solution components and problem dimensions (in case of inductive design)

Figure 5 abstracts the concepts and relationships illustrated in Fig. 4 to a meta model. It only depicts intra-statement and instantiation relationships. It should be noted that relationships, in general, can have attributes. Exemplary attributes of the intra-statement relationships depicted in Fig. 5 (in oval shape) are explanatory power for explanatory statements, claimed utility for design statements, and observed utility for observational statements.

Since all proposed inter-statement relationships relate only the detailed concepts in statements, and abstract concepts are related only by (obvious) instantiation and association relationships, we will drop the abstract statement concepts in the following. Figure 6 illustrates the resulting simplified PDKA meta model.

Figure 6 does not depict potential inter-statement relationships between explanatory and observational statements because this type of relationships is sometimes implied, but rarely explicitly covered in DSR methodology literature—a notable exception being Drechsler and Hevner (2018).

According to our understanding of architecture outlined in Sect. 1, PDKA not only covers structural components and their relationships, but also guidelines for

---

[2] Structural differences result from the different nature of explanatory models and design statements (effects may be related to several problem dimensions, a cause may relate to several solution components) and the different nature of design statements and observational statements (a solution component may be implemented in different design features, a requirement may be integrating several problem dimensions). In Fig. 4, this structural "mismatch" is illustrated by an overlay of primary concept structures and corresponding structures from related concepts. For example, the structuring of solution components of s deviates from the structure of the underlying causes x; The structuring of problem dimensions of p deviates from the structure of the underlying effects y; The structuring of solution instance design features of situated solution instance si deviates from underlying solution components s; The structuring of problem instance requirements pi from underlying problem dimensions p.

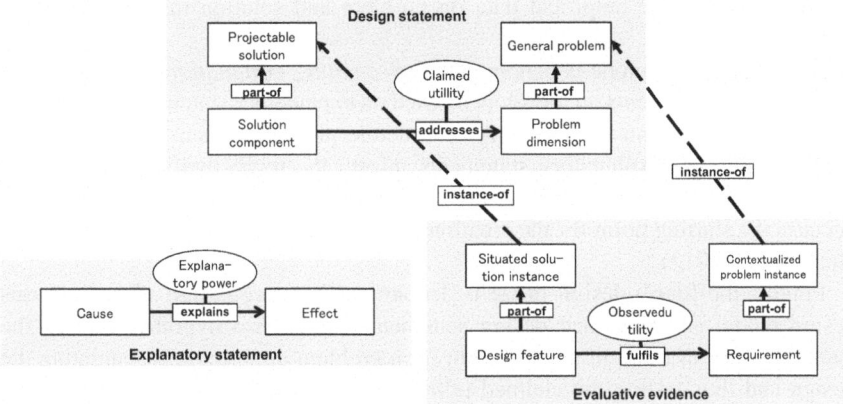

Fig. 5 PDKA meta model (focus on intra-statement relations)

designing and evolving a particular PDKA. Building on the structural PDKA model, we propose four different *design modes* for contributing PDK.

The first design mode is denominated *aligning knowledge components*. This design mode aims to strengthen the fit and thus consistency among existing design statements, explanatory statements, and/or observational statements. Existing knowledge gaps between statements shall be addressed or even closed. Such alignment may also contribute to one of those statements—in DSR, it is usually the design statement. Avdiji and Winter (2019) describe those knowledge gaps and general strategies for aligning knowledge components in detail.

The second design mode is denominated *theorizing design observations*. This design mode focusses on abstracting observational statements to design statements. For doing so, researchers often cumulate existing empirical knowledge from designed instances. Such an abstraction constitutes, for example, the core of an action design research process (Sein, Henfridsson et al. 2011). Often such a research setting is also referred to as data-driven design because the starting point for the

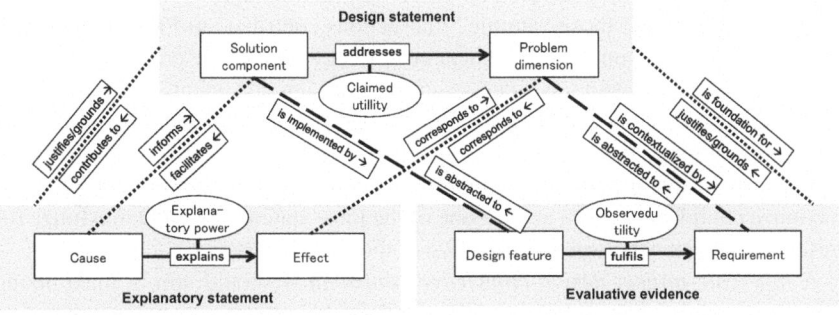

Fig. 6 Simplified PDKA meta model

creation of PDK are empirical data on problem and solution instances (Fischer et al., 2012).

The third design mode is denominated *effectuating explanations*. In this design mode, design statements are developed based on explanatory statements. Very often explanatory statements help identify or structure problem dimensions in complex problem settings. Explanatory statements inform the respective solution components as well. Such a research setting is also referred to as theory driven design because the starting point for the creation of PDK are descriptive theories (Fischer, Gregor et al. 2012).

Finally, the fourth design mode is denominated *testing design visions*. In this design mode, an envisioned design statement represents a hypothesis about the claimed utility of a solution component for a problem dimension. Instantiating the design and thus testing the claimed utility closes a build-evaluate cycle (Hevner, March et al. 2004).

The four design modes represent archetypes of DSR projects. As a consequence, complex DSR projects may instantiate components from different modes of design.

The proposed structure of PDKA is open for diverse approaches to develop PDK and thus caters the diversity of DSR approaches and settings. Yet, it provides a common ground for a broad range of DSR endeavours. While it defines the core components of DKA, its few proposed guidelines for the design and evolution of DK allow for a flexible application. The model and its application are also artefact-agnostic, i.e. leave the choice of a specific solution artefact type open for later stages of the DSR process. These guidelines specifically focus intra- and inter-statement coherency, because coherency of PDK contributions is particularly valuable in the light of the often-cumulative nature of DK development.

Improving intra- and between-statement coherency between PDK components can be decomposed into basic, yet abstract *transactions*. Within a design statement, explanatory statement, and/or observational statement (intra-statement consistency), a transaction may either focus on establishing a hypothesized relationship between existing knowledge components—or it may validate such a hypothesis in an artificial or natural evaluation setting. Between two of those statements (between-statement consistency), the basic transactions are identifying suitable kernel theory that informs design statements, evaluating designs through instantiated artefacts, and developing new designs based on observed instantiations.

However, not all of those "atomic" transactions contribute to PDK. Particularly transactions focusing on intra-statement consistency may solely create design entities (observational statements), design visions (design statements), or descriptive knowledge (explanatory statements). We consider none of those to constitute a valid PDK contribution as they do not cover a minimum set of relevant concepts. Instead, it seems reasonable to require a *minimal project design knowledge contribution* to maximize confidence within at least one of the three statements AND maximize (or preserve) coherency between at least two of the three layers.

A *full-scale project design knowledge contribution* should aim at maximizing confidence within all three layers AND maximize (or preserve) coherency between all three layers.

4 Demonstration

For the purpose of demonstrating our PDKA model proposal, we use a published DSR artefact design for *informal control in Enterprise Architecture Management* (EAM) (Schilling et al., 2019). The authors of that study propose the so-called *Enterprise Architecture Label* aimed at influencing decision-makers in their decision-making processes, so that IS designs that are preferable from an enterprise-wide perspective appear to be more attractive than alternative designs that are preferable from their local (e.g. department) perspective only. While the problem of insufficient alignment of local business and technology initiatives with enterprise-wide objectives is well-known in IS research (e.g. Malaurent & Avison, 2016), the authors propose the employment of labels as a novel solution. Their proposed design aims at complementing well-developed formal modes of control by *facilitating informal modes of control* (Cram et al., 2016; Kirsch, 1997; Ouchi, 1979) in EAM. Their design is not only informed by *control theory*, but also by more specific research on *institutional theory* (DiMaggio & Powell, 1983; Meyer & Rowan, 1977). In the context of EAM, institutional theory explains the factors fostering the compliance with EAM interventions (Weiss et al., 2013) as well as their effects (Brosius et al., 2018).

Figure 7 illustrates how the study uses PDKA concepts and relationships. The artefact development was part of an action design research (Sein, Henfridsson et al. 2011) setting, i.e. the authors developed situated solution instances in contextualized problem instances. While the contextualized problem instances defined the boundaries of what has been feasible within the organization, the explanatory statements informed the researchers of the possible levers for potential solution components. Based on the specific instances they abstracted the generalized design.

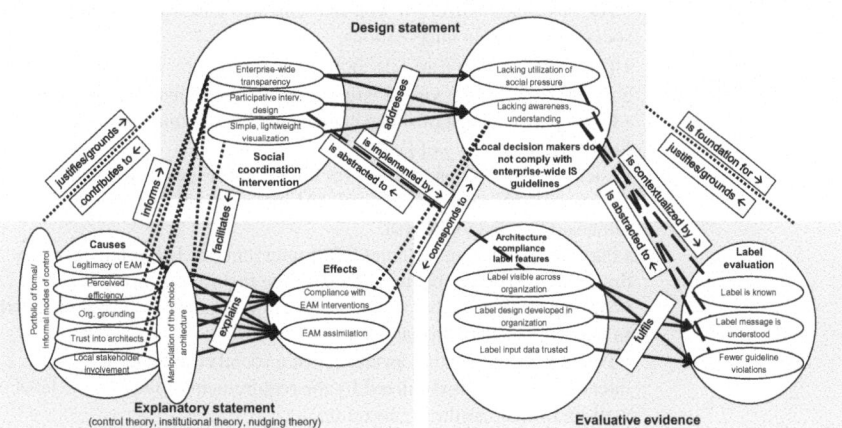

Fig. 7 PDKA of social coordination intervention to improve the alignment of local IS decisions with enterprise-wide IS guidelines

Figure 7 remains illustrative because it does not cover all the components and relationships that are described in the original publication and the literature it references (Schilling et al., 2019). Still, it illustrates the multitude of components and their relationships that comprise the intended PDK. Indeed, there were a number of follow-up publications later on. Cahenzli et al. (2022) extended the explanatory statements along *nudging theory* (Thaler & Sunstein, 2008). Buchmann and Haki (2021) and later Haki et al. (2023) added evaluative evidence by instantiating a similar situated solution in a different contextualized problem instance (technical debt management).

An interesting feature of the proposed conceptualization of PDKA is that, like other conceptual information models, a PDKA model instance can be directly translated into natural language for validation purposes. For the social coordination intervention illustrated in Fig. 7, a "translation" is presented in Table 1.

From this excerpt of the demonstration example's PDKA, it becomes clear that a textual "translation" of PDKA is helpful in validating and communicating

Table 1 Natural language "translation" of PDKA model instance illustrated by Fig. 7

Statements (levels)	• A higher trust into architects **explains** (together with other factors) increased EAM assimilation. • Designing interventions in a participative way **addresses** the need for increasing awareness and understanding by decision-makers. • Achieved trust in EAM label data **fulfils** the requirement that EAM guideline violations need to be reduced.
Selected relationships between statements	• Social coordination interventions **are justified by** the need to complement formal by informal control modes. • Social interventions to create EAM compliant behaviour **contribute to** the institutionalization of EAM. • Innovative social interventions to create EAM compliant behaviour **are the foundation for** successful interventions based on labels. • The observable effects of well-implemented labels **justify** innovative social coordination interventions.
Selected relationships between concepts	• The need to create trust into architects **informs** the necessity to aim at a simple, lightweight visualization of social coordination interventions. • Participative design of social coordination EAM interventions **facilitates** legitimacy of EAM. • Lacking assimilation of EAM (as effect) **corresponds to** lacking awareness and understanding of EAM interventions (as a problem dimension)—and vice versa. • Participative design of social EAM interventions **is implemented by** designing an EAM label together with the (using) organization. • Making the EAM label visible in the entire organization **is abstracted to** enterprise-wide transparency. • The problem of lacking awareness of a social coordination intervention **is contextualized by** the requirement of making the label well-known across the organization. • The requirement of sufficiently understanding the EAM label **is abstracted to** the problem of lacking utilization/effectivity of social coordination interventions.

design—and that, vice versa, a detailed textual description of design projects provides a good basis for conceptualizing PDK.

5 Evaluation

Our objective is to inform design researchers by proposing a PDKA model that provides

1. On the "complete artefact" level: Guidance on how to fulfil quality, completeness, and coherency requirements in early stages of designing PDK.
2. On the "artefact component" level: Guidance on how important components of PDK need to be designed in order to fit the overall design.

As architectural considerations promise to be particularly valuable in situations with significant levels of design complexity, the analysis of the PDKA model's utility should analyse complex DSR processes that lead to complex IS artefacts. Moreover, those artefacts ideally are considered to represent significant DK contributions in the DSR community (indicated by, e.g., publication in renowned outlets). To obtain insights into the artefact development process beyond what is documented in published papers, we selected publications whose lead authors would be available for personal interviewing. Three studies were chosen:

(1) "A Design Theory for Visual Inquiry Tools" by Avdiji et al. (2020) delivers DK in the form of a design theory for visual inquiry tools. The design theory is based on a theorizing process for three existing visual inquiry tools that are developed in dedicated design science research projects and tested in the real world with practitioners. The authors perform a within- and cross-projects analysis of the three DSR projects and generalize the PDK into 12 design principles to guide the design of visual inquiry tools. Their PDK covers observational statements (from developing and evaluating the Business Model Canvas, Value Proposition Canvas, and Team Alignment Map artefacts), a design statement (design principles for visual inquiry tools), and explanatory statements (about ontology development, shared visualization, joint inquiry, and decision-making in strategic management).

(2) "Monitoring the Complexity of IT Architectures: Design Principles and an IT Artefact" by Widjaja and Gregory (2020) aims at providing tool support for IT architects who need to monitor the structural and dynamic complexity of a firm's IT architecture in the context of digital business strategy. In the form of design principles inferred by heuristic theorizing, the DK they propose is accumulated over three cycles and several iterations with five large companies over eight years. During the evolution of this PDK, both fitness and confidence (more cases, more evaluative evidence) are increased in parallel. Also, the understanding of the problem improves by moving from a standardization focus via a heterogeneity focus to a complexity focus (the most comprehensive form).

Their PDK covers observational statements (from developing several complexity analysis tools), a design statement (design principles for complexity management support), and explanatory statements from various IS theories.

(3) In their study "Designing Process Guidance Systems: The Case of IT Service Management", Morana and Maedche (2020) start with a real-world problem in a specific case (observation), decontextualize the problem, successively identify theories on "guidance systems" (taxonomy of design features, spatial and navigational theory), evaluate their design proposal by lab experiments, and finally add instantiations in a real-world context. Their PDK covers observational statements (from both real-world problems and real-world design instantiations), a design statement (design principles for process guiding systems), and explanatory statements (about spatial and navigational theory).

Since all publications focus on results and explicate artefact evolution and coherency only to a limited extent, we decided to conduct semi-structured interviews with lead authors for collecting and analysing qualitative data. Our questions address artefact components and their relations, the development process, and the perceived value the proposed PDKA would have had in supporting their DSR study. Each interview comprised a short introduction where the interviewers summarize their understanding of the paper in focus. This provided the opportunity to detect and sort out any misunderstanding about the interviewee's research early in the interview. After that introduction, Part 1 focused on the process of building and iterating the DK contribution, the role of descriptive theory and of instantiations of the design. In Part 2, the interviewers presented and discussed their proposed conceptualization of PDKA to assure that PDK and its usage in DSR is understood. The final Part 3 focused on the perceived utility and their dimensions that PDKA would have had for the respective DSR study.[3]

In the following, we summarize the interviews for each of the three parts described above. I1, I2, and I3 indicate whether the statements were made in the context of study (1), (2), or (3).

In Part 1, all interviewees mentioned the importance of descriptive theory. Descriptive theory has been helpful for structuring the design process as well as for analysing instances in the field (I1). Descriptive theory has also been reported helpful for arguing, presenting, and justifying the design. In general, theory was perceived a source of inspiration (I3). Even though theory has been reported to be crucial in the design process, its importance is not always prominently discussed in the final manuscript (I2).

Next to descriptive theory, design instantiations were reported to be the core of developing the design statement (I1). Design instantiations were also considered a means for testing explanatory statements (I2).

The responses in Part 1 generally support the need of PDKA to cover all three types of *statements*, i.e. explanatory statement, design statement, and observational statement. In Part 2, the interviewees commented on the various PDKA *components*

---

[3] For details of the interview guideline see Appendix 1.

and their *relationships*. While these comments did not change the basic structures within or between statements, they had large impact on developing the used terminology to the state that has been presented in the current version of this chapter. Those adaptations of terminology not only were based on the interviewees' understanding of the underlying terms and concepts, but they were also a result of deeply engaging with the research presented in the selected papers, its underlying research processes including the papers' revisions, and the experiences that interviewees made in papers that are considered direct predecessors of the focal studies.[4]

In Part 3, all three interviewees were rather positive on the utility PDKA would have had in their DSR study. They highlighted a common terminology among authors, reviewers, editors, and readers for presenting knowledge contributions as a major source of utility (I1, I2). The PDKA components were perceived helpful for meeting expectations of the community and thus justifying why certain components are reported on. Thus, PDKA components are not (just) a checklist, rather they hint at opportunities for potential contribution areas (I2).

Thus, PDKA may also guide young as well as experienced researchers in arguing for their research design and the respective procedural standards (I3).

Finally, PDKA explicates, how observational statements, on the one hand, help materialize descriptive statements and thus also guides researchers in contributing descriptive knowledge as part of a DSR project (I1).

6   Discussion and Conclusion

This chapter proposes a conceptualization of PDK that provides a foundation (i) for understanding the variety of relevant concepts related to the early stages of developing IS artefacts, (ii) for understanding the relationships between these concepts, and (iii) for providing architectural guidance in early, artefact-agnostic stages of creating, evolving, and publishing DK.

Focusing on the discussed concepts and relationships not only supports the consistency among the components of a full or partial PDK contribution; it also caters the systematic integration of PDK contributions into the DSR knowledge base and thus fosters DK accumulation.

We demonstrated that the PDKA model not only affords to document complex PDK in a comprehensive yet compact semiformal way, but that the "essence" of PDK also can be represented by textual documentations. Based on the correspondence between semiformal and textual representations, PDKA allows to "translate" DK in both directions in addition to systematically comparing and integrating PDK. Our PDKA proposal advances existing discourses by being based on a

---

[4] For details of those changes, see Appendix 2.

consolidation of several methodological streams of DSR, and moving beyond checklists and generic PDK conceptualizations.

We call design researchers to apply the structural and prescriptive aspects of PDKA for conducting early, artefact-agnostic phases of DSR studies more effectively or more efficiently:

- The proposed PDK structure can be applied to systematically assess and compare existing DK, e.g. in state of research and/or state of practice reviews
- The implied PDKA guidelines can be applied to explore and assess potential avenues for PDK development (e.g. empirical grounding of theoretically grounded design statements vs. theoretical grounding of empirically grounded design statements)
- The proposed PDK structure can be applied for maximizing coherency when developing and assessing DK (e.g. by systematically understanding and minimizing knowledge gaps)
- The proposed PDK structure can be applied for claiming consistency of DK contributions
- The proposed PDK structure can be applied for presenting, validating (translation into text), and communicating PDK in a structured way.

Since the proposed PDKA model should be parsimonious and implications should be as actionable as possible, we needed to scope out certain aspects that have been covered in some related work. Future research may aim at incorporating goals, stakeholders, objectives, concerns, requirements, etc., into PDKA and may also want to differentiate between features, properties, capabilities, etc., of projectable solution artefacts—instead of generalizing these aspects to *solution component*. We also believe that, as a consequence of differentiating between static and actionable properties of a design solution, it may be useful to integrate events or states into extended models of PDKA. Moreover, aspects such as desirability, values, concerns, or legitimacy could be investigated regarding their potentials to constitute relevant extensions to the PDKA model. Regarding the descriptive foundations of designing, more detailed conceptualizations of causation (e.g. probabilities), design effectiveness, and observed performance could be considered. Possible further additions to PDKA could result from integrating intermediate solution artefacts (Tuunanen, Winter et al. 2024), different scopes of descriptive statements (midrange theory, cf. Kuechler & Vaishnavi, 2012), different levels of confidence (nascent vs. full-scale design theory, cf. Gregor & Hevner, 2013), or alternative justifications/designs (e.g. design theory nexus, cf. Pries-Heje & Baskerville, 2008).

To enhance PDKA's utility from a processual (rather than structural) perspective, PDK gaps (Avdiji & Winter, 2019) could be related to the PDKA model so that such gaps could be addressed in early stages of design.

While the presented evaluative evidence collected from authors of selected complex DK contributions is encouraging and helped to advance our conceptualization, broad empirical evidence for the specific utility of the proposed artefact for improving DK accumulation and evolution in DSR needs to be collected by future application studies.

For advancing DSR methodology beyond the specific contribution of our PDKA proposal, design researchers may

- Analyse the role of architectural design conceptualizations for supporting *DK accumulation and evolution* (e.g. partial contributions, aggregation of PDK, dynamics of knowledge creation processes)
- *Explore conceptual alignment* between explorative and design statements (i.e. better understanding and using semantics of "corresponds", "informs", "facilitates" relations between concepts)
- *Explore potential specifics of artefact types* or DSR reference processes beyond the artefact-agnostic view of the proposed PDKA
- Investigate potential of architectural design conceptualizations for *more efficient organization of DK* on the DSR community level
- Further explore the potential of such conceptualizations for *"closing the loop"* with explanatory statements, i.e. design instantiations as manifestations/materializations of explanatory statements.

Appendix 1: Interview Guideline

Introduction (5 min): Interviewers provide a short summary of how they understand the respective study from a DKA perspective (artefact and its components, coherency, design process, justification).

Part 1 (15 min)

- Please describe the process of building, developing, iterating your design/artefact

  - Were there earlier versions of the paper or related (even non-DSR) papers?
  - Were there projects/industry collaborations related to the paper?
  - Inductive or deductive, formative or summative evaluation ...
  - Which role had artefact complexity and related challenges (coherency)
  - Was there a "blueprint" during the evolution or was it driven by opportunities?

- How and when did you employ descriptive theories?

  - For justification after the design or its iterations?
  - For improving the design?
  - Informing the design in the beginning?
  - Did you consider alternative theoretical justifications? How did you make a selection?

- How and when did you employ instantiations?

  - Only for evaluation?
  - For inspiring/informing your design?
  - For extending the projectability of your design?

Part 2 (5 min): Presentation of the proposed DKA artefact; Discussion to assure that DKA and its usage in DSR is understood.

Part 3 (30 min)

- Would the proposed DKA have been useful...

  - To build the artefact?
  - To assess qualities of the "complete artefact" (coherency)?
  - To guide the evolution of the artefact?
  - To justify the artefact?
  - To evaluate the artefact?
  - To publish the research?
  - To communicate the research?
  - To embed the research in related work?

- Which aspects would have helped in particular?

  - DKA components -> artefact completeness
  - DKA guidelines -> artefact design, process guidance
  - Guidance on «complete artefact» level vs. guidance on «artefact component» level
  - Guidance for positioning and further developing the artefact

Appendix 2: Design Iterations

This appendix documents how the PDKA conceptualization has evolved through comments by and discussions with the evaluation interview partners (see Sect. 5). For reasons of clarity and comprehensibility, Table 2 reports on two states only, that is pre and post interviews, even though there have been more iterations driven by discussions among authors before and during the evaluation phase.

Table 2 Artefact design iterations

	Authors' original version	Version post interviews	Interviewee proposing/ triggering change	Comments/rationale
Concepts	"Means"	"Projectable Solution" and "Solution Component"	1 and 3	The interviewees generally missed the concept of a "Problem", which they found to be central in DSR. The potentially more general concept of "Ends" has therefore been replaced by "Problem". As a consequence, "Means" has been replaced by "Solution". Moreover, interviewees discussed the granularity of those concepts which led to the additions of "Component" and "Dimension". Similarly, "Requirement" not better represents the instantiation of a "Problem".
	"Ends"	"General Problem" and "Problem Dimension"		
	"Achieved Effect"	"Requirement"	3	
Statements	"Descriptive statements"	"Explanatory statement"	1	In the DSR context such statements are valuable, since they do not just relate causes and effect but also explain why certain effects occur.
Relations	"Causality", "Effectivity", "Performativity"	"explains", "addresses", "fulfils"	1	Instead of introducing yet another rather complex construct for describing the relations between concepts we rather focus on describing the relation between those concepts.
	<none>	Relations between Explanatory and Observational Statements and their respective concepts	2	Even though our focus is on the design statement and its foundations, interviewees mentioned, on the one hand, the importance of instances as "materialization" of explanatory statements, and, on the other hand, the importance of empirical observations for not only design theorizing but also for explanatory theory. Starting with these to statements we did not only introduce relations between the concepts of the statements but also between the statements as such. We added the relations between the other statements, too.

References

Aier, S., & Fischer, C. (2011). Criteria of progress for information systems design theories. *Information Systems and E-Business Management, 9*(1), 133–172.

Avdiji, H., Elikan, D., Missonier, S., & Pigneur, Y. (2020). A design theory for visual inquiry tools. *Journal of the Association for Information Systems, 21*(3), 695–734.

Avdiji, H., & Winter, R. (2019). Knowledge gaps in design science research. *International Conference on Information Systems*. Munich, Germany.

Braun, C., Wortmann, F., Hafner, M., & Winter, R. (2005). Method construction – A core approach to organizational engineering. In H. Haddad, L. M. Liebrock, A. Omicini, & R. L. Wainwright (Eds.), *ACM symposium on applied computing* (Vol. 2, pp. 1295–1299). ACM.

Brosius, M., Aier, S., Haki, K., & Winter, R. (2018). Enterprise Architecture Assimilation: An Institutional Perspective. In *Proceedings of the 39th International Conference on Information Systems (ICIS 2018), San Francisco, USA.*

Buchmann, L., & Haki, K. (2021). Digital nudging for technical debt management: Insights from a technology-driven organization. In *54th Hawaii International Conference on System Sciences (HICSS 54). Maui, Hawaii, USA* (pp. 4094–4103).

Cahenzli, M., Deitermann, F., Aier, S., Haki, K., & Budde, L. (2022). Intra-organizational nudging: Designing a label for governing local decision-making. In R. Cuel, D. Ponte, & F. Virili (Eds.), *Exploring digital resilience - challenges for people and organizations* (pp. 232–246). Springer Nature.

Cram, W. A., Brohman, M. K., & Gallupe, R. B. (2016). Information systems control: A review and framework for emerging information systems processes. *Journal of the Association For Information Systems, 17*(4), 216–266.

Denyer, D., Tranfield, D., & van Aken, J. E. (2008). Developing design propositions through research synthesis. *Organization Studies, 29*, 393–413.

DiMaggio, P. J., & Powell, W. W. (1983). The iron cage revisited: Institutional isomorphism and collective rationality in organizational fields. *American Sociological Review, 48*(2), 147–160.

Drechsler, A., & Hevner, A. R. (2018). Utilizing, producing, and contributing design knowledge in DSR Projects. In S. Chatterjee, K. Dutta, & R. P. Sundarraj (Eds.), *Designing for a digital and globalized world* (pp. 82–97). Springer.

Fischer, C., Gregor, S., & Aier, S. (2012). Forms of Discovery for Design Knowledge. In *The 20th European Conference on Information Systems, Barcelona.*

Gleiniger, A., Vrachliotis, G., Bellut, C., Feichter, J., Mainzer, K., Brown, D. S., Terzidis, K., & Venturi, R. (2012). *Complexity: Design Strategy and World View*. Birkhäuser.

Goldkuhl, G. (2004). Design theories in information systems – A need for multi-grounding. *Journal of Information Technology Theory and Application, 6*(2), 59–72.

Gregor, S., Chandra Kruse, L., & Seidel, S. (2020). The anatomy of a design principle. *Journal of the Association for Information Systems, 21*(6), 1622–1652.

Gregor, S., & Hevner, A. R. (2013). Positioning and presenting design science research for maximum impact. *MIS Quarterly, 37*(2), 337–355.

Gregor, S., & Jones, D. (2007). The anatomy of a design theory. *Journal of the Association for Information Systems, 8*(5), 312–335.

Haki, K., Rieder, A., Buchmann, L., & Schneider, A. W. (2023). Digital nudging for technical debt management at credit suisse. *European Journal of Information Systems, 32*(1), 64–80.

Hevner, A. R., March, S. T., Park, J., & Ram, S. (2004). Design science in information systems research. *MIS Quarterly, 28*(1), 75–105.

IEEE. (2000). *IEEE Recommended Practice for Architectural Description of Software Intensive Systems* (IEEE Std 1471-2000).

Kirsch, L. J. (1997). Portfolios of control modes and is project management. *Information Systems Research, 8*(3), 215–239.

Kuechler, W., & Vaishnavi, V. (2012). A framework for theory development in design science research: Multiple perspectives. *Journal of the Association for Information systems, 13*(6), 395–423.

Malaurent, J., & Avison, D. (2016). Reconciling global and local needs: A canonical action research project to deal with workarounds. *Information Systems Journal, 26*(3), 227–257.

Meyer, J. W., & Rowan, B. (1977). Institutionalized organizations: Formal structure as myth and ceremony. *American Journal of Sociology, 83*(2), 340–363.

Morana, S., & A. Maedche (2020). Designing process guidance systems the case of IT service management. Design science research. Cases. J. vom Brocke, A. Hevner and A. Maedche. , Springer: 177-203.

Ouchi, W. G. (1979). A conceptual framework for the design of organizational control mechanisms. *Management Science, 25*(9), 833–848.

Peffers, K., Tuunanen, T., Rothenberger, M. A., & Chatterjee, S. (2007). A design science research methodology for information systems research. *Journal of Management Information Systems, 24*(3), 45–77.

Pries-Heje, J., & Baskerville, R. (2008). The design theory nexus. *MIS Quarterly, 32*, 731–755.

Schilling, R. D., Aier, S., & Winter, R. (2019). Designing an artifact for informal control in enterprise architecture management. In *International Conference on Information Systems*.

Sein, M. K., Henfridsson, O., Purao, S., Rossi, M., & Lindgren, R. (2011). Action design research. *MIS Quarterly, 35*(1), 37–56.

Thaler, R. H., & Sunstein, C. R. (2008). *Nudge. Improving decisions about health, wealth and happiness*. Penguin.

Tuunanen, T., Winter, R., & Vom Brocke, J. (2024). Dealing with complexity in design science research - A methodology using design echelons. *MIS Quarterly, 48*(2), 427–458.

Venable, J. R. (2006). The role of theory and theorising in design science research. In S. Chatterjee & A. Hevner (Eds.), *International conference on design science research in information systems and technology* (pp. 1–18).

vom Brocke, J., Winter, R., Hevner, A., & Maedche, A. (2020). Special issue editorial – Accumulation and evolution of design knowledge in design science research: A journey through time and space. *Journal of the Association for Information Systems, 21*(3), 520–544.

Weiss, S., Aier, S., & Winter, R. (2013). Institutionalization and the effectiveness of enterprise architecture management. In *34th International Conference on Information Systems (ICIS 2013). Milano, Italy*.

Widjaja, T., & Gregory, R. W. (2020). Monitoring the complexity of IT architectures: Design principles and an IT artifact. *Journal Of The Association For Information Systems, 21*(3), 664–694.

Abstraction and Abstraction Levels in Design Science Research

Robert Winter and Antonia Albani

1 Introduction

In general, design proposals in design science research (DSR) claim utility by associating a problem and a solution (Venable, 2006), i.e., by providing a solution that can be applied to solve a relevant problem—or to solve a number of relevant problems which share certain characteristics.

Routine problem-solving in business practice aims at developing *contextualized* solutions for *situated* problems—and may reuse successful solutions to address similar situated problems. In contrast, DSR aims at developing solution artefacts that can be *projected* to a problem *class* rather than a situated problem. The obvious difference between problem-solving practice and DSR is that in DSR (i) addressed problems have a higher level of abstraction (problem class instead of situated problem), (ii) designed solutions need to have a higher level of abstraction (applicability to a problem class instead of a situated problem), and (iii) the design proposal thus is "projectable" (Baskerville & Pries-Heje, 2019).

From a knowledge creation (and not just practical value) perspective, the contribution of a design proposal is the higher, the more "abstract" it is (Gregor & Hevner, 2013, p. 352).

When designing, however, researchers cannot focus on high levels of abstraction only. The instance level needs also to be considered to (i) sufficiently understand the addressed design problem instances (and characterize the problem class accordingly) and (ii) evaluate the proposed design solution's utility when instantiated and applied to problem instances in context (Hevner et al., 2004). Consequently, DSR always operates on at least two levels of abstraction, both for problems and for

R. Winter (✉) · A. Albani
Institute of Information Systems and Digital Business, University of St. Gallen,
St. Gallen, Switzerland
e-mail: Robert.Winter@unisg.ch

© The Author(s), under exclusive license to Springer Nature
Switzerland AG 2025
R. Winter (ed.), *Designing the Information Systems Artefact*, Progress in IS,
https://doi.org/10.1007/978-3-031-98311-5_3

solutions. Figure 1 illustrates a simplified DSR object model that spans two levels, the instance level and an abstract level. When abstract problems (i.e., problem classes) and abstract solutions (i.e., projectable designs) are involved, contextualized problems can be understood as problem instances and situated solutions can be understood as solution instances.

Different types of DSR outcomes have different "built-in" abstraction characteristics:

Solution *instances* (e.g., implemented information systems or implemented workflows) can usually be projected to a very small set of very similar problem instances (e.g., plant steering in specialty chemical industry)—and sometimes they may even usefully address only one unique problem instance.

Methods, (reference) models, frameworks, or *technological rules* are designed to be projectable to a broader yet specified range of problem instances (e.g., control of standard business processes, management of software development projects). Artefacts of these types need to be contextualized and/or instantiated to become applicable to actual problem instances. Methods are instantiated to contextualized workflows (e.g., for conducting a specific development project), reference models are instantiated to represent contextualized solutions (e.g., an implemented process or organizational structure), etc.

Design principles or *design theories* are usually designed to be projectable for a very large range of problems (e.g., agile organization). For artefacts of these types, a multi-step contextualization is necessary to "apply" them to represent useful solutions for actual problems.

As a consequence of the quest for projectability and many potentially relevant context dimensions, there exists not only one "abstract level" and one "instance level" in DSR. A DSR study may touch—particularly when artefacts of different types are designed in one project—different levels of abstraction. Figure 2 illustrates this situation.

Surprisingly, there is not much specific artefact-agnostic, methodological guidance available for understanding and navigating artefact abstraction. While the typology of design artefacts has been investigated thoroughly (see, e.g., chapter "Typology of IS Artefacts: Providing an Organizing Foundation for Design Science

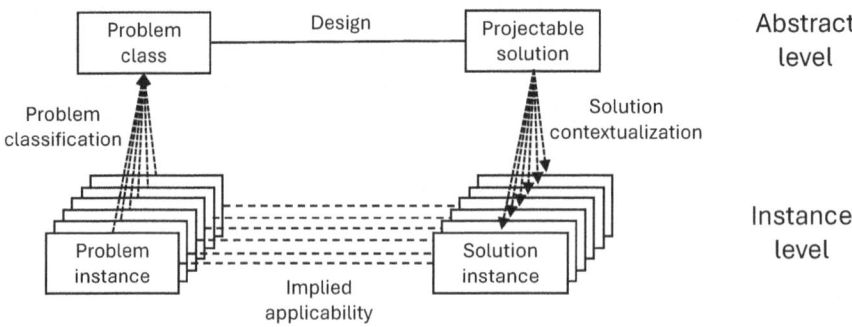

Fig. 1 Problem class, projectable solution, and design

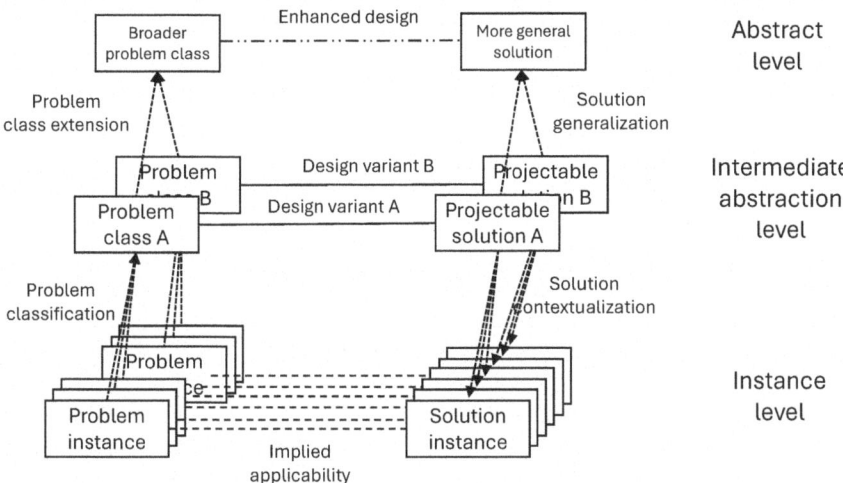

Fig. 2 Multiple levels of abstraction in DSR

Research Outcomes" in this book), their potential abstraction levels—and thus the projectability of the proposed designs—are often only regarded implicitly, if at all. Since researchers need to work both on the instance level and often on several levels of abstraction, and designs need to traverse different abstraction levels when conducting a DSR study or applying projectable designs, more guidance on *dealing with artefact abstraction* is needed.

The goal of this chapter is to

• Explore the role and significance of abstraction in DSR
• Demonstrate how abstraction works for important DSR outcome types
• Generalize abstraction in DSR and specify elementary operations to increase or reduce the abstraction level of problems, solutions, and designs
• Demonstrate how abstraction levels are traversed in DSR methods
• Discuss which guidelines are needed for dealing with abstraction in DSR

The chapter is structured as follows: In the next section, existing contributions on artefact abstraction in DSR are discussed. On this basis, we conceptualize DSR from an abstraction perspective and summarize related work on abstraction hierarchies in Sect. 3. Exemplary problem/solution abstraction hierarchies for important IS design artefacts are presented in Sect. 4. In Sect. 5, we generalize artefact abstraction in DSR and present five fundamental activities for increasing or decreasing the level of abstraction in DSR projects. In Sect. 6, we discuss which role abstraction has in different DSR process models.

2   Coverage of Artefact Abstraction in Design Science Research

"Abstraction and representation of appropriate means, ends, and laws are crucial components of design-science research" (Hevner et al., 2006, p. 88). Consequently, many methodological contributions to DSR address this aspect (e.g., Baskerville & Pries-Heje, 2010; Gregor & Hevner, 2013; Sein et al., 2011).

When analyzing extant DSR methodology discourses, a clear notion of abstraction and guidance on how to deal with abstraction in DSR is however missing. "While researchers widely regard the artifact as central in the paradigm, they have diverse opinions about what it is and how it matters" (Baskerville & Pries-Heje, 2019, p. 54). With the notion and typology of the IS artefact still being discussed among DSR scholars (see chapter "Typology of IS Artefacts: Providing an Organizing Foundation for Design Science Research Outcomes" in this book), it is difficult to clarify artefact abstraction and how to deal with it. While early contributions classify DSR artefacts as constructs, models, methods, and instances (Hevner et al., 2004; March & Smith, 1995), more recent discourses (such as Wieringa, 2014, p. 29: "[…] something created by people for some practical purpose") take a very broad view on what an artefact is, making it even more difficult to conceptualize abstraction and provide guidance on how to deal with it. Nevertheless, Gregor and Hevner emphasize the importance of understanding and defining the artefact to appreciate the various levels of artefact abstractions that may constitute DSR contributions. As stated in Gregor and Hevner (2013, p. 253), "An artifact that is presented with a higher level degree of abstraction can be generalized to other situations." Consequently, design theories have been proposed to be included in the DSR artefact typology (e.g., by Winter, 2008). Beyond typologies, Weigand et al. (2021) have proposed to introduce an artefact ontology to clarify its notion for use in DSR. They state that the DSR artefact should have at least a certain level of rigor and generalizability and should generalize over multiple use contexts (Weigand et al., 2021).

Although generalization and abstraction issues (as well as, related to that, reflection, theorizing, and projectability) are often discussed in DSR, only a few contributions can be found that conceptualize generalization or abstraction in a way that allows us to navigate between levels and to systematically understand these aspects beyond the context of a specific artefact type.

Design theories have been introduced to encapsulate abstract knowledge regarding the design and development of IS artefacts. Since there was little guidance on how to develop design theories in DSR, Gregor et al. introduced a framework to assist researchers in abstracting design knowledge for the creation of design theories, which give explicit prescriptions on how to design and develop an artefact (Gregor et al., 2013). *Theorizing* is achieved through inductive processes of reflection and abstraction. "…abstraction refers to the process of deriving abstract concepts (e.g., generic features) from observed instances (e.g., instances of a class of artifacts). Reflection, in broad terms, refers to contemplating about, and learning from, experiences made in the past. Together, these mental activities offer the potential to generate generic knowledge out of design practice" (Gregor et al., 2013, p. 2). Details about the levels of abstraction that can be reached through theorizing, however, are not presented. The authors only state that the abstraction levels very much depend on the nature of the artefacts, resulting in more- or less-formal design theories.

Lee et al. (2011) elaborate in their *idealized design theory framework* on the abstraction levels of theorizing. They introduce two levels of abstraction, the instance and the abstract domain. The framework goes along with four theorizing activities: abstraction, solution search, de-abstraction, and registration. Abstraction is realized by deriving common concepts while removing context-specific details from the instance problem. In the abstract domain, an explanatory design theory results from the abstract solution search process. Design practice theories are used in the transition from the abstract domain to the instance domain to bring a proposed artefact to life (de-abstraction). Registering is the evaluation of the solution instance. In their application of the framework in two cases it becomes clear that abstraction levels of instance problems may differ from case to case. In case 2 the abstraction activity cannot be observed because the case already started with an abstract problem. Further elaboration on the levels of abstraction of DSR instances and the generalized conceptualization of level navigation is therefore needed.

To reduce confusion about abstract knowledge contributions (e.g., design theories), Gregor and Hevner (2013) develop a *DSR knowledge contribution framework and schema*. They introduce three levels of artefact abstraction. On level 1, more specific and less mature knowledge can be found. Artefacts on this level are instantiations such as software products or implemented processes. More "abstract, complete, and mature" is located on higher levels of abstraction. For example, on level 2 artefacts such as constructs, methods, models, design principles, and technological rules are mentioned. Design theories are presented as artefacts on level 3. Using this framework, researchers can roughly classify their DSR contribution by understanding the general abstraction level of their designed artefact. However, level 2 is quite "crowded" with many different artefact types and not much specified abstraction sub-levels, and no guidance for abstraction (or de-abstraction) activities is given.

For specific artefact types, many abstraction levels have been reported. For *explanatory design theories,* a hierarchical arrangement of abstraction levels of the theories can be listed, where more specific theories inherit from more general theories (Baskerville & Pries-Heje, 2010). These authors divide design theory in design practice theory and explanatory design theory. The artefact type explanatory design theory "...prescribes principles that relate requirements to an incomplete description of an object" (Baskerville & Pries-Heje, 2010, p. 273). The more general the explanatory design theory is, the more critical is the degree of its incomplete description. Further, Wache et al. (2022) state that, given the fact that many abstraction levels can be seen in *design principles*, there still is limited knowledge available about advantages or disadvantages of using a certain level of abstraction. This fact hinders not only researchers in making informed decisions about the level of design principle abstraction, but also practitioners in applying the "best fitting" design principles. The authors illustrate such challenges by positioning design principles for chatbots in four quadrants. The dimensions of their positioning model are (i) abstraction level and (ii) the density of distinct concepts used in a design principle. This illustration nicely highlights the diversity of abstraction levels. However, what is still missing are guidelines for deciding about the required abstract levels for given design problems.

Approaches which set out to guide the *generalization* process are sparse but of great relevance. Mullarkey and Hevner (2019) elaborate on the Action Design Research (ADR) method (Sein et al., 2011) by including an artefact abstraction activity and adding the DSR principle *abstraction*. This allows us to highlight the DSR build activity and states "… that every ADR intervention cycle will introduce an artefact at the appropriate level of abstraction for the stage of project activity and goals" (Mullarkey & Hevner, 2019: 15). Cronholm et al. (2024), however, claim that there is no detailed guidance in the abstraction process activity. Seeing that necessity for detailing guidance in abstraction, they define prescriptive guidelines for the process of generalization. Those guidelines help to generalize design knowledge and to find the right level of abstraction. The guidelines have been derived by the analysis of three DSR projects and based on theoretical literature work. It is a first step in the right direction, but they are focusing on a specific DSR process model (see chapter "Function-Construction Patterns for Designing IS Artefacts" in this book) and need to be extended and validated beyond this specific process model and generalized across artefact types.

Another view on generalization in DSR is *projectability* (Baskerville & Pries-Heje, 2019). While generalization is often based on descriptive knowledge, gained from analyzing existing problems or class of problems, projection is concerned with prescriptive knowledge about future solutions. Baskerville and Pries-Heje (2019) name generalization also the backward-looking concept of generalization, whereas projection provides a "…forward-looking means to frame the future" (Baskerville & Pries-Heje, 2019, p. 54).

In summary, while there are several mindful contributions to dealing with abstraction and abstraction levels in DSR, one can state that there still is a lack of clarity regarding understanding abstraction levels beyond specific artefact types and regarding a complete set of activities to navigate between abstraction levels. This conclusion is underlined by the work of Seddon and Scheepers (2015), who state that the use of generalization in IS is often unsatisfactory. The authors criticize the conflicting positions of Lee and Baskerville (2003) and Tsang and Williams (2012) regarding generalization. While design theories and design principles are in the focus of abstraction activities, work on abstraction concerning other artefacts, e.g., methods, models, or constructs, is hard to find. In the following sections, we set out to close this gap by providing a conceptualization of artefact abstraction that can be applied to a broad range of artefact types and by proposing a set of artefact-agnostic activities that facilitate to navigate between different levels of artefact abstraction.

3   Conceptual Foundations

3.1   *Problem Abstraction vs. Solution Abstraction vs. Design Abstraction*

As discussed, both problems (classes) and solutions exist on various levels of abstraction. A problem class can comprise everything between one, few, and a very large number of problem instances. A solution may be usefully applicable to address one, relatively few, or a very large number of problems. Ideally, design should relate a problem class (which is addressed on a certain abstraction level) to a solution on *corresponding* abstraction levels. It is, however, possible that an abstract design (theory) is associated with a comparably narrow defined problem class or that a broad problem class is associated with a comparably specific solution.

As indicated earlier, during the DSR process it often is necessary to "navigate" between abstraction levels. Such a navigation is possible in two different directions:

1. Starting from more specific levels, more abstract problem classes can be derived by extension (considering additional problem instances) and/or generalization (relaxing the characteristics filter). They usually create a need for more abstract solutions—which allow them to be projected to a larger set of problem instances.
2. Starting from more abstract levels, it is also possible to narrow down the focus to more specific problem classes. This usually allows us to specialize solutions that need to be projected to fewer problem instances (e.g., to achieve higher utility by reducing problem variety).

Since *design* in DSR is understood as an association between a problem class and a projectable solution, design contributions aiming at *improvement* (Gregor & Hevner, 2013) will generally (i) extend or generalize the addressed problem class, (ii) consequently require the solution to be developed to be projectable to that extended/generalized problem class—and the widened utility claim will need to be (iii) increased by adding evaluative evidence (vom Brocke et al., 2020).

In Fig. 3, problem class β denotes an extension/generalization of problem class α; solution B is designed to be projectable to more problem instances than solution A. Consequently, the enhanced design proposal (associating B with β) would be considered an improvement of the initial design proposal (associating A with α). It should be noted that both design proposals are based on analyses that cannot cover all possible problem instances in α, β and all possible solution contextualizations. In every specific study, only a (small) fraction of possible problem instances can be analyzed, only a (small) fraction of potential solutions can be contextualized ("demonstrated"), and even fewer contextualized solutions can be evaluated.

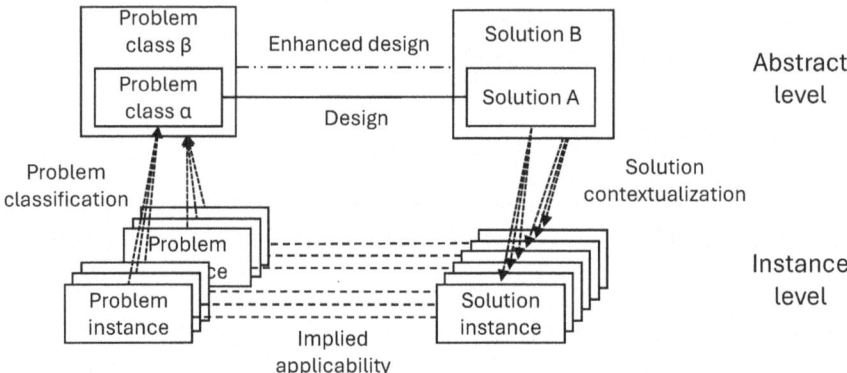

Fig. 3 Enhancing projectabilty in DSR

3.2   Abstraction in Other Fields

In DSR, problem classes and solutions can be interpreted as *object references* of design proposals. If multiple levels of abstraction have to be regarded, such references form an *abstraction hierarchy*. Abstraction hierarchies have been investigated in various fields, including hierarchical production planning (cf., e.g., Winter, 1996) or multidimensional data analytics (cf., e.g., Pedersen & Jensen, 1999).

In DSR, designs reference the problem space and the solution space. In production planning, in contrast, (planned or actual) production references the product space, the time space, the resource space, and maybe even other reference spaces. Any item of interest (e.g., planned or actual production) is referring to a product on some level of aggregation (item, product family, product group/category, etc.), a time unit on some level of aggregation (shift, day, week, etc.), a resource on some level of aggregation (machine, production line, plant, etc.), and maybe other relevant reference objects. These references can be to any level of abstraction. Figure 4 illustrates how plan data on different levels of precision refer to two abstraction hierarchies. Using the aggregation or decomposition dependencies implied by the abstraction hierarchies, plans on different abstraction levels can be kept consistent and changes can be propagated (Winter, 1996). It should be noted that plan data may be associated with references on different aggregation levels at the same time (e.g., weekly production plan for product variants, daily production plan for product groups).

In multidimensional data analytics, analysis objects reference a wide range of potential context dimensions—often up to eight or more dimensions whose combination promises to create relevant insights. Any item of interest (e.g., planned or actual sales) can be related to a product on some level of aggregation (item, product family, product group/category, etc.), a time unit on some level of aggregation (hour, day, week, etc.), a location on some level of aggregation (store, region, market, etc.), and/or many other references whose combination may allow insights. These

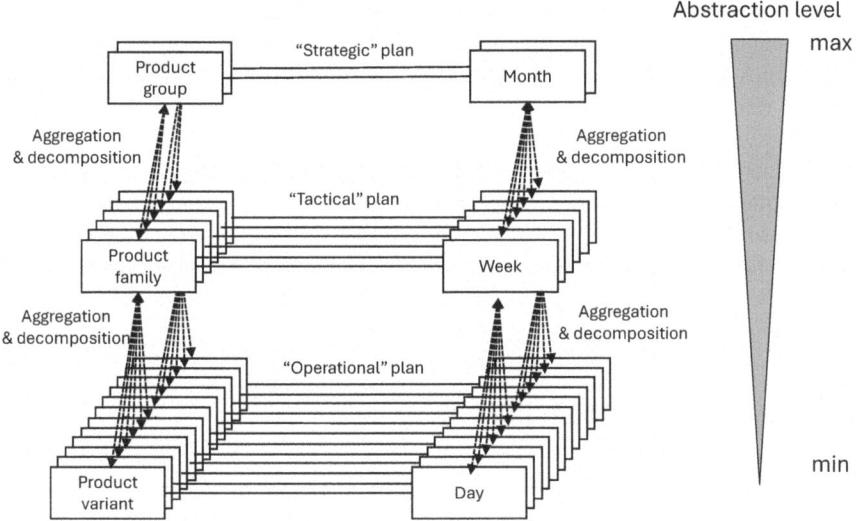

Fig. 4 Hierarchical production planning

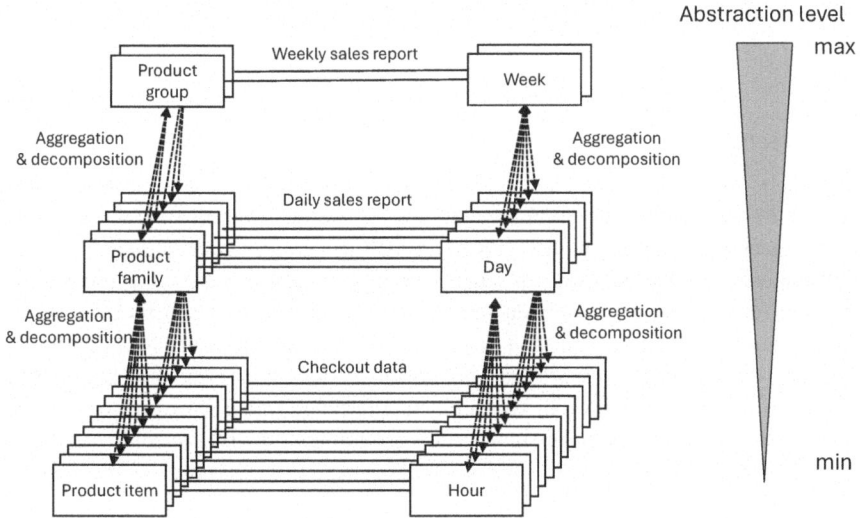

Fig. 5 Multidimensional data analysis

references can be to any level of abstraction. Figure 5 illustrates how sales analyses on different levels of abstraction refer to two abstraction hierarchies. Using the aggregation or decomposition dependencies implied by the abstraction hierarchies, analyses on different abstraction levels can be kept consistent and changes can be propagated. It should be noted that sales data may be associated with references on different aggregation levels at the same time (e.g., daily sales per product group, weekly sales for select product items). In online analytical processing, often many concurrent abstraction hierarchies are used to support a large variety and flexibility of analytics (Codd et al., 1993). In addition to product and time, more- or less-abstract references could be to sales location, campaign, customer (segment), or other possibly relevant contexts.

Abstraction hierarchies can be found in different domains. Based on the aggregation/decomposition semantics between their levels, the semantics of the item of interest can be managed when traversing different levels of aggregation or precision. We believe that this fundamental concept can also be useful for dealing with abstraction levels in DSR.

4 Artefact Abstraction in DSR

In this section, we demonstrate how abstraction works for important types of DSR outcomes (see chapter "Typology of IS Artefacts: Providing an Organizing Foundation for Design Science Research Outcomes" in this book). Referring to the conceptualizations introduced in the preceding section, the "item of interest" is the design proposal. Design proposals always reference a problem class (on various levels of abstraction) and a more- or less-abstract solution.

4.1 Method

As a well-understood example of a method, we illustrate different abstraction levels for a project management method (PMM). PMBOK (Project Management Institute, 2008) intends to cover all kinds of (change) projects and all aspects of project management for companies in all industries. More specific PMMs will focus, e.g., on technochange projects as a class of projects or on a specific industry (e.g., utilities). Even more specific PMM methods may cover certain subclasses of technochange projects (such as introducing or replacing standard enterprise software) or may be tailored to legislative conditions in a certain geography. Finally, a specialized PMM may be configured to be applicable for small organizations that replace their enterprise software.

The resulting abstraction hierarchy for methods is illustrated in Fig. 6. It combines different abstraction dimensions: focus (when, where, and by whom is method used), depth (which aspects of the problem are covered), and projectability (range of the addressed problem class).

It should be noted that, on every mentioned level of abstraction, the designed artefact is still a method, i.e., a generic artefact that becomes instantiated by applying it in a concrete context, resulting in concrete schedules, task assignment, and analysis/design documents.

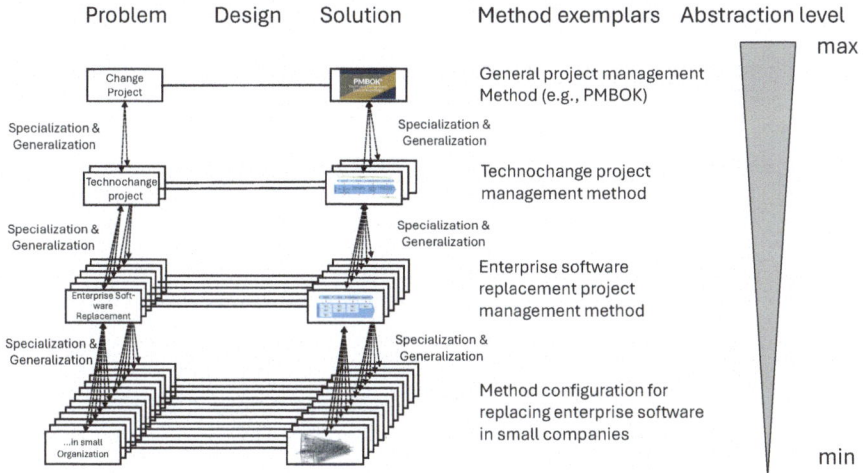

Fig. 6 Abstraction of (project management) method

It should also be noted that the abstraction levels are not linked by aggregation or decomposition relationships, but instead by specialization or generalization relationships, respectively.

4.2 Model

As a well-understood example of a model, we illustrate different abstraction levels for a reference process model (RPM). Generic RPMs, e.g., for the order-to-cash process (https://www.salesforce.com/sales/cpq/what-is-order-to-cash/), intend to cover all kinds of business models, all kinds of products, all potential channels, etc. More specific RPMs may focus, e.g., on a type of business model (e.g., retail, wholesale, platform), a customer segment (e.g., public administration), or a legal context (e.g., WTO-governed business). More specific RPMs may then cover certain subtypes of products such as perishable foods. An even more specific RPM can be tailored to certain product sub-categories and/or specific demand patterns (such as small conveniences stores).

The resulting abstraction hierarchy for RPM is illustrated in Fig. 7. It combines different abstraction dimensions: focus (when, where, for what, and by whom is model used), depth (which aspects of the problem are covered), and projectability (range of the addressed problem class).

It should be noted that, on every level of abstraction, the designed artefact is still a reference model, i.e., a generic artefact that becomes instantiated by applying it in a concrete context, resulting in concrete workflow models, task definitions, and analysis/design documents.

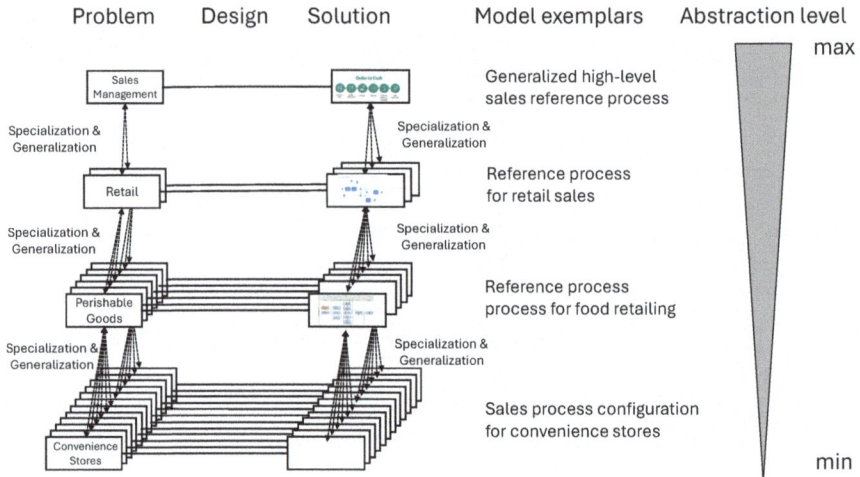

Fig. 7 Abstraction of (reference process) model

Also, for models, the abstraction levels are not linked by aggregation or decomposition relationships, but instead by contextualization or decontextualization relationships, respectively.

4.3 Construct

As an example of a construct, the typology of DSR artefacts is chosen (cf. chapter "Typology of IS Artefacts: Providing an Organizing Foundation for Design Science Research Outcomes" in this book). The most generic artefact typology (AT) intends to cover all kinds of DSR artefacts. More specific ATs focus, e.g., on a certain type of artefacts (e.g., models or methods). Even more specifically, an AT may focus on subtypes of one specific type (e.g., maturity models). An even more specific AT can be tailored to certain maturity models, e.g., by capability maturity models or maturity models for a certain domain.

An abstraction hierarchy for DSR artefact typology is illustrated in Fig. 8. It combines different abstraction dimensions: focus (for which application area is typology used), depth (to which level of detail are artefacts covered), and projectability (range of the classified artefacts).

It should be noted that, on every level of abstraction, the solution artefact is still a typology/taxonomy, i.e., a generic artefact that becomes instantiated by applying it in a concrete context, resulting in concrete assignment of artefact instances to certain types.

Also, for constructs, the abstraction levels are not linked by aggregation or decomposition relationships, but by contextualization or decontextualization relationships, respectively.

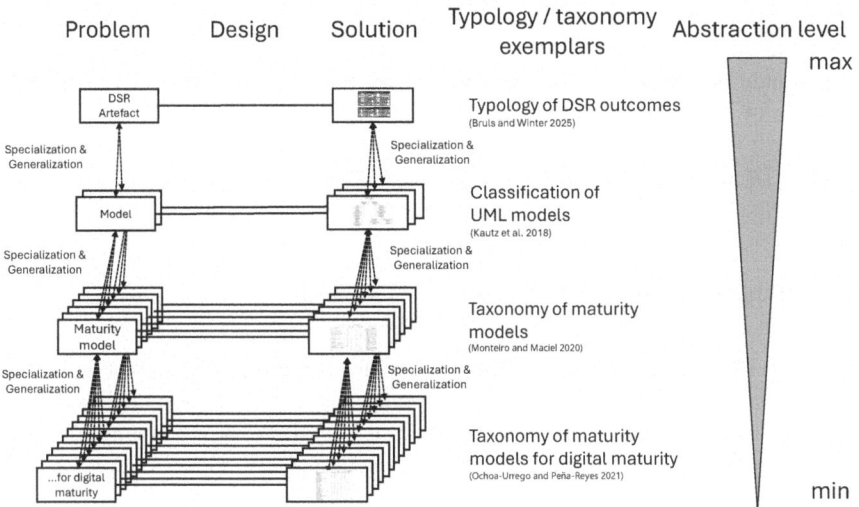

Fig. 8 Abstraction of (typology) construct

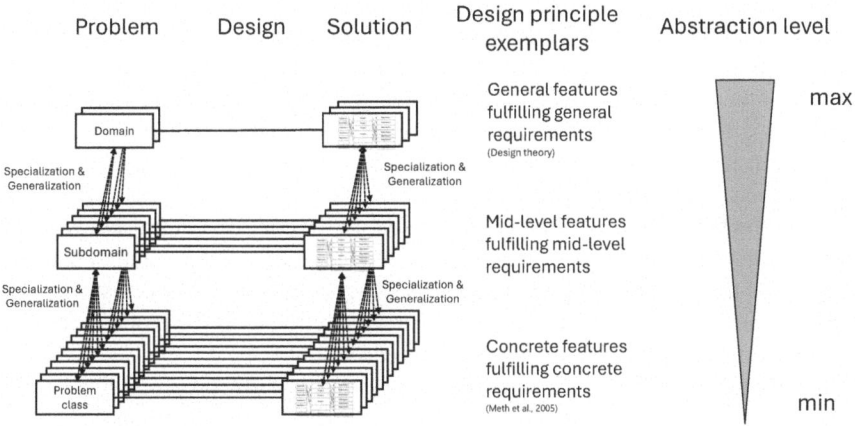

Fig. 9 Abstraction of design principle

4.4   Design Principle

As an example of design knowledge, we illustrate an artefact abstraction hierarchy for design principles (DP) in Fig. 9. Abstract DPs show how general requirements can be fulfilled by generalized solution features—the essential property of "explanatory design theory" (Baskerville & Pries-Heje, 2010). Concrete DPs show how concrete requirements (for situated solutions) can be fulfilled by contextualized solution features (Meth et al., 2015). In between coverage of an entire domain and coverage of a specific problem class, many intermediate levels of abstraction are thinkable for design principles.

It should be noted that, on every level of abstraction, the design knowledge has the form of a design principle, i.e., a generic artefact that becomes instantiated by applying it in a concrete context, resulting in realized features of concrete solution entities (Drechsler & Hevner, 2018).

5 Navigating Between Abstraction Levels

In the preceding section, we have demonstrated for common DSR artefact types that the problem space and the solution space can be structured as abstraction hierarchies. When analyzing problems, constructing solutions, or evaluating designs, designers often need to navigate between abstraction levels. Some examples are:

1. If a solution does not sufficiently address all problems in a problem class, the problem class may need to be reduced (specialization) to increase design utility.
2. If a solution works well for a given problem class, the design contribution may be increased by extending the problem class (abstraction).

During all phases of the DSR process, abstraction levels are implied by differences in focus (when, where, and by whom is the design needed), depth (which aspects of the problem are covered), and projectability (range of the addressed problem class). Designs exist on different levels of abstraction, determined by the abstraction level of the addressed problem and the abstraction level of the solution—which can be different.

From the perspective of artefact abstraction, the overall design process is separated into (i) the sub-process of creating or selecting an abstract solution and (ii) "applying" this abstract solution to address the problem class of interest. For the "application," i.e., the adaptation of the abstract solution to fit the problem (class), five fundamentally different transformations can be used.

In his analysis of reference modeling, vom Brocke (2007) proposed five design "principles for reuse" of abstract ("reference") models. From an artefact-agnostic abstraction perspective in this chapter, these principles can be understood as fundamental specialization operations. Table 1 illustrates these operations, i.e., transitions from a more abstract to a less abstract level in the abstraction hierarchy of solutions.

In principle, these operations can be applied to other types of artefacts. Becker et al. (2007), for example, describe these five operations for specializing methods.

Progress in DSR often means to create more abstract problem–solution associations based on a set of more specific problems and solutions (cf., e.g., Sein et al., 2011). Consequently, we do not only need to apply specialization operations in DSR abstraction hierarchies like the five ones presented in Table 1—we also need to move into the opposite direction, i.e., we need *abstraction operations*.

By *reverting* the five artefact specialization operations, we propose the following five abstraction operations for DSR:

Table 1 Fundamental options for specialization/contextualization of abstract artefacts (inspired by vom Brocke, 2007, pp. 58–68)

Specialization operation	Visualization	Description
Analogy		The abstract artefact serves as a means of orientation for the construction of a specialized/contextualized artefact. The relation between the artefacts is based on a perceived similarity of both regarding a certain aspect.
Specialization		The specialized/contextualized artefact is characterized by adding (but not replacing) components to the abstract artefact that make it better suitable for a certain context.
Aggregation		The specialized/contextualized artefact is created by a combination of one or more abstract artefact (or artefact components.
Instantiation		The specialized/contextualized artefact is created by integrating one or several extensions into appropriate generic place holders of the abstract artefact.
Configuration		The specialized/contextualized artefact is created by following configuration rules provided by the abstract artefact that define how to select and combine certain of its components.

(1) *Pattern-oriented* **generalization:** If different "similar" artefacts appear to have been developed by following certain solution patterns, they may be replaced by the underlying patterns (for pattern identification, see Lösser & Winter, 2025).

For the RPM example, sales processes for different payment options may result from applying a common process design pattern or adapting an original process model to cover alternative payment options.

(2) *Commonality* **generalization:** If different "similar" artefacts can be interpreted as *specializations* of a more abstract artefact, this abstract artefact can be created by concentrating on common components and ignoring components that differ between artefacts (for generalization, see Smith & Smith, 1977).

For the RPM example, different payment options in otherwise similar sales processes can be ignored to create a general process model that has to be complemented by a "payment" component in an application context.

(3) *Compositional* **generalization:** If different "similar" artefacts can be interpreted as *compositions* from a set of more abstract building blocks, this set of abstract (building block) artefacts can be constructed by systematically analyzing identical and different components and deriving combination rules (for building block identfification, see Aporntewan & Chongstitvatana, 2003).

For the RPM example, different payment options in otherwise similar sales processes can be generalized to a payment-agnostic process building block model and different payment-specific process building blocks. Together with composition rules, the combination of payment-agnostic and payment-specific modules makes up an abstract RPM.

(4) *Fusion* **generalization:** If different "similar" artefacts can be interpreted as *instantiations* of a more abstract artefact, this abstract artefact can be constructed

by concentrating on common properties and ignoring differentiating properties (for generalization, see Smith & Smith, 1977).

For the RPM example, different payment options in otherwise similar sales processes can be generalized to a generic "payment" step in a unified, general process model.

(5) *Configurative* **generalization:** If different "similar" artefacts can be interpreted as *configurations* of a more abstract artefact, this abstract artefact can be constructed by systematically analyzing identical and different properties and deriving respective configuration rules. In some way, this "reverse pattern" resembles the Quantitative Comparative Analysis approach (for QCA, see Rihoux & Ragin, 2009).

For the RPM example, different payment options in otherwise similar sales processes can be generalized giving a unified, general process model which "branches" internally to the different options within.

The proposed abstraction operations are illustrated in Table 2. Although most generalization operations appear to be applicable across most types of design artefacts, this claim needs to be supported by future research and DSR practice. Together, the ten artefact operations (five for specialization/contextualization and five for generalization) form a "vocabulary" for navigating the solution space and deriving design propositions in DSR on the desired level of abstraction.

Table 2 Fundamental options for artefact abstraction

Abstraction operation	Visualization	Description	Corresponding generalization
Pattern-oriented generalization		Four different forms of temple fronts are generalized to one generic temple facade.	Analogy
Commonality generalization		Four different types of rectangles are generalized to a generic rectangle.	Specialization
Compositional generalization		Three symbols that combine certain graphical elements are transformed into the set of elements from which they are composed.	Aggregation
Fusion generalization		Four rectangles with different fill patterns are generalized to a generic rectangle with "fill pattern" as a property.	Instantiation
Configurative generalization		Four graphical elements with different numbers of angles and different colours are related to a table that lists the respective number of angles and the respective colour for every element.	Configuration

6 Conclusions: Recommendations for Dealing with Abstraction in DSR

Different DSR process models imply different paths through abstraction levels. The widely adopted design science process model (Peffers et al., 2007) implies that analysis, design, and conclusion take place on the highest justifiable level of abstraction (= intended projectability), while demonstration and evaluation are based on artefact instances. The typical "movement pattern" starting with specialization (for instance-level demonstration and evaluation) and abstraction (for publishing the abstract contribution) is illustrated in the upper left corner of Fig. 10.

The Action Design Research process (Sein et al., 2011) starts with actual solution instances addressing contextualized problems which ultimately support a final "learn and theorize" phase that generalizes the design on the highest justifiable level of abstraction (= intended projectability). The typical "movement pattern" starting

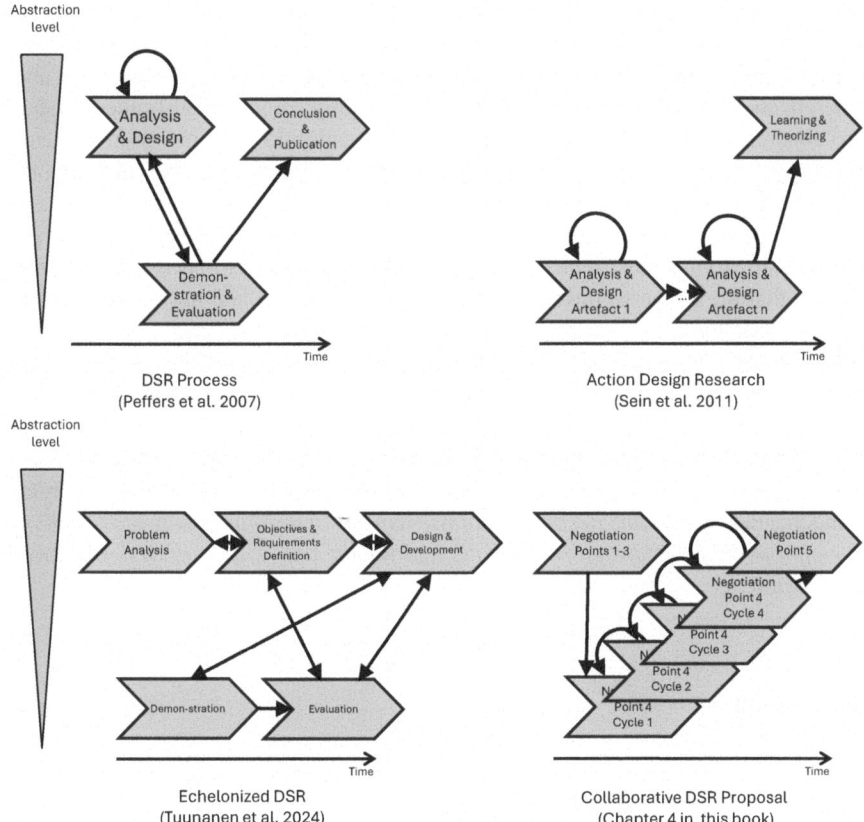

Fig. 10 Implied abstraction levels for selected DSR process models

with solution instances and finishing with abstraction (for learning and theorizing) is illustrated in the upper right corner of Fig. 10.

The echelonized DSR approach (Tuunanen et al., 2024) starts with problem analysis which is followed by several instances of objectives and requirements and design and development echelons on higher levels of abstraction as well as several instances of demonstration and evaluation echelons on instance level. Its typical "movement pattern" is illustrated in the lower left corner of Fig. 10.

In chapter "Collaborative Evolution of the IS Artefact: Negotiating Research/ Practice Tensions" of this book, a collaborative research-practice DSR process is proposed that successively increases design projectability while preserving usefulness and confidence. In contrast to the other two approaches that basically differentiate only an instance and an abstract level of design, this DSR process proposal successively increases the level of abstraction, thereby trying to combine usefulness objectives (for practice stakeholders) and contribution objectives (for research stakeholders) according to the "managed evolution" approach (Murer et al., 2010). The resulting "movement pattern" is illustrated in the lower right corner of Fig. 10.

While the sequence of abstraction levels depends on the chosen DSR process model, the design proposal's claim as well as the evaluative evidence, specialization, and generalization is essential in all approaches. The presented exemplary artefact abstraction hierarchies and the proposed artefact-agnostic specialization and generalization operations promise to provide not only a conceptual framework but also concrete guidance for (i) understanding abstraction in DSR in a more systematic way, (ii) choosing appropriate forms and levels of abstraction, and (iii) supporting the researcher's navigation in that space.

We are aware that the usefulness of the presented approach to separate abstraction/specialization from artefact type-specific design considerations is not evaluated yet. We therefore plan to raise more interest in abstraction and abstraction hierarchies in DSR by, e.g., including these aspects in methodology teaching. We hope that DSR projects in complex contexts will pick up our suggestions and apply the proposed concepts and operations, which will allow us to gain evaluative evidence. The selection of a promising solution artefact type (see chapter "Function-Construction Patterns for Designing IS Artefacts" of this book for design patterns) and the choice of a most appropriate level of abstraction can and should be regarded as independent—*and this decoupling of two aspects of designing may also open up new options both for design researchers and for the application of designed artefacts in practice.*

References

Aporntewan, C., & Chongstitvatana, P. (2003). Building-block identification by simultaneity matrix. *Soft Computing, 11*, 214–214.

Baskerville, R. L., & Pries-Heje, J. (2010). Explanatory design theory. *Business and Information Systems Engineering, 2*, 271–282.

Baskerville, R., & Pries-Heje, J. (2019). Projectability in Design science research. *Journal of Information Technology Theory and Application, 20.*

Becker, J., Janiesch, C., & Pfeiffer, D. (2007). Reuse mechanisms in situational method engineering. In J. Ralyté, S. Brinkkemper, & B. Henderson-Sellers (Eds.), *IFIP WG8.1 Working Conference on Situational Method Engineering - Fundamentals and Experiences (ME07).* Springer.

Codd, E. F., Codd, S. B., & Salley, C. T. (1993). *Providing OLAP to user-analysts: An IT mandate.* E.F. Codd & Associates.

Cronholm, S., Göbel, H., Sjöström, J., & Juell-Skielse, G. (2024). Generalisation of *design science research.* In *32nd European Conference on Information Systems (ECIS 2024).* Paphos.

Drechsler, A., & Hevner, A. R. (2018). Utilizing, producing, and contributing design knowledge in DSR projects. In S. Chatterjee, K. Dutta, & R. P. Sundarraj (Eds.), *Designing for a digital and globalized world.* Springer.

Gregor, S., Müller, O., & Seidel, S. (2013). Reflection, abstraction and theorizing in design and development research. In *Twenty First European Conference on Information Systems (ECIS) 2013*, Paper 83. Utrecht.

Gregor, S., & Hevner, A. R. (2013). positioning and presenting design science research for maximum impact. *MIS Quarterly, 37,* 337–355.

Hevner, A. R., March, S. T., Park, J., & Ram, S. (2004). Design science in information systems research. *MIS Quarterly, 28,* 75–105.

Hevner, A. R., March, S. T., Park, J., & Ram, S. (2006). Design science in information systems research. In J. L. King & K. Lyytinen (Eds.), *Information systems: The state of the field.* Wiley & Sons.

Lee, A. S., & Baskerville, R. L. (2003). Generalizing generalizability in information systems research. *Information Systems Research, 14,* 221–243.

Lee, J. S., Pries-Heje, J., & Baskerville, R. (2011). Theorizing in design science research. In *Service-Oriented Perspectives in Design Science Research, 6th International Conference on Design Science Research in Information Systems and Technology (DESRIST 2011).* Springer.

Lösser, B., & Winter, R. (2025). Towards design patterns – finding suitable artefact type candidates for a design problem. In *HICSS-58* (pp. 5365–5374). Waikoloa Village, HI.

March, S. T., & Smith, G. F. (1995). Design and natural science research on information technology. *Decision Support Systems, 15,* 251–266.

Meth, H., Müller, B., & Maedche, A. (2015). Designing a requirement mining system. *Journal of the Association of Information Systems, 16,* 799–837.

Mullarkey, M. T., & Hevner, A. R. (2019). An elaborated action design research process model. *European Journal of Information Systems, 28,* 6–20.

Murer, S., Bonati, B., & Furrer, F. J. (2010). *Managed evolution: A strategy for very large information systems.* Springer, Heidelberg.

Pedersen, T. B., & Jensen, C. S. (1999). Multidimensional data modeling for complex data. In *Proceedings 15th international conference on data engineering* (pp. 336–345). IEEE.

Peffers, K., Tuunanen, T., Rothenberger, M. A., & Chatterjee, S. (2007). A design science research methodology for information systems research. *Journal of Management Information Systems, 24,* 45–77.

Project Management Institute. (2008). *A guide to the project management body of knowledge.* Project Management Institute.

Rihoux, B., & Ragin, C. C. (2009). *Configurational comparative methods: Qualitative comparative analysis (QCA) and related techniques.* Sage, London.

Seddon, P. B., & Scheepers, R. (2015). Generalization in IS research: a critique of the conflicting positions of Lee & Baskerville and Tsang & Williams. *Journal of Information Technology, 30,* 30–43.

Sein, M. K., Henfridsson, O., Purao, S., Rossi, M., & Lindgren, R. (2011). Action design research. *MIS Quarterly, 35,* 37–56.

Smith, J. M., & Smith, D. C. P. (1977). Database abstractions: Aggregation and generalization. *ACM Transactions on Database Systems (TODS), 2*, 105–133.

Tsang, E. W. K., & Williams, J. N. (2012). Generalization and induction: Misconceptions, clarifications, and a classification of induction. *MIS Quarterly, 36*, 729–748.

Tuunanen, T., Winter, R., & Vom Brocke, J. (2024). Dealing with complexity in design science research - A methodology using design echelons. *MIS Quarterly, 48*, 427–458.

Venable, J. R. (2006). The role of theory and theorising in design science research. In S. Chatterjee & A. Hevner (Eds.), *International conference on design science research in information systems and technology* (pp. 1–18). CA, USA.

vom Brocke, J. (2007). Design principles for reference modeling - reusing information models by means of aggregation, specialization, instantiation, and analogy. In P. Fettke & P. Loos (Eds.), *Reference modeling for business systems analysis*. Hershey.

vom Brocke, J., Winter, R., Hevner, A., & Maedche, A. (2020). Special issue editorial – accumulation and evolution of design knowledge in design science research: A journey through time and space. *Journal of the Association for Information Systems, 21*, 520–544.

Wache, H., Möller, F., Schoormann, T., Strobel, G., & Petrik, D. (2022) Exploring the abstraction levels of design principles: The case of chatbots. In *WIRTSCHAFTSINFORMATIK*.

Weigand, H., Johannesson, P., & Andersson, B. (2021). An artifact ontology for design science research. *Data & Knowledge Engineering, 133*.

Wieringa, R. J. (2014). *Design Science Methodology for Information Systems and Software Engineering*.

Winter, R. (1996). Continuous abstraction hierarchies in hierarchical production planning. *Journal of Decision Systems, 5*, 11–34.

Winter, R. (2008). Design science research in Europe. *European Journal of Information Systems, 17*, 470–475.

Collaborative Evolution of the IS Artefact: Negotiating Research/Practice Tensions

Robert Winter and Alan Hevner

1 Tensions Between Research and Practice in Design Science Research

Balancing practical artefact development and theoretical contributions is essential for design-oriented research (Baskerville et al., 2018). Since practitioners and researchers have different objectives and concerns, balanced outcomes can however only be achieved through close and continuous collaboration. While general methodological guidance for DSR is available, mature, and widely adopted, recent studies (Cronholm et al., 2024; Haj-Bolouri et al., 2018) state persistent challenges not only for producing generalizable knowledge from situationally developed solutions that can be transferred to other organizational contexts (see chapter "Abstraction and Abstraction Levels in Design Science Research" of this book) but also for dealing with different stakeholder intentions. Current DSR process models, such as the Design Science Research Methodology (Peffers et al., 2007) and Action Design Research (Mullarkey & Hevner, 2019; Sein et al., 2011), provide epistemological approaches that call for integrating the activities of researchers and practitioners but do little (i) to reconcile project tensions due to their differing project goals and (ii) to provide methodological actionable guidance for coordinating activities and balancing mutually successful research outcomes.

Fundamental tensions arise among varied stakeholders due to different backgrounds, expectations, constraints, aspirations, and skillsets that key stakeholder

R. Winter (✉)
Institute of Information Systems and Digital Business, University of St. Gallen,
St. Gallen, Switzerland
e-mail: Robert.Winter@unisg.ch

A. Hevner
School of Information Systems and Management, Muma College of Business, University of
South Florida, Tampa, FL, USA

© The Author(s), under exclusive license to Springer Nature
Switzerland AG 2025
R. Winter (ed.), *Designing the Information Systems Artefact*, Progress in IS,
https://doi.org/10.1007/978-3-031-98311-5_4

groups bring to a collaborative project team. In particular, we emphasize the different goals of practitioners and researchers in a DSR project. Practitioners desire situated design solutions with measurable impacts for intervention and use in practice as artefact instantiations. To meet utility and sustainability goals, effective solutions should be as application specific (i.e., situated, contextualized) as possible. Such design solutions are only abstracted to serve as reference artefacts (e.g., constructs, models, methods) to be reused in the solution of similar application problems. In contrast, researchers look to generate novel design knowledge (DK) through the creation, evaluation, and use of artefacts that can be generalized in the form of design postulates (Drechsler & Hevner, 2015). To achieve a scientific contribution, internal and external validity measures are of paramount importance. Generalized design postulates are contextualized to validate problem understanding and evaluate solution goodness.

Although preferred artefact abstraction levels (see chapter "Abstraction and Abstraction Levels in Design Science Research" of this book) and design knowledge goals are different, successful outcomes of a DSR project must satisfy both practitioners and researchers. This requires a project management approach that supports close collaboration and negotiation at key points in the project process. Practitioners and researchers bring specific knowledge and distinct capabilities to the project and must work together effectively in close collaboration.

In most documented DSR projects (see Sect. 3), practitioners and researchers collaborate mainly at the beginning (problem analysis) and the end (solution evaluation) of the research. Effective alignment and an efficient collaboration however cannot be achieved with attention at only the preliminary and concluding phases. The iterative nature of design requires *evolutionary, continuous* collaboration throughout the DSR project. While the different aspirations of practitioners and researchers are not incompatible, a full understanding of how best to trade off budget, schedule, resources, and staffing to achieve both in a solution is rarely seen in DSR projects and is not specifically supported in current DSR methods. Instead, design projects often place attention on only one of the two outcomes: (i) practice impacts or (ii) knowledge contributions. Consequently, there are different ideas about the importance and representation of DSR artefacts as design knowledge research contributions (system instantiations vs. abstract generalizations). Both perspectives overlap and compete in the research/practice interspace of collaboration. Aiming at both, achieving a practice impact and making a knowledge contribution, DSR projects need to navigate important tensions in this complex interspace of research and practice (as shown in Fig. 1).

The *practice perspective* of the DSR project centers on the application environment with a grounded understanding of the problems and opportunities to be addressed. Project resources of systems, technologies, human stakeholders, budgets, and schedules constrain and bound feasible solutions. Pragmatic goals of utility provide an effective, efficient, and situated solution with sufficient sustainability to support the solution's adaptability to change in the environment. These practice impacts are evaluated rigorously in context during each iteration of the DSR project cycles.

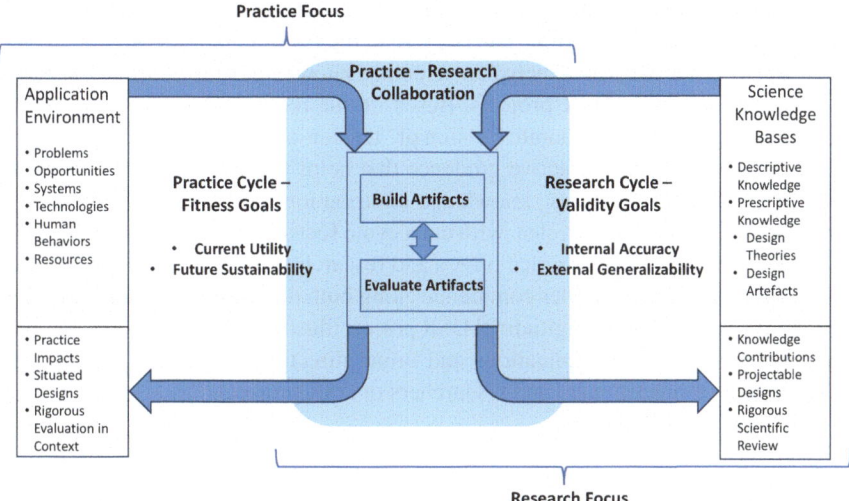

Fig. 1 Practice and research collaboration in a design science research project

Occurring simultaneously, the *research perspective* of the DSR project has its focus on consuming existing and producing new design knowledge during the DSR cycles. Researchers appropriate and apply extant knowledge via rigorous methods of design and evaluation to grow new knowledge in the application context of the project. Research goals balance the internal validity of the knowledge to accurately solve the specific problem and the external validity to extend the knowledge in the form of projectable (i.e., generalizable) outcomes in the form of design principles or theories for broader and different application contexts. Rigorous scientific evaluation methods are applied to assess the achievement of these goals during each iteration of the DSR project cycles.

As shown in Fig. 1, the intersection of practice and research foci requires close stakeholder collaborations in the build/evaluate DSR cycles of the project. Each cycle should produce artefacts that satisfy both practice and research goals. However, we must recognize that progress on each of these dimensions will vary based on the design/evaluate activities of that cycle (vom Brocke et al., 2020). While some cycles will produce greater progress on practice goals (e.g., increasing solution fitness), other cycles will produce greater progress on research goals (e.g., increasing solution projectability). Managing progress in this collaborative project intersection to satisfy both stakeholder groups is the research objective of this chapter. We propose to elaborate the functional (black-box) perspective of complex DSR projects, to decompose knowledge and impact improvements into perspectives that are not only instrumental for a better understanding of the objectives of knowledge accumulation and evolution in DSR, but also to provide a basis for guiding mixed practitioner/researcher teams to more effectively balance their differing goals and objectives.

We begin by introducing two concepts which we believe are fundamental to address tensions in the collaborative evolutionary DSR process, *tension-aware management techniques* and the concept of *managed evolution*. We then summarize a literature survey that identifies current research gaps of comprehensive guidance for navigating the interspace between scientific knowledge contribution and practice impact creation in DSR projects. Based on the requirements identified in the literature discussion, we elaborate a vision of "tension-aware managed evolution"—an innovative artefact with active guidance that helps to achieve improvements in both areas of project success (knowledge contribution and impact creation) by a staged sequence of design cycles, with each cycle focusing on measurable progress among the dimensions of practice fitness and research validity with rigorous evaluations that provide stakeholder confidence along both dimensions. A demonstration case study grounded on a longitudinal DSR project illustrates the proposed approach. We close with research implications and future directions to achieve an effective collaboration of practitioners and researchers in DSR projects.

2 Conceptual Foundations

Our evolutionary model for practitioner/research collaboration is grounded in the applications of tension-aware management theories and concepts of managed project evolution.

2.1 Tension-Aware Management

Tensions among human actors are decomposed into various competing demands or opposing elements in different dimensions or levels (e.g., standard vs. variety of output; control vs. autonomy of actors; collective vs. individual identification) (Smith & Lewis, 2011; Wareham et al., 2014). Referring to Mini and Widjaja's (2019) comprehensive literature review of tensions in digital platform business models, tensions can be classified as either *dilemmas* or *paradoxes*. In general, dilemmas denote tensions in which each element is imposed with clear advantages and disadvantages (Smith & Lewis, 2011). Weighing advantages and disadvantages of each element and then making a trade-off or "either-or" decision could resolve dilemmas (Lüscher & Lewis, 2008; Smith, 2014). Dilemmas may become paradoxical if "contradictory yet interrelated elements (dualities) [...] exist simultaneously and persist over time; such elements seem logical when considered in isolation, but irrational, inconsistent, and absurd when juxtaposed" (Smith & Lewis, 2011:387 cited in Mini & Widjaja, 2019). Mini and Widjaja (2019) distinguish:

1. *Organizing* tensions (surfacing when complex organizational systems create competing designs and processes)
2. *Performing* tensions (arising when a plurality of actors seek action for conflicting goals)

3. *Learning* tensions (involving using and often destroying past practices to create new ones)
4. *Belonging* tensions (stemming from competing identities among stakeholders)

Putnam et al. (2016) present three broad management strategies to cope with tensions: either-or, both-and, and more-than. "Either-or responses seek to resolve paradoxes by, for example, choosing one element to the detriment of the other or spatially and/or temporally separating tensions. [...] Both-and strategies [...] explicitly consider the interdependence of contradictory elements [...] More-than responses consider, for example, reframing and transcendence of tensions such that the elements of a tension become encompassed inside each other to form a new perspective or the introduction of a third element that goes beyond the existing elements" (Mini & Widjaja, 2019).

Through the lens of *tension-aware management*, we observe primarily *performing* and *belonging* tensions in DSR projects between practice and research stakeholders due to their different backgrounds and objectives. These tensions can be considered as a *paradox* because, in the long run, the perceived dilemma in expectations and rewards may result in only temporary resolutions, but in the long run DSR projects require that both practitioners and researchers reach satisfactory goal states. Satisfying both sets of stakeholders presents a complex paradox requiring a long-term, sustainable solution. An *either-or* management approach appears not useful as both researcher and practitioner capabilities and contributions are needed for successful DSR contributions, as stated in the introduction. Although a *more-than* response would be desirable, the conceptual differences between abstraction levels and success measures seem to impede a new distinct and integrative DSR project management perspective beyond emphasizing both "rigorous relevance" and "relevant rigor." Consequently, we set out to develop a *both-and* management approach. Acknowledging the strong interdependence of utility and validity goals in developing innovative, rigorous solutions to relevant problems, we propose a process model providing a steering mechanism for coordinating validity-focused with utility-focused activities along the artefact evolution process.

2.2 Managed Project Evolution

For guiding the evolutional progress of activity portfolios in the context of goal tensions, the concept of managed evolution has been proposed (Murer et al., 2010). Important aspects that need to be addressed are (i) identifying diverse stakeholder goals and their interdependencies, (ii) negotiating goal conflicts, (iii) understanding the possible actions and the effects the actions have on all relevant project goals, (iv) iteratively selecting and combining actions to ensure overall project progress, (v) managing changes in the problem and solution spaces, (vi) measuring progress in both research and practice goals, and (vii) determining when a satisfactory solution across all goals is achieved and can be implemented and published.

One particularity of managed evolution is that the coordinated activities may not only have impacts on more than one goal—some activities may have a negative impact on a certain goal while contributing to another goal (Murer et al., 2010). The application of managed evolution for a project with the goal of improving the alignment of IT agility with business value is illustrated by Fig. 2. The guidance is provided by delineating an "evolution channel" of acceptable deviation from the targeted relation between agility improvements and added business value. If change activities (e.g., system modifications) do not leave the channel and lead to overall project progress regarding *either* business value *or* agility, they are conducted with well-defined measures of progress on each of the dimensions.

The managed evolution concept can be easily extended to more than two competing goals (Furrer, 2019). Figure 3 illustrates a transformation program where changeability, dependability, and business value are to be improved together, with each change project having a different contribution, including sometimes even negatively affecting one or more of the three concurrent objectives.

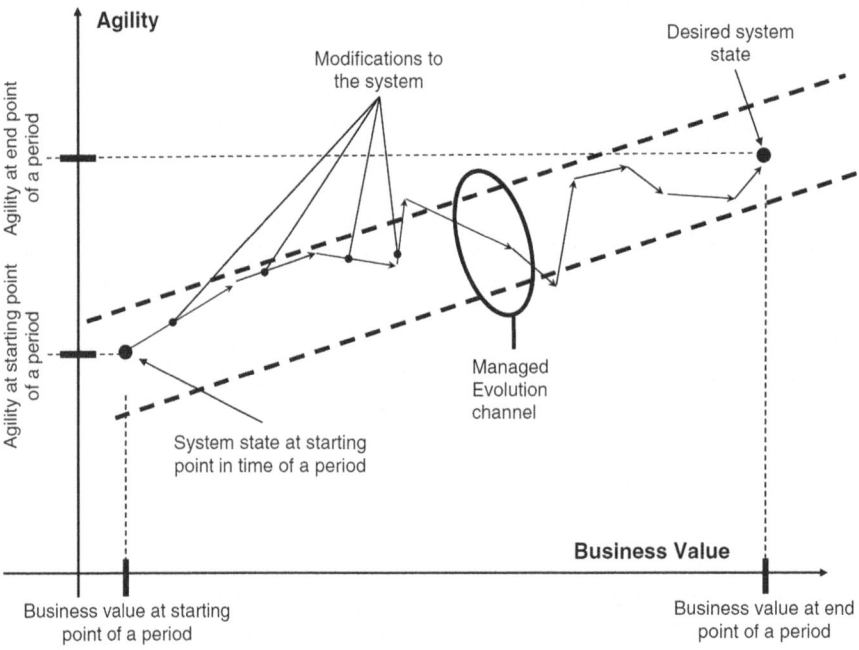

Fig. 2 Managed evolution in IT/business alignment (Murer et al., 2010)

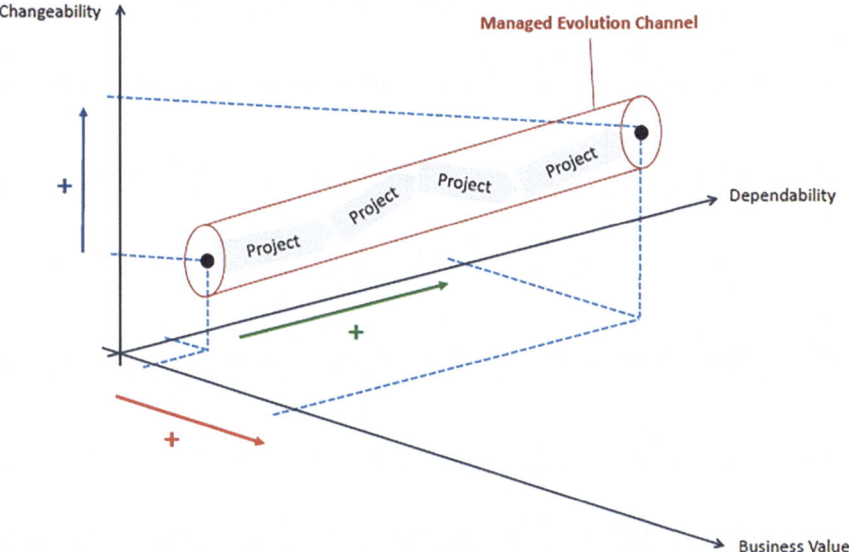

Fig. 3 Managed evolution trajectory with three competing objectives (Furrer, 2019)

2.3   *Managed DSR Project Evolution*

Having been successfully adopted for different types of problems, we posit that the concept of managed evolution can also be applied to guide multiple stakeholders to navigate in the practice/research intersection of DSR projects. The objective is to achieve overall progress toward both practical impact and knowledge contribution by choosing an appropriate sequence of *cycles* of design activities, even if single activities contribute to very different changes (including negative) to one of the goal dimensions. To better understand the character of DSR activities regarding practice impacts and design knowledge creation, we present a systematic conceptualization of the DSR managed evolution model as seen in Fig. 4. The two dimensions show the progress of a DSR project journey as it evolves with increases in the validity of the scientific contributions and the fitness of the practice impacts of the designed artefacts (vom Brocke et al., 2020).

While, in general, longitudinal DSR projects aim to maximize results in both dimensions, single design cycles may contribute to one dimension while holding steady or even reducing performance in the other. For example, adding configurative components to an artefact may increase its projectability (i.e., extend the covered problem class), but at the same time may reduce practical utility because not all new potential use situations have been thoroughly evaluated in all contexts. Thus, the results of a DSR design cycle can be:

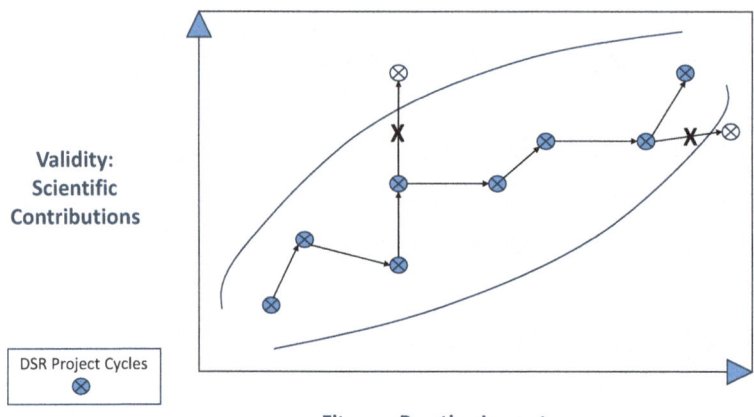

Fig. 4 DSR project journey in a managed evolution channel

- To increase solution validity (e.g., improved projectability with more general problems addressed) while such a solution may decrease or maintain the current level of fitness
- To increase fitness (e.g., greater contextualization with more specific problems addressed) while such a solution may decrease or maintain the current level of validity
- To increase both fitness (contextualized solution more complete) and validity (solution is more projectable to additional contexts)

Any of these alternative effects can occur in combination. In the light of such a diversity of possible moves in the two dimensions, the need for steering project progress becomes apparent. However, guidance for identifying or defining desirable project cycles is not necessarily provided when the reference system and the evolution channel are solely defined in terms of either validity by the researchers or fitness by the practitioners. We therefore propose to define and bound the DSR managed evolution channel (that implies managing both dimension boundaries) based on an assessment of which validity and fitness levels are desirable from a feasibility and desired impact perspective. Trade-offs between research and practice perspectives may be required. An effective approach to manage a collaborative DSR project would need to assess effects of every planned iteration on the relevant IS artefact evolution channel and prevent iterations from being conducted that increase validity too greatly at the expense of fitness progress or increase fitness too greatly at the expense of validity (as illustrated in Fig. 4 with points that fall outside of the managed evolution channel).

Another factor that must be considered in managed evolution trade-offs is the selection and rigor of evaluation method applied to assess the fitness and validity of the designed artefacts in each DSR cycle. Instead of a separate dimension of project progress (i.e., stakeholder confidence) as presented in (vom Brocke et al., 2020), we find that the level of evaluation in each cycle is more appropriately viewed as an integral component in each of the two dimensions. Different evaluation methods will provide greater progress and stakeholder confidence to either or both the fitness dimension and the validity dimension. It may be quite difficult to decide on a single evaluation method that will satisfy both researchers and practitioners. This is a critical negotiation point for each DSR cycle to decide on rigorous and feasible evaluation methods to satisfy both stakeholder groups. For example, researchers may desire to perform rigorous evaluations within the narrow contextual bounds required to achieve significant, generalizable results via methods such as controlled experiments. On the other hand, practitioners may argue that the costs of time and money do not allow full access to the practice application environment to perform rigorous controlled experiments and may prefer more feasible and cost-effective simulations of artefact intervention or the use of qualitative methods such as focus groups or user interviews. Thus, compromises on the rigor, feasibility, and costs of evaluation methods must be assessed in each project design cycle.

The sketched evolution channel in Fig. 4 aims to illustrate these considerations. In concrete DSR projects, it may be difficult to exactly predict such a channel. Thus, we propose that the growth of the evolution channel will be emergent during the project with each design cycle negotiated based on the results of the previous cycles and any changes in the problem and solution spaces. However, project planning targets for each of the dimensions can be set at the beginning of the project and revised continually as the project channel evolves over time. The project impact considerations and proposed research contributions may be very well introduced as an important component of project planning to communicate goals and expectations appropriately to all stakeholders.

3 Practitioner/Researcher Collaboration in DSR: Approaches and Issues

Tensions between pragmatic goals for practice and theoretical goals for research in DSR have been widely recognized in the field (Gregor & Hevner, 2013). Here, we briefly summarize several recent efforts to study practitioner and research collaboration in DSR projects.

Schmid (forthcoming) investigates DSR literature to identify how and when practitioners and researchers work together in DSR. While not finding a general pattern, he identifies some typical forms. Practitioners are consistently engaged in the evaluation of design artefacts (100% of the analyzed cases) and are almost always involved during initial problem analysis (75% of cases), mainly by interviews or various workshop formats. However, their involvement in defining objectives of solutions is rare (12%). Therefore, Schmid suggests that researchers often set the methodological framework of studies, whereas practical aspects are only sporadically introduced. Collaborations in artefact design and development are observed in about 50 percent of cases, often in the form of iterative processes between the two stakeholder groups. Interestingly, the intensity of such collaborations varies depending on the complexity of the artefact to be developed. Regarding the continuity of collaborative interactions, Schmid observes a tendency toward researchers leading the primary artefact development with practitioners providing periodic feedback. The participation of practitioners during the demonstration stage of the developed artefact is relatively limited (approximately 31% of cases). In summary, researchers typically conduct the artefact development independently, while practitioners provide initial input (focused on requirements) and later periodic feedback on the artefact's practical utility (evaluation).

Based on his literature review, Schmid (forthcoming) concludes that the relationship between researchers and practitioners in DSR can be examined along three dimensions:

- Artefact type—Technical artefacts (e.g., software prototypes, IT system instances) usually require frequent and iterative feedback during the development (from end users or IT experts), while models or methods typically involve less (or at least less continuous) collaboration. In the latter case, the focus lies on conceptual work, which researchers can often do independently if the requirements are clear at the beginning.
- Sociotechnical problem focus—The requirement for both technical and human behavior designs in the solution artefact requires more intense and continuous collaboration from practitioners and researchers. For this class of problems, researchers often must systematically elicit contextual knowledge from practitioners (e.g., by means of workshops or interviews) to prepare for organizational acceptance and possibly reconcile divergent concerns of stakeholder groups. Close collaborations are particularly needed in the early phases of problem understanding and requirements definition. More technical problems (e.g., improving a software solution or algorithm), on the other hand, can often be addressed with targeted input from specific persons. In many such cases, only the specialist department or internal expert is involved.
- Wickedness of the problem space—Solutions in a wicked problem space will require a diversity of experiences, expertise, and new ideas from both practitioners and researchers. The need for intensive and flexible collaboration is emphasized. This is where the entrepreneurial principle of effectuation can come into play (Drechsler & Hevner, 2015), in which researchers and practitioners proceed step by step together in uncertain environments. Iterative, fast design cycles with "take along" resources will build to a satisfactory set of artefacts that meet both practice and research goals (Schmid, forthcoming). This approach requires flexible, opportunistic collaboration that may require the involvement of new partners depending on emerging requirements.

While Schmid's analysis provides an overview of stakeholder collaboration patterns, other DSR studies underscore the importance of effective practitioner–researcher interaction in DSR and sometimes propose concrete recommendations or even solution aspects. Vom Brocke and Lippe (2010) recommend integrating a project management approach into DSR projects to manage stakeholder roles explicitly, improve communication, and align expectations systematically. Similarly, the DSR Grid proposed by vom Brocke and Maedche (vom Brocke & Maedche, 2019) introduces a canvas with six components in early phases of designing a DSR study. The holistic yet simple overview facilitates a shared understanding between researchers and practitioners, thereby supporting design and communication and increasing the chances of project success. Baskerville et al. (2018) emphasize the importance of balancing practical artefact development and theoretical contributions, highlighting that maintaining this balance is essential for successful DSR projects. They call for mechanisms that simultaneously advance practical artefacts and theoretical insights. This is particularly relevant for collaboration, as the required balance typically emerges through regular interactions between practitioners and researchers during project execution. However, they do not propose concrete concepts or artefacts that enable improved collaboration.

Österle et al. (2011) underline the critical importance of practitioner engagement to ensure real-world applicability of developed solutions and mutual benefits for researchers and practice partners. More concretely, Otto and Österle (2012) not only provide methodological principles for successful knowledge creation by researcher–practitioner collaborations in DSR, but also present an organizational setting for defining common goals, shared activities, iterative knowledge-generation cycles (based on the SECI model), and mutual commitment of resources.

While the general need has been discussed and important components such as objectives, underlying mechanisms, and organizational settings for effective researcher–practitioner collaboration in DSR have been proposed in extant discourses, DSR process models do not explicitly support such collaboration considerations. Widely adopted reference process models such as the Design Science Research Methodology (Peffers et al., 2007) or Action Design Research (Sein et al., 2011; Mullarkey & Hevner, 2019) provide no significant support to coordinate activities and balance interests of practitioners and researchers—also more recent approaches for complex DSR endeavors such as echelonized DSR (Tuunanen et al., 2024) do not provide specific mechanisms for managed evolution or deal with tensions between stakeholder group concerns.

In a recent paper, Cronholm et al. (2024) analyze collaboration challenges in Action Design Research and identify three critical themes: (i) shape IT artefacts based on organizational interventions, (ii) exploit the mutual dependency between developing design principles and IT artefacts, and (iii) contextualize and generalize learning. To deal with the first challenge, design sessions with multiple organizations and researchers were organized that prevented problem understanding being too closely driven by specific problem instantiations to maintain a useful level of projectability of design. To deal with the second challenge, a number of joint meetings were organized where solution instance design(s) and design principle formulation were aligned. To deal with the third challenge, both bilateral meetings between researchers and practitioners and multilateral workshops with all involved organizations were organized to ensure coherency and mutual inspiration between solution instances and generalized learnings.

Cronholm et al. (2024) propose ways to overcome collaboration challenges and balance practitioner with researcher outcomes of DSR projects. Their analysis and proposals are, however, set in the context of Action Design Research. We aim at extending DSR guidance beyond the chosen process method by proposing a general organizational model that integrates practitioner–researcher collaboration and negotiation into all essential DSR activities. Our proposal supports the need for rigor-relevance balancing not only to be negotiated in early project phases, but re-negotiated and used for steering a managed evolution path throughout the project across all traversed levels of problem and solution generalization (or specialization; see chapter "Abstraction and Abstraction Levels in Design Science Research" of this book).

4   Negotiation Points for Research/Practice Collaboration

Figure 5 illustrates the proposed dynamic DSR process model with five key negotiation points that support the researcher/practitioner team to navigate the DSR project journey through the managed evolution channel. We detail the issues and the expected results of each of the negotiations during the DSR project journey from start to end. During the journey, a progress map with dimensions of validity and fitness will emerge along with the project's accumulation of design knowledge contributions to practice and theory.

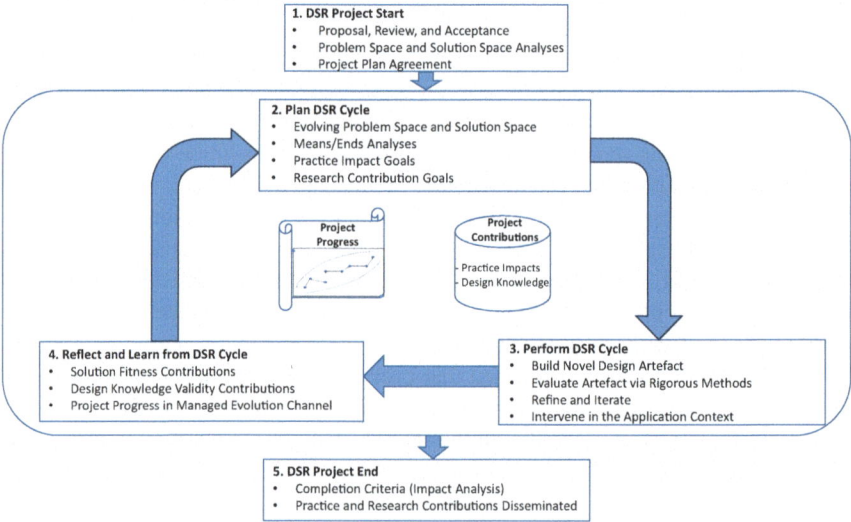

Fig. 5 Practice/research negotiation points in a DSR project journey

4.1   Negotiation Point 1: DSR Project Start

The genesis of a DSR project is the recognition that an opportunity exists to transform an existing system state or to create a new system for the benefit of targeted groups, organizations, and society. A detailed project proposal provides a strategic vision and a tactical mission statement for the project. The proposal will identify key stakeholders who will be impacted by the implemented design artefacts and who must buy into the execution of the project for its success. The negotiations at the project start will require that the goals of both researchers and practitioners be clearly stated in the project proposal to establish common expectations across all stakeholders. All voices must be heard in the proposal during its review. Appropriate signoffs are required before the project is commenced.

The first point of negotiation is a detailed Project Plan with initial agreements of the required means to perform the project and the needed ends for project success. This negotiation begins with cataloging available resources (e.g., budget, schedule, human capabilities, technologies, data) and engaging project stakeholders. A key starting activity for the DSR project is the acquisition of sufficient resources in the form of human capabilities, design knowledge bases, data repositories, and system technologies to achieve both practice and research contributions.

Next, project ends are defined as stakeholder goals, objectives, and values that must be managed via negotiated trade-offs to define a set of measurable success goals for the design artefacts that will provide the functions and qualities leading to an innovative solution and implementation that meets stakeholder needs. When determining the goodness criteria for solution acceptance, we recognize the socio-technical aspects of any practical solution. Project ends should, therefore, include a rich mix of practice and research goals related to technology (e.g., security, reliability, performance), information quality (e.g., accuracy, timeliness), human interaction (e.g., usability, user experience) (Adam et al., 2021), and societal needs (e.g., accessibility, fairness, ethics) (Hevner et al., 2018). Since researchers and practitioners may have different "value systems," both a significant knowledge contribution and a significant solution potential are to be achieved. Together, respective assessment criteria of potential design solutions establish guidance for both formative and summative evaluations (Venable et al., 2016). The negotiation points of means and ends will inform each other during the initial project startup and during planning for each of the design cycles. For example, certain goals may not be feasible unless sufficient resources (e.g., expertise, schedule, budget) are provided to the project team.

This point of negotiation will focus on achieving a clear representation of the complex problem space along with the innovative opportunities (e.g., new technologies) of the solution space. The project problem space and solution space will evolve continually over each of the iterative DSR process cycles in reaction to the emergent project progress.

4.2   Negotiation Point 2: Plan DSR Cycle

The execution of the project is made up of multiple incremental DSR cycles defined as sub-projects that together constitute the DSR project journey. Based on one or several build–evaluate iterations, each cycle shall produce design contributions to both practice and theory. The first critical practice/research negotiation point for each DSR cycle is collaborative planning and risk assessment to initiate the cycle. The results of the previous DSR cycles are reviewed in terms of the current state of project progress and the accumulated contributions of contextual artefacts and abstract design knowledge. Project means and ends are re-negotiated and the overall project plan revised before the start of each cycle to plan the desired incremental results for the next DSR cycle in terms of contributions and progress. Updates to the evolving problem space and solution space are performed. Cycle risks are thoroughly assessed and contingencies are planned if risks are encountered (Venable et al., 2019).

4.3   Negotiation Point 3: Perform DSR Cycle

The most essential point of negotiation and collaboration occurs during the performance of the build and evaluate iterations in the DSR cycle. As seen in the shaded area of Fig. 1, practitioners and researchers work together closely to generate novel ideas in the artefact build and to assess the effectiveness of the artefact with rigorous evaluation methods and demonstrations.

- **Build artefact:** Solution artefacts are built and evaluated in rapid formative iterations. Design solutions are built via creativity, intuition, experience, theory, theoretical frameworks, and trial and error; however, there should be a logic and rationale behind the choices made. The collaborative team creates many potential design candidates and then uses ranking based on goals satisfaction to narrow the focus to a small set of emergent solution design artefacts to move forward to rigorous evaluation and demonstration.
- **Evaluate artefact:** *Formative* evaluations refine the design artefact to an effective solution that meets the goals of the DSR cycle. Selections of the appropriate evaluation methods in each cycle are based on the needs of the project and the skillsets of the project team (Sonnenberg & vom Brocke, 2012). Evidence produced by evaluations promotes stakeholder confidence in the DSR cycle results. The level of research confidence assesses such qualities as the types of evaluation performed, the rigor of the evaluation methods, and the convincing nature of the evaluation results.
- **Demonstrate artefact:** If deemed important, the design artefact may be demonstrated for a *formative* proof of concept in a simulated application context. The costs of prototyping and constructing the demonstration environments are negotiated among the project stakeholders.

- **Intervene with artefact:** At the completion of multiple iterations the artefact will reach a stable point for intervention in application context. A negotiated decision point for the artefact solution intervention and *summative* evaluation must be based on information that matches the research questions to the operational possibilities for evaluation (Prat et al., 2015). The DSR project team will identify an appropriate set of evaluation methods to align with the opportunities and constraints of the operational environment. The application environment impacts and restricts the experimental controls that can be put into place, given the context within which the evaluation is carried out. The stakeholders within the application domain must sign off on experimental evaluation within that domain.

4.4 Negotiation Point 4: Reflect and Learn from DSR Cycle

Upon satisfactory completion of the build/evaluate iterations, the project team reflects on both the theoretical and the practical contributions of the DSR cycle. The team records project progress in the managed evolution channel by measuring movements in validity and fitness from the current DSR cycle. Practitioners reflect on improvements made to building effective solutions to the contextual problem space. Researchers reflect on the new design knowledge added to the prescriptive and descriptive knowledge bases. Contributions to the knowledge base may include extensions to prior theories and methods used during the research, the created design solution/artefacts, nascent design theories surrounding the use of the solution artefacts, and the experiences gained from performing the research. These contributions to the knowledge base are essential for reception by the academic audience and are useful for providing relevant value to the stakeholder audiences.

Upon completion of the DSR cycle, the emergent state of the DSR project is assessed and the negotiation points of project means and ends are engaged for the next DSR cycle. The project returns to Negotiation Point 2 for planning of the next DSR cycle. If the design solutions are a satisfactory conclusion to the project, then the project is completed, and the final negotiation point of project end is performed.

4.5 Negotiation Point 5: DSR Project End

The DSR research/practitioner team will negotiate a project completion with satisfactory results for all stakeholders based on the emergent research goals, practice goals, and progress goals. The impacts of the project are analyzed, and publications and products are produced to disseminate the project contributions to wider communities of practice and scientific research. The implementation and evolution of effective and reusable artefacts (e.g., sociotechnical systems and processes) for business problems are an essential outcome of the DSR project.

4.6   Negotiation Point Summary

Table 1 provides a summary of the negotiation points of the managed evolution DSR project process. The table highlights examples of the expertise brought to the negotiations by researchers and practitioners, along with prominent trade-offs in the negotiations.

5   Demonstration

We present a concise proof-of-concept case study of how the proposed collaboration process model and its actionable negotiation point guidance can be applied in an actual complex, multi-cycle DSR project. By reimagining a completed longitudinal project, we demonstrate what benefits are achieved by "managing the evolution" of both knowledge contribution and impact creation over multiple DSR cycles. Movements along the dimensions of validity and fitness are identified and analyzed to demonstrate the progress of the overall project.

5.1   Project Domain: Enterprise-level IT Coordination
       in Decentralized Organizations

The general problem addressed by the demonstration DSR study is the limited ability of large, decentralized organizations to achieve enterprise-wide IT benefits by leveraging synergies via sharing software solutions and harnessing the complexity of IT application landscape across the full organization. One specific aspect of this challenge is that local decision-makers are likely to focus on project-, unit-, or function-specific short-term *local* benefits instead of focusing on enterprise-wide, *global* benefits (Brosius et al., 2019). As root cause for insufficient "coordinate ability" in decentralized organizations, a lack of institutionalization of enterprise-level coordination by most local decision-makers has been identified (Ross & Quaadgras, 2012). Local decision-makers' institutionalization deficits can be traced to inadequate consideration of social legitimacy, efficiency, organizational grounding, and trust in the classical canon of coordination interventions, e.g., Enterprise Architecture Management (Weiss et al., 2013). The prioritization of local practice goals also limits the project's ability to achieve research goals of generalizing the solutions to broader application contexts. Formalizing design principles and design theories as research goals is often not considered important and, thus, important design knowledge is lost.

To solve these problems, an Action Design Research project was formed to design and implement novel coordination interventions to improve local decision-makers' institutionalization of enterprise-level coordination. Stakeholders included

Table 1 Negotiation points, expertise, and trade-offs

Negotiation point	Practitioner expertise	Negotiation trade-offs	Researcher expertise
1. Project start	• Relevance from application context • Impact goals • Practice resources	• Capture problem space • Analyze solution space • Balance relevance and rigor goals • Build project plan • Acquire resources	• Rigor from knowledge bases • Scientific goals • Research resources
2. Plan DSR cycle	• Assess evolving project progress and contributions based on impact goals • Identify changes in application context • Provide additional practice resources	• Capture changes in problem space and solution space for new DSR cycle • Rebalance relevance and rigor goals • Build project plan for new DSR cycle • Acquire additional resources	• Assess evolving project progress and contributions based on scientific goals • Identify changes in knowledge bases • Provide additional research resources
3. Perform DSR cycle	• Creativity and reasoning based on practice expertise and experience • Collaboration motivation • Knowledge of operational context for demonstration and intervention	• Collaborate to build novel solution artefacts • Collaborate to evaluate artefacts • Perform demonstrations of artefacts in formative evaluations • Perform interventions in operational summative evaluations • Provide evidence for practice impacts and research contributions	• Creativity and reasoning based on research expertise and experience • Collaboration motivation • Knowledge of rigorous research methods for evaluation
4. Reflect and learn from DSR cycle	• Assess project progress and impact contributions from practice view • Communicate with practice stakeholders and judge satisfaction • Determine impact goals for the next DSR cycle	• Did DSR cycle provide an appropriate balance of fitness and validity? • Map current project progress in managed evolution channel • Contribute new artefact and evaluation evidence to knowledge bases • Decide if DSR project is complete, else • Determine goals for next DSR cycle	• Assess project progress and scientific contributions from research view • Communicate with research stakeholders and judge satisfaction • Determine scientific goals for the next DSR cycle
5. Project end	• Implement solution artefacts in the application environment • Assess achievement of practice impact goals • Perform return on investment from DSR project	• Capture new problem and solution spaces upon completion of DSR project • Recognize limitations of DSR project • Assess successes and failures of collaboration between practice and research stakeholders	• Disseminate and publish research contributions in conferences and archival journals • Assess achievement of research contribution goals • Plan for future research based on contributions from DSR project

several large, decentralized organizations in Europe and a team of academic researchers with expertise in the development and use of IT/business alignment, enterprise-level IS management, and organizational decision-making. Informal interventions in the form of nudge incentives (Thaler & Sunstein, 2021) were identified as particularly promising interventions because they do not directly manipulate the choice architecture of decentralized decision-makers (better acceptance), can be designed in a way that uses the existing social system (perceived legitimacy), support local objectives (perceived efficiency), are grounded in organizational values (decentralized decision-making), and can be developed in a form that is perceived to be trustworthy (Winter, 2022). The following sections reimagine the progress of this AR/DSR project by overlaying the managed evolution process as proposed in this chapter.

5.2   Starting the DSR Project (Negotiation Point 1)

The project team, composed of engaged practitioners and researchers, described the design problem initially in terms of very general issues of harnessing IS complexity and addressing local–global conflicts among decision-makers. Kernel theory candidates were identified as control theory, institutionalization theory, and nudge theory. The project started with the project team envisioning a solution that applied informal coordination interventions with nudge incentives. It was recognized that this type of solution is very generic, and a big conceptual distance would need to be bridged between the desired (valid, projectable) research solution and the effective (fit, useful) system instantiation for implementation. Multiple DSR cycles of building and evaluating design candidates with situated problems and contextualized solutions would be needed to demonstrate and achieve satisfactory system designs, implementations, and research contributions.

At the start of project planning (Negotiation Point 1), the team recognized the inherent complexity of the problem space. An initial research strategy was determined to be mostly inductive with experimental studies to be performed at various situated organizations. Research aspirations for generalizable design theories were tempered by understanding that design knowledge will emerge over multiple cycles and design sub-projects in different companies will create only little or heterogeneous evaluative evidence. For those early project phases, it will be hard to claim sufficient research contributions due to the situatedness of the respective project settings. Moreover, during the extended project period, structural changes in the practice partner panel or at specific partner companies may threaten the collection of sufficient evaluative evidence, and the diversity of practice partners could make it difficult to generalize insights into formal design principles and theories.

Project preparations included many of the actions presented in Table 1 and will not be detailed. The team produced an initial understanding of the problem space, a vision of the solution space opportunities, usable practice relationships with intervention opportunities, and required resources in terms of time, space, and staff.

Table 2 DSR cycles in demonstration study

Cycle		Relative fitness (scale 1–10)	Relative validity (scale 1–10)
1	Compliance label in company A unit X	4	3
2	Compliance label in company A unit Y	4 (+ 0)	4 (+1)
3	Complexity cost internalization in company B	5 (+ 1)	5 (+1)
4	Social system nudges in company C	8 (+3)	7 (+2)
5	Informal intervention design evaluated by expert panel	10 (+2)	10 (+3)

Project means and ends were detailed and negotiated between practice and research stakeholders. It was quickly recognized that a long-term project setup was needed with sub-projects (multiple DSR cycles) to focus on several different aspirational objectives, such as better demonstrating the intervention solution's performance efficiency or improving the social legitimacy of enterprise-wide coordination. By testing the effectiveness of different novel interventions to reach the desired DSR objectives, it would then be possible to successively generalize effective intervention designs to design principles that link generalized design requirements to generalized design features—while building up sufficient overall evaluative evidence and applying intermediate insights to design more effective and/or more general solutions along the DSR cycles.

5.3 Sub-Projects as Iterative DSR Cycles (Negotiation Points 2–4*)

The longitudinal DSR project emerged as a series of sub-projects which we can interpret as DSR cycles in the managed evolution process model. Each cycle built on the results of the previous cycles in the project. Table 2 provides an overview of the project as it evolved over time with progress measured in terms of increased (or decreased) contextual fitness and scientific validity measures.[1] It should be noted that, in compliance with the managed evolution concept, not every cycle contributed to progress on all dimensions (see negative or zero change deltas in Table 2). A more detailed summary of each DSR cycle (i.e., sub-project) is provided in the Appendix.

For each of the DSR cycles, specific aspects of the design vision were contextualized to demonstrate their potential to address overall goal improvements in the problem solution. For every proposed set of design requirements, the analysis of

---

[1] In the interests of illustration and brevity, we measure each of the progress dimensions on a subjective scale of 1–10. A future research direction is to investigate appropriate measures and measurement techniques for each dimension of project progress.

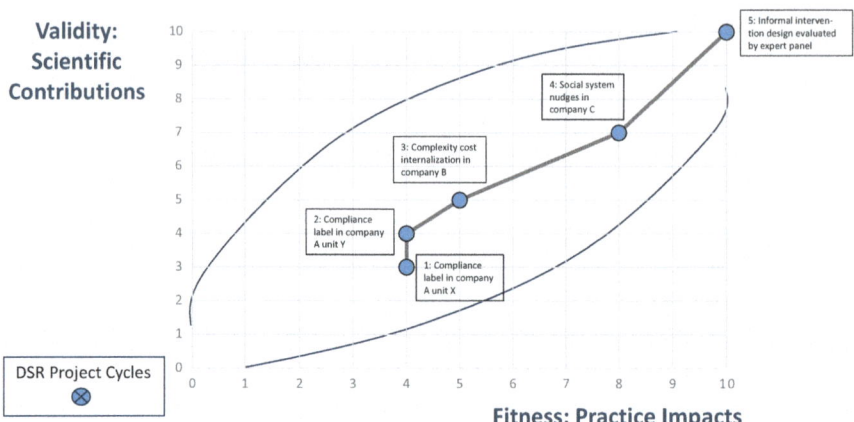

Fig. 6 Managed evolution in demonstration study

extant research as well as the state of practice resulted in distinct sets of solution components that would then be integrated and tailored to the problem at hand.

Each DSR cycle contributed an innovative artefact and (except the inductive generalization in cycle 5) its evaluation. In addition, each cycle made well-defined research and practice contributions to the respective knowledge bases. For the impacts of practice, three large organizations were involved in the first three DSR cycles and the pilot study in DSR cycle 4. Real practitioners were involved who have real stakes in the project outcomes (Nunamaker et al., 2015).

In summary, the project executed five DSR cycles, each involving the three Negotiation Points 2–4. The sequence of cycles ("the sub-project journey") emerged with each cycle planned based on the results of the previous cycles. Each cycle made a distinct artefact contribution (e.g., architecture compliance labels, costing and charging models, data quality improvement nudges) designed and implemented in a real-life organization. Over the course of the sub-projects, the application scope was increased (one business unit, a second business unit, several companies in an industry, and finally several industries). For securing sufficient support for the iterative sequence of DSR cycles, an (organized) panel of practice partners and a dedicated project planning process are important. An ideal setting for such an ambitious endeavor is consortium research (Österle & Otto, 2010) as more project options reduce risk and stakeholders with similar objectives can be used as sounding board/ focus group. In analogy to Fig. 4, the evolution of validity and fitness in the demonstration project is illustrated in Fig. 6.

5.4   Consolidation and Completion of Project (Negotiation Point 5)

When either the desired amount of insights and evaluative evidence is created—or resources are used up or practice support ends, the generalization of effective design features and design requirements can take place, e.g., in the form of formulating design principles (Winter, 2022). In this phase, longitudinal aspects of the project can be studied, and summative, more ambitious publications can be created. For this demonstration project, archival publications (e.g., Beese, Aier, et al., 2023; Beese, Haki, et al., 2023) were prepared at the conclusion of the DSR project journey. It must be mentioned that this stage of reflection and academic journal writing has only limited support from the practitioner side (long writing/revision cycles without perceived practice values) so that publishing activities that need active practice support should be conducted as early as possible.

In summary, ambitious DSR projects can create value both in terms of knowledge contribution and practical impact. These two output types, however, occur at different times and on different levels of abstraction. Organizing design work, design contextualization, and rigorous evaluation is a complex, long process whose organizational challenge goes far beyond predicted project plans. The DSR case study has, partly intentional and partly accidental, followed our managed evolution proposal and nicely demonstrates the usefulness of such guidance for coordinating fundamentally different objectives, stakeholders, abstraction levels, and design aspects.

6   Conclusions and Directions for Future Research

We propose and demonstrate a rigorous and actionable managed evolution DSR process model to support practitioner and researcher negotiations that achieve balanced project contributions between scientific theory and practical impacts. The process model tracks project progress along the dimensions of validity and fitness. A simple planned sequence of DSR cycle iterations is often insufficient to consider the diversity of contexts (for high validity), the complex interplay between problem space, solution space, and design (for high fitness), or the different forms of evaluative evidence (for high confidence in the validity and fitness measures). A managed and emergent evolution of DSR cycles promises to guide such endeavors not unlike sprints in an agile solution development project. The effective use of managed evolution in DSR projects provides the following key implications.

(1) To support researcher goals, the bounded application context of the complex artefact and its intervention environment need to be well understood for rigorous design theory development. Contextualization and abstraction have multiple dimensions, such as application scope (e.g., a team, a business unit, a

company, an industry, cross-industry), aspect focus (e.g., a nudge, a class of nudges, a type of informal interventions, the entire class of informal interventions), and aspirational purpose (e.g., avoid certain behaviors, change mindset, coordinate toward a certain set of objectives). Thus, the first negotiation point requires the project stakeholders to come to a common representation of the problem space with a well-defined understanding of the starting point of the research project and the aspirational ends of theory contributions.

(2) To support practitioner goals, the interplay of problem space, solution space, and creative design for the composition of the artefact needs to be understood and negotiated to achieve satisfactory solutions with fitness impacts. Project artefacts are comprised of a problem specification (i.e., representation of the problem space is an intermediate artefact—that can be validated with stakeholders), specific and generic design solutions, and the association of the design artefacts with the problem specification. The wicked complexity of the project must be managed in an incremental emergent process of iterative DSR cycles that produce measured goal improvements that demonstrate increasing fitness of the solution in the problem space.

(3) To provide confidence in the design artefacts across all project stakeholders, the multidimensionality of goals needs to be well understood, negotiated, and communicated. The confidence placed on complex artefacts is not exclusively dependent on perceived or actual use value (e.g., increased effectivity, efficiency, or sustainability of a design), but also on the consensus between stakeholders regarding utility dimensions and on the degree of justification that is implied by validity causalities that underlie the proposed intervention. Establishing clear research goals (i.e., aspirations) and agreeing on the evaluative methods during interventions of design artefacts in context support growing confidence in the project solutions.

(4) To maintain continuous project progress, the implications of each progress dimension in isolation are important for the respective practitioner and researcher stakeholders, but it is equally important to assess the trade-offs among the two dimensions when planning for the next DSR cycle as shown in Table 1. An important contribution of the managed evolution process approach is the ability to assess these fitness vs. validity trade-offs. It is often necessary to temporarily focus on one dimension at the expense of the other as we saw demonstrated in the case study. For example, if the next DSR cycle expands the problem scope to multiple organizations (increasing validity and projectability), the design solution may be less fit to a specific context. In addition, the selection of possible evaluation opportunities in the DSR cycle may also decrease fitness confidence due to the increased complexity of the varying application contexts. Therefore, the balance of validity vs. fitness contributions has also to be steered in a way that DSR cycles do not leave the acceptable "channel" of managed evolution.

(5) To manage the dynamic nature of the DSR project, the negotiated decision model must be adaptive to changes in the problem and solution spaces and to the emergent discoveries of successes and failures in each of the rapid, iterative

DSR cycles. The concept of the managed evolution DSR process model supports the emergence of well-defined iterative DSR cycles in a longitudinal project. Each DSR cycle must therefore not be too complex and time-consuming but rather should focus on comparably fast results to allow for evolutionary development within reasonable periods acceptable to both practitioners and researchers. The project team will have opportunities to identify stable points in the emergent process when design artefacts can be introduced into actual use (practice contributions) and when research papers can be produced and published (theory contributions).

(6) DSR project researchers must perform an initial selection of a research strategy and adapt this strategy through project evolution. Once the problem space is bounded and an interesting research problem is posed, a decision on research strategy is made. Will the creative design artefacts be grounded in extant knowledge from descriptive and prescriptive theories (deductive reasoning) or will creative solutions be designed and implemented with reflective growth of design theories as a result (inductive reasoning)? Or the DSR project may be driven by a combination of research strategies viewed as more intuitive where purer approaches are precluded by problem complexity (abductive reasoning). A longitudinal DSR project will have inflection points where the team goes from building a contextualized solution to reflecting on results and generating an abstract design theory. The negotiation points on means, end, and planning for the next DSR cycle provide support for identifying these important inflection points of movement on research strategy during the project.

(7) DSR project practitioners must operationalize the design artefacts through the dynamic movements of increased or decreased solution fitness and evaluation confidence that will occur during the DSR project. The agility inherent in the rapid, iterative DSR cycles supports practitioners to quickly identify designs that do not fit the application context or do not produce strong improvements with resulting low confidence in the design artefact. The objective then is to fail fast and plan for the next cycle with a different set of fitness progress goals (Abraham et al., 2014). The project will often learn much from cycle failures and capturing design knowledge from all DSR cycles is essential.

In conclusion, DSR projects feature unique challenges due to the collection of varied stakeholders with different requirements and goals for project success. While practitioners desire contextualized solutions for complex, real-world problems, researchers aspire to develop generalized design theories that contribute to a broader understanding of descriptive and prescriptive knowledge. Both groups desire rigorous and effective evaluations of design artefacts that provide high levels of confidence in the validity and fitness of the design solution. Actionable guidance toward balancing stakeholders' goals and achieving satisfactory levels of theory and practice contributions in a DSR project is the purpose of this chapter. Points of practitioner and research negotiation during the project are highlighted and demonstrated in a retrospective case study.

The DSR managed evolution process model is a conceptual proposal that is yet to be fully tested in the planning and execution of an actual DSR project. We find the potential advantages of the new model to be compelling, but many details of its adaptation and use will need to be considered and implemented (Lukyanenko & Parsons, 2020). Future research on how best to assess progress along the dimensions of validity and fitness with high levels of evaluation confidence applying both quantitative and qualitative measures is needed. The adaptation of project management environments and tools to agile, managed evolution processes will support the capture of project contributions and progress tracking (see, e.g., vom Brocke et al., 2017; Morana et al., 2018; Herwix & Rosenkranz, 2019; vom Brocke et al., 2021). Actual experience with the use of the managed evolution DSR process model will provide evidence for refining the model and improving the guidance for its use in impactful DSR projects with effective support from research environments and toolsets.

Acknowledgment The authors wish to thank Simon Michael Schmid for sharing his literature analysis of practitioner–researcher collaboration in DSR and contributing to Sect. 3.

Appendix: Overview of DSR Cycles in Demonstration Project

DSR Cycle 1: The project team designed a Compliance Label model artefact as a vehicle for communicating IT integration and coordination across distributed project teams and organization sites. The goals were to improve messaging (e.g., showcasing successful solution sharing, see Schilling et al., 2019) and to engineer social pressure (e.g., by making non-compliant projects transparent across the organization, Winter, 2022). The artefact was implemented and evaluated in one country unit of Company A as a possible foundation for improving the social legitimacy of enterprise-wide coordination ("why should I comply?").

DSR Cycle 2: The Compliance Label artefact was implemented and evaluated in another country unit of Company A to extend the dimensions of validity/projectability (e.g., more general solution across multiple units) with increased confidence (e.g., additional evaluation evidence).

DSR Cycle 3: The project team designed an artefact to estimate integration Complexity Cost aimed at supporting the cost-calculation and charging of technical debt to non-compliant change projects and to allow the provision of cost-reduction project support (e.g., by supporting architects or reduced costs of shared software solutions). This artefact was used as foundation to demonstrate coordination efficiency ("what's in it for me?") (Aier et al., 2015). The artefact was implemented and evaluated in Company B. Positive movements in both validity and fitness were found, but questions on how the cost model would extend to other company environments caused the confidence in the validity dimension to decrease.

DSR Cycle 4: Based on the results of the initial three cycles, the team designed a nudge-based sociotechnical system artefact to improve the integration quality of critical corporate data. Relation Manager Guilds were created across the multiple units where know-your-customer data quality issues could be discussed and a common sense of regulatory compliance could be institutionalized (Cahenzli, 2020). A pilot of the system was implemented in Company C with rigorous evaluation of its impacts via qualitative user surveys. By extending the project to a different type of intervention, a different setting (data quality management), and a different industry, this DSR cycle provided significant advances in along both dimensions of validity and fitness with increased confidence in both dimensions for the designed solution.

DSR Cycle 5: To conclude the project, the design artefacts were integrated into a comprehensive design approach for informal coordination interventions. The results of the previous four cycles were analyzed and a framework was proposed to develop such interventions for different types of coordination problems and organizations. For that purpose, additional evaluative evidence and expanded coherent design guidance from other interventions and case companies were considered. The results constituted strong evidence that the overall project had achieved its desired measures of validity and fitness with an acceptable level of confidence.

References

Abraham, R., Aier, S., & Winter, R. (2014). Fail early, fail often: Towards coherent feedback loops in design science research evaluation. In *35th International Conference on Information Systems (ICIS 2014)*. Association for Information Sytems.

Adam, M. T., Gregor, S., Hevner, A., & Morana, S. (2021). Design science research modes in human-computer interaction projects. *AIS Transactions on Human-Computer Interaction, 13*(1), 1–11.

Aier, S., Labusch, N., & Pähler, P. (2015). *Implementing Architectural Thinking: A Case Study at Commerzbank AG*. Proceedings of the CAiSE 2015 Workshops, Stockholm, Sweden.

Baskerville, R., Baiyere, A., Gregor, S., Hevner, A. R., & Rossi, M. (2018). Design science research contributions: Finding a balance between artifact and theory. *Journal of the Association For Information Systems, 19*(5), 358–376.

Beese, J., Aier, S., Haki, K., & Winter, R. (2023). The impact of enterprise architecture management on information systems architecture complexity. *European Journal of Information Systems, 32*(6), 1070–1090.

Beese, J., Haki, K., Schilling, R., Kraus, M., Aier, S., & Winter, R. (2023). Strategic alignment of enterprise architecture management – How a decade of corporate transformation shaped the portfolio of control mechanisms at Commerzbank. *European Journal of Information Systems, 32*(1), 92–105.

Brosius, M., Aier, S., Haki, K., & Winter, R. (2019). The institutional logic of harmonization: Local versus global perspectives. In D. Aveiro, G. Guizzardi, S. Guerreiro, & W. Guédria (Eds.), *Advances in Enterprise Engineering XII. EEWC 2018. LNBIP* (Vol. 334, pp. 3–17). Springer.

Cahenzli, M. (2020). Guiding the Institutionalization of Behaviour: Designing a Nudging-inspired Solution.

Cronholm, S., Göbel, H., & Shrestha, A. (2024). Researcher-practitioner collaboration in action design research. *Australasian Journal of Information Systems, 28*, 1–32.

Drechsler, A., & Hevner, A. (2015). Effectuation and its implications for socio-technical design science research in information systems. In *Proceedings of the Design Science Research in Information Systems and Technology (DESRIST 2015)*. Dublin.

Furrer, F. J. (2019). Evolution strategies. In *Future-proof software-systems: A sustainable evolution strategy* (pp. 57–89). Springer Fachmedien Wiesbaden.

Gregor, S. and A. R. Hevner (2013). "Positioning and Presenting Design Science Research for Maximum Impact." *MIS Quarterly 37*(2): 337–355.

Haj-Bolouri, A., Purao, S., Rossi, M., & Bernhardsson, L. (2018). Action design research in practice: Lessons and concerns. In *European Conference on Information Systems*, Paper 131.

Herwix, A., & Rosenkranz, C. (2019). A multi-perspective framework for the investigation of tool support for design science research. In *Proceedings of the 27th European Conference on Information Systems (ECIS)*. Sweden.

Hevner, A., Prat, N., Comyn-Wattiau, I., & Akoka, J. (2018). A pragmatic approach for identifying and managing design science research goals and evaluation criteria. In *Proceedings of the SigPrag Workshop*. San Francisco.

Lukyanenko, R., & Parsons, J. (2020). Research perspectives: Design theory indeterminacy: What is it, how can it be reduced, and why did the polar bear drown? *Journal of the Association for Information Systems, 21*(5), 1343–1369.

Lüscher, L. S., & Lewis, M. W. (2008). organizational change and managerial sensemaking: Working through paradox. *Academy of Management Journal, 51*(2), 221–240.

Mini, T., & Widjaja, T. (2019). Tensions in digital platform business models: A literature review. In *40th International Conference on Information Systems (ICIS 2019)*, Munich, Germany.

Morana, S., vom Brocke, J., Maedche, A., Seidel, S., Adam, M. T. P., Bub, U., Fettke, P., Gau, M., Herwix, A., Mullarkey, M. T., Nguyen, H. D., Sjöström, J., Toreini, P., Wessel, L., & Winter, R. (2018). Tool support for design science research—Towards a software ecosystem: A report from a desrist 2017 workshop. *Communications of the AIS, 43*(17).

Mullarkey, M. T., & Hevner, A. R. (2019). An elaborated action design research process model. *European Journal of Information Systems, 28*(1), 6–20.

Murer, S., Bonati, B., & Furrer, F. J. (2010). *Managed evolution: A strategy for very large information systems*. Springer.

Nunamaker, J. F., Briggs, R. O., Derrick, D. C., & Schwabe, G. (2015). The last research mile: Achieving both rigor and relevance in information systems research. *Journal of Management Information Systems, 32*(3), 10–47.

Österle, H., Becker, J., Frank, U., Hess, T., Karagiannis, D., Krcmar, H., Loos, P., Mertens, P., Oberweis, A., & Sinz, E. (2011). Memorandum on design-oriented information systems research. *European Journal of Information Systems, 20*(1), 7–10.

Österle, H., & Otto, B. (2010). Consortium research. A Method for researcher-practitioner collaboration in design-oriented IS research. *Business and Information Systems Engineering, 2*(2), 273–285.

Otto, B. and H. Österle (2012). Principles for knowledge creation in collaborative design science research. In *33rd International Conference on Information Systems (ICIS)*, Orlando, FL.

Peffers, K., Tuunanen, T., Rothenberger, M. A., & Chatterjee, S. (2007). A design science research methodology for information systems research. *Journal of Management Information Systems, 24*(3), 45–77.

Prat, N., Comyn-Wattiau, I., & Akoka, J. (2015). A taxonomy of evaluation methods for information systems artifacts. *Journal of Management Information Systems, 32*(3), 229–267.

Putnam, L. L., Fairhurst, G. T., & Banghart, S. (2016). Contradictions, dialectics, and paradoxes in organizations: A constitutive approach. *Academy of Management Annals, 10*(1), 65–171.

Ross, J. W., & Quaadgras, A. (2012). *Enterprise architecture is not just for architects*. Center for Information Systems Research Sloan School of Management Massachusetts Institute of Technology.

Schilling, R. D., Aier, S., & Winter, R. (2019). Designing an artifact for informal control in enterprise architecture management. In *International Conference on Information Systems*. Munich, Germany.

Schmid, S. M. (forthcoming). Bridging the gap: Analyzing collaboration between practitioners and researchers across different stages of the design science research process. In *itAIS 2024*. Piacenza.

Sein, M. K., Henfridsson, O., Purao, S., Rossi, M., & Lindgren, R. (2011). Action design research. *MIS Quarterly, 35*(1), 37–56.

Smith, W. K. (2014). Dynamic decision making: A model of senior leaders managing strategic paradoxes. *Academy of Management Journal, 57*(6), 1592–1623.

Smith, W. K., & Lewis, M. W. (2011). Toward a theory of paradox: A dynamic equilibrium model of organizing. *Academy of Management Review, 36*(2), 381–403.

Sonnenberg, C., & vom Brocke, J. (2012). Evaluations in the science of the artificial – Reconsidering the build-evaluate pattern in design science research. In K. Peffers, M. Rothenberger, & B. Kuechler (Eds.), *Design science research in information systems. Advances in theory and practice* (Vol. 34, pp. 381–397). Springer.

Thaler, R. H., & Sunstein, C. R. (2021). *Nudge: The final edition*. Penguin Books.

Tuunanen, T., Winter, R., & Vom Brocke, J. (2024). Dealing with complexity in design science research - A methodology using design Echelons. *MIS Quarterly, 48*(2), 427–458.

Venable, J. R., Pries-Heje, J., & Baskerville, R. (2016). FEDS: A framework for evaluation in design science research. *European Journal of Information Systems, 25*(1), 77–89.

Venable, J. R., Vom Brocke, J., & Winter, R. (2019). Designing TRiDS: Treatments for risks in design science. *Australasian Journal for Information Systems, 23*.

vom Brocke, J., Fettke, P., Gau, M., & Seidel, S. (2017). Tool-support for design science research: Design principles and instantiation. *SSRN Electronic Journal*.

vom Brocke, J., Gau, M., & Maedche, A. (2021). Journaling the design science research process. Transparency about the making of design knowledge. In L. C. Kruse, S. Seidel, & G. I. Hausvik (Eds.), *The Next Wave of Sociotechnical Design. DESRIST 2021* (Lecture Notes in Computer Science, vol 12807). Springer.

vom Brocke, J., & Lippe, S. (2010). Taking a project management perspective on design science research. Global perspectives on design science research: *5th international conference, DESRIST 2010*. St.Gallen, Switzerland, pp 31–44.

vom Brocke, J., & Maedche, A. (2019). The DSR grid: Six core dimensions for effective capturing of DSR projects. *Electronic Markets, 29*, 379–385.

vom Brocke, J., Winter, R., Hevner, A., & Maedche, A. (2020). Special Issue editorial – Accumulation and evolution of design knowledge in design science research: A Journey through time and space. *Journal of the Association for Information Systems, 21*(3), 520–544.

Wareham, J., Fox, P. B., & Giner, J. L. C. (2014). Technology ecosystem governance. *Organization Science, 25*(4), 1195–1215.

Weiss, S., Aier, S., & Winter, R. (2013). Institutionalization and the effectiveness of enterprise architecture management. In *34th International Conference on Information Systems (ICIS 2013)*. Milano, Italy.

Winter, R. (2022). Designing Informal EAM Interventions – A Complementary Approach for Managing Enterprise Architecture Complexity. In *Proc. 55th Hawaii International Conference on System Sciences (HICSS 55)*, pp 7244–7253.

Function-Construction Patterns
for Designing IS Artefacts

Simon Michael Schmid, Benedict Lösser, and Robert Winter

1 Introduction: Navigating the Diversity of Solution Space and Functional Requirements

Throughout the past two decades, there has been a growing interest to establish Design Science Research in Information Systems (DSR) as an approach that combines the creation of relevant design knowledge with the rigor of scientific inquiry. The core of DSR is the construction and evaluation of innovative artefacts that constitute useful solutions to relevant real-world problem classes (Hevner et al., 2004; Peffers et al., 2007). Gregor and Hevner (2013) conceptualize different types of artefacts as contributing to knowledge at varying levels of abstraction, contingent upon the maturity of both the problem domain (i.e., the application context) and the solution domain. As such, a DSR project may yield artefacts that range from concrete instantiations (such as implemented products or operational processes) to abstract theoretical contributions, including nascent forms of design theory (e.g., design principles). Given the growing diversity and complexity of DSR artefacts

Simon Michael Schmid, Benedict Lösser and Robert Winter contributed equally to this chapter.

S. M. Schmid
Institute of Information Systems and Digital Business, University of St. Gallen, St. Gallen, Switzerland

DHBW Ravensburg, Baden-Wuerttemberg Cooperative State University, Stuttgart, Germany

B. Lösser · R. Winter (✉)
Institute of Information Systems and Digital Business, University of St. Gallen, St. Gallen, Switzerland
e-mail: Robert.Winter@unisg.ch

© The Author(s), under exclusive license to Springer Nature Switzerland AG 2025
R. Winter (ed.), *Designing the Information Systems Artefact*, Progress in IS, https://doi.org/10.1007/978-3-031-98311-5_5

over the past 25 years (Engel et al., 2019; Tuunanen et al., 2024), researchers often find it challenging to identify suitable directions for solution construction, delineating the projectability of their design proposals, and providing sufficient evaluative evidence to support their claims. To better understand these challenges, we examine existing approaches for organizing both the solution space and the functional requirements of the problem space, considering them separately as well as in relation to each other.

The Solution Space To provide an ontological and organizing foundation for DSR outcomes, various artefact classification proposals have been made. The major share of classifications (Gregor & Hevner, 2013; Drechsler & Dörr, 2014; Drechsler & Hevner, 2018; Vaishnavi et al., 2019; Weigand et al., 2021; Offermann et al., 2010) reflects mainly the solution space. The proposed classifications largely refine the very generic classification scheme introduced by March and Smith (1995) which itself draws on the foundational work of Nunamaker Jr et al. (1991). In addition to design entities that address specific problems or problem classes of smaller scale, design knowledge may take the form of generic problem solutions (Winter, 2008), design principles (Chandra Kruse et al., 2015) or even elaborated design theories (Gregor & Jones, 2007). With growing level of abstraction and maturity of the proposed outcome (design entity or design knowledge), the scientific contribution of a DSR study increases (Gregor & Hevner, 2013). A more comprehensive and systematically constructed typology of DSR artefacts is discussed in depth in Chapter "Typology of IS Artefacts: Providing an Organizing Foundation for Design Science Research Outcomes" of this book. With growing heterogeneity and complexity of possible design outputs, it becomes increasingly difficult for researchers to identify appropriate solution construction strategies.

Functional Requirements of the Problem Space Not only the diversity of artefacts/DSR outcomes in the solution space needs to be structured by referring to (construction) typologies. While IT-related organizational problems were dominant in the early years of DSR, the problem space has widened and now also comprises predominantly organizational design problems (e.g., DSR in entrepreneurship) or people-oriented design problems (e.g., transformation management). From a design perspective, one common denominator for different design problems are functional requirements. An existing classification of IT artefacts that clearly references the functional requirements has already been proposed by Iivari (2007). The types of IT artefacts in his work are based on the intended use (e.g., "to artisticize"). The proposed dimensions in Iivari (2007) are however rather high-level and conceptually unclear for abstract DSR artefacts—and further steps need to be taken to improve tangibility and consequences for the construction of artefacts. Another approach to grasp the concept of functionality is offered by Weigand et al. (2021). They use different levels and divide artefacts into primary, action-oriented, and secondary, support-oriented, artefacts. As subtypes they offer algorithms, programs, and IS applications for primary artefacts—and formal languages, constructs, and methods for secondary artefacts. These considerations focus however very strongly on rather "technical" artefacts and are not yet fine-grained enough to provide actual guidance for the construction of IS artefacts, in particular for the selection of a suitable artefact type.

Only if the complexity of both "reference worlds" of design, the problem space and the solution space, is reduced by referring to simplifying structure models, the inherent relationships between functional and construction-oriented properties of these spaces become tangible. While Offermann et al. (2010) assign simple usage scenarios (i.e., support and description) to fixed artefact (construction) types, Lösser and Winter (2025) proposed to simplify design guidance in the form of "design patterns." Design patterns aim at representing frequent (actual or possible) designs by aggregate associations between a functional type and a construction type. Constituting aggregate relationships between the "functional and the construction perspective" (2025:5365), DSR design patterns would provide actionable guidance for designers in two directions: (1) For a class of functional requirements, patterns can point to suitable or unsuitable types of "fitting" solution artefacts. (2) For a type of solution artefacts, patterns can point to suitable or unsuitable classes of "fitting" functional requirements. The differentiation of the design space into a "functional" and a "construction" perspective draws on the distinction proposed by Weigand et al. (2021) between "use" and "make." This differentiation is also well-established in engineering science as "functional" vs. "construction" perspectives (Pahl et al., 2007).

As illustrated before, many classification proposals for DSR outcomes (particularly for the solution space) exist. However, there is still little knowledge on types of functional requirements (i.e., referring to the problem space). Against this backdrop, we propose the first research question:

Research Question 1: What classes of functionality requirements should be differentiated because they imply different solution approaches?

Based on a functional clustering of design problems, typical associations between these classes and solution types could be identified. Such associations, when empirically validated and semantically making sense, can then be proposed as design patterns. The second research question is:

Research Question 2: Which pattern candidates can be proposed from analyzing empirical associations between functional problem clusters and solution types?

Conceptually, this study builds on the exploratory analysis of Lösser and Winter (2025) who pioneered this stream of research with an initial dataset and a conceptual distinction between functional and construction perspectives. To build on this foundation and respond to the authors' call for a broader empirical sample of DSR studies, we first review existing classifications of DSR artefacts and conceptualize relevant dimensions for evaluating their underlying design logic. We focus on top-ranked journals and conferences in the field of IS, as identified by the VHB publication outlet rating to explore associations between functional problem types and construction types. Our exploratory study aims to support DSR researchers by offering design hypotheses, highlighting challenges and broadening the empirical basis for artefact theorization.

To that end, we introduce two candidate types to support artefact reasoning in DSR: (i) problem-construction (PC) pattern candidates, which support the search for suitable solution artefacts for given functional requirements, and (ii) problem analysis (PA) pattern candidates, which enable reflection on whether a specific artefact type has the potential to address a certain class of functional requirements. By proposing pattern candidates, we contribute to a deeper design understanding of problem and solution spaces which is particularly valuable in the early stages of DSR projects and for novice design researchers.

In the following, we refer to function-construction patterns simply as "patterns." We are aware that different types of patterns may be useful in DSR, including but not limited to design activity patterns or problem-solution patterns. In the tradition of engineering disciplines where construction support relies on functional analysis and associating construction types with functional requirements (see, e.g., Pahl et al., 2007), we focus on this type of pattern.

The remainder of this chapter is structured as follows: Section 2 discusses conceptual foundations, Section 3 details the chosen methodology for our study, Section 4 presents our empirical findings, and Sect. 5 discusses contributions and implications.

2 Conceptual Foundations

2.1 Types of Functional Requirements (Problem Space)

The functional perspective in our study builds on the discussion in Lösser and Winter (2025) who characterize design problems along three functional dimensions: (A) abstraction level, (B) knowledge type, and (C) contextualization. This perspective is particularly useful as it sharpens the previously ambiguous space of functional requirements and allows it to be structured. The functional categories are described below and illustrated by Fig. 1.

A) Abstraction Level
"While design research is aimed at creating solutions to specific classes of relevant problems by using a rigorous construction and evaluation process, design science reflects the design research process and aims at creating standards for its rigour" (Winter, 2008: 471). A design problem may be directly addressable by a solution artefact (referred to as *primary artefact*) or by an artefact that supports the process of designing (referred to as *secondary artefact*). While Winter (2008) distinguishes these forms of designing using the terms "design research" and "design science," vom Brocke and Maedche (2019) distinguish the same issue using the terms "design processing" and "design theorizing."

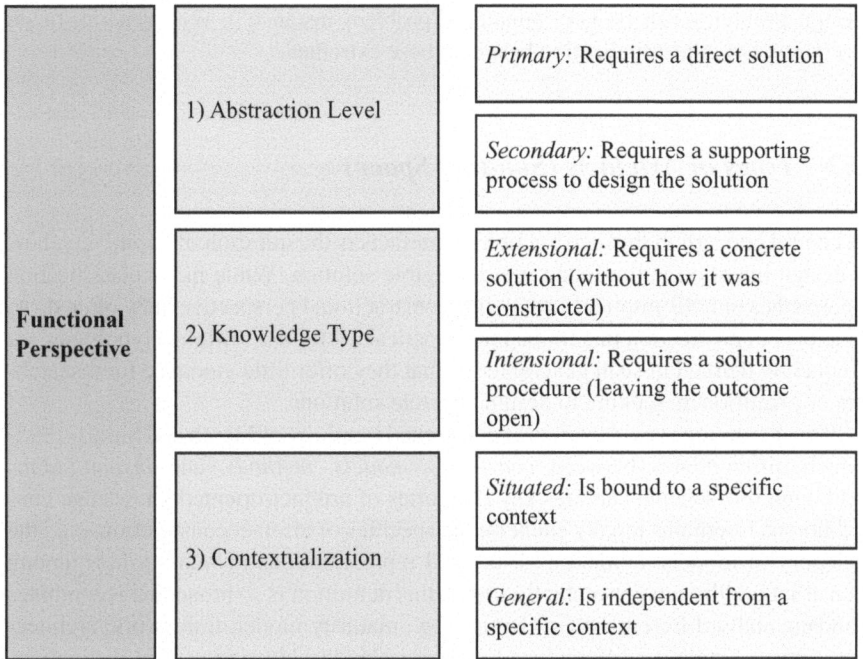

Fig. 1 Categories of functional perspective (Adapted from Lösser & Winter, 2025)

B) Knowledge Type
"Artefacts that already represent a solution to a problem (while leaving the solution process open) should be differentiated from artefacts that represent a solution process (while leaving the result open)" (Lösser & Winter, 2025: 5368). This distinction aligns with the complementary perspectives described in Winter et al. (2009: 9) where an activity view (which outlines the procedures to be followed) and a result view (which focuses on the intended outcomes) are differentiated. According to this understanding, some design problems may require a concrete solution without describing how it is constructed—or may require a solution procedure while leaving the specific outcome open. As both forms can be meaningful ways of designing, Winter et al. (2009: 1) describe them as "two sides of the same coin." Samuel et al. (2018) refer to the respective forms of designing as *extensional* (solves the problem directly) and *intensional* (solution process).

C) Contextualization
"Depending on the level of situatedness of the problem and the level of contextualization of the solution, design knowledge can exist on many different levels of abstraction (or contextualization)" (Lösser & Winter, 2025: 5368). Design, in this view, concerns the relationship between a problem and a solution space, where the problem class can be more or less general and the solution can be more or less projectable (Venable, 2006; vom Brocke et al., 2020). From a functional perspective,

design problems can be very situated ("problem instance"), very general, or on every level of contextualization between these extremes.

2.2   Types of Artefacts (Solution Space)

A central concern in the construction of artefacts is the question of "*how*," i.e., how a design intention is translated into a tangible solution. While many classification approaches in DSR implicitly adopt this constructional perspective, they often do so at a level of abstraction that limits their practical usefulness: Artefact typologies are frequently defined in such general terms that they offer little guidance for researchers or practitioners seeking to design concrete solutions.

This limitation is evident in the widely cited typology of March and Smith (1995) which differentiates between *constructs, models, methods,* and *instantiations.* Although this schema captures key categories of artefact-oriented knowledge contributions, it remains largely silent on the specifics of artefact construction, e.g., the category of models, defined as structured representations of relationships among constructs. Although conceptually sound, this definition is so broad that it combines fundamentally different artefact forms (e.g., maturity model, framework, architecture) into a single, undifferentiated category, thereby blurring critical distinctions that are highly relevant for solution construction.

More recent classification efforts have responded to the growing breadth and complexity of DSR outcomes by proposing extended sets of artefact types. Even if such classifications are not functionally exhaustive, they represent a useful starting point for structuring the design space. For our analysis, we adopt the artefact categories proposed by Vaishnavi et al. (2019) (see Table 1), as they offer a well-balanced conceptual foundation: broad enough to capture meaningful variation and identify recurring design patterns, yet sufficiently structured to avoid an overly fine-grained fragmentation that would hinder pattern recognition. We do not assume that

Table 1 Solution artefact types following Vaishnavi et al. (2019:16)

	Output	Description
1	Construct	The conceptual vocabulary of a domain
2	Model	Sets of propositions or statements expressing relationships between constructs
3	Framework	Real or conceptual guides to serve as support or guide
4	Architecture	High-level structures of systems
5	Design principle	Rules that guide design translating general requirements into general design features
6	Method	Sets of steps used to perform tasks—How-to knowledge
7	Instantiation	Situated implementations in certain environments that address contextualized design problems
8	Design theory	A prescriptive set of statements on how to construct solutions for a (usually) large problem class

artefacts can be unambiguously assigned to a single type. On the contrary, overlaps are not only possible but often desirable, as they reflect the multifaceted nature of artefact design.

2.3   Design Patterns

Design patterns document projectable solutions to recurring problems in a given context which have proved successful in practice. Originating from built environment architecture (Alexander et al., 1977) when already the problem, the context, and the solution were differentiated (Alexander, 1979: 247), the idea of patterns has gained popularity when being applied to software engineering by Gamma et al. (1995). For designing in DSR, patterns could provide projectable constructional guidance when associating a problem class with a generic solution.

As the main challenge for identifying design patterns in DSR, the complexity and diversity of problem space, solution space, and designs has been discussed above. The functional (problem) categories provide a foundation to create functional problem classes. The artefact typology provides a foundation to create solution artefact classes. With both "sides" of the design space aggregated by functional and constructional clusters, respectively, associations should be easier to identify and design patterns easier to be derived. Figure 2 illustrates the principle of this simplification.

An important precondition for identifying associations between functionally defined classes and construction-oriented classes is that both perspectives are represented by an appropriate set of empirically observed data points which are clustered in an appropriate way (see Fig. 3). Published DSR studies serve as data points.

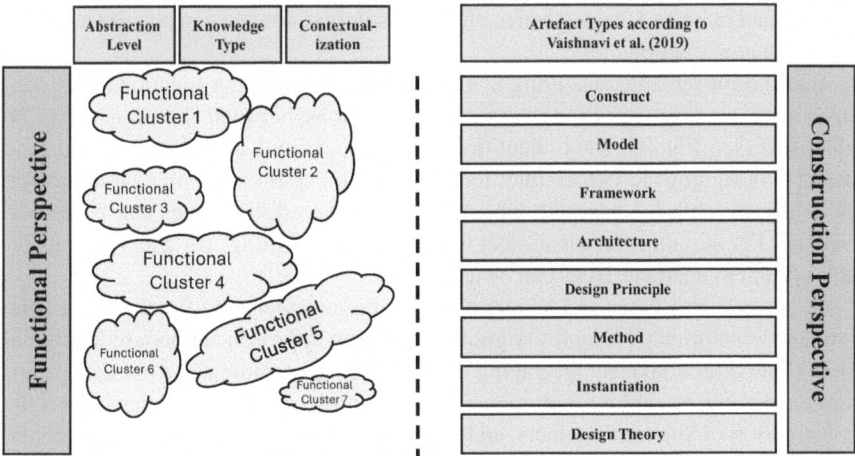

Fig. 2 Functional vs. construction perspective

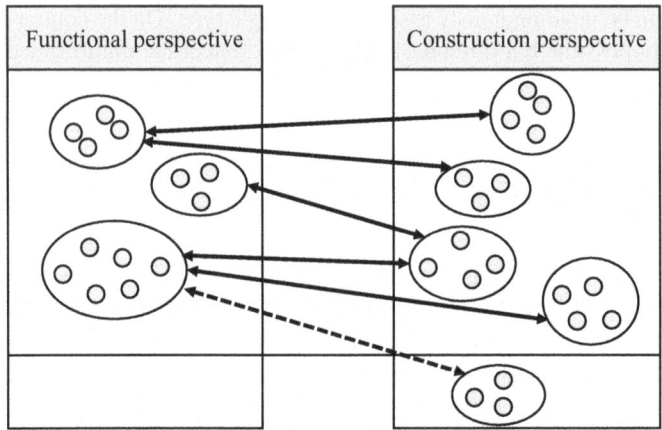

Fig. 3 Functionally defined classes vs. construction-oriented classes of designs

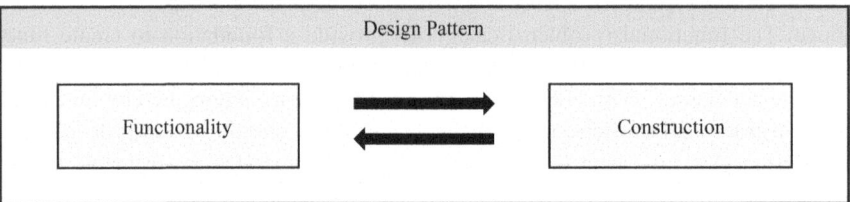

Fig. 4 Association-based design pattern

Since we primarily consider independent artefacts in the description of scientific outlets, the relationship to less abstract (auxiliary) artefacts is usually not considered. The respective design requirements can be used to assign them to a functionally defined class and the respective choice of solution artefact can be used to assign them to a construction class.

Based on a sensible clustering of DSR studies from both a functional and constructional perspective, strong or weak associations between the classes can be identified (see Fig. 4). Once identified, such associations can be interpreted (and used for designing) in two distinct forms: (i) With certain problem characteristics, generally suitable (or generally unsuitable) solution artefact types can be associated. (ii) For certain solution artefact types, generally "fitting" (or generally unsuitable) problem characteristics can be associated.

In contrast to Lösser and Winter (2025) who consider only the direction from problem to solution (from left to right in Fig. 4), our approach adopts a bidirectional view (both directions). By leveraging the identified associations, we use design pattern candidates to explore both directions: how problem characteristics inform the construction of solution artefacts, and conversely, how solution concepts shape the analysis and framing of functional requirements. This dual orientation reflects the inherently iterative nature of DSR, where understanding and shaping co-evolve throughout the design process. Building on this perspective, we distinguish between two complementary types of design pattern candidates: PC patterns, which support the transition from problem space to solution space (left-to-right), and PA patterns, which facilitate reflection on how solution artefacts relate back to problem formulation (right-to-left). This conceptual differentiation enables potentially a more flexible and reflective use of design patterns in DSR, offering guidance whether a project starts with a well-understood problem or with a preliminary solution idea.

3   Methodology

We first conducted a structured literature review to identify relevant DSR studies from the past five years. A subsequent multi-stage screening process was applied to exclude papers that did not meet the predefined inclusion criteria. In the second part of this section, we describe the coding procedure used to extract artefact characteristics and classify them into functional and constructional clusters.

3.1   Literature Search

The objective of the structured literature review was to identify recent DSR studies that explicitly report the development of artefacts, thereby providing empirical observations how functional and constructional aspects are associated. The review was limited to the five-year period from 2020 to 2024 to capture the most mature stages of extant discourses. The search strategy employed a structured query applied to titles and abstracts, combining terms related to DSR, artefact construction, and the Information Systems (IS) context:

("DSR" OR "Design Science Research") OR ("Artefact" AND "Design*" AND "IS").

The review was restricted to peer-reviewed, English-language publications; Research-in-Progress (RIP) and short papers were systematically excluded due to the typically incomplete state of artefact development and often missing evaluation in such contributions. We focused on top-ranked journals and conferences in the field of IS, as identified by the VHB publication outlet rating.[1] Specifically, we analyze DSR contributions presented in the European Conference on IS (ECIS), the International Conference on IS (ICIS), and the AIS Basket of eleven leading journals. An initial sample of 163 publications was retrieved, containing a total of 191 artefact references. The screening procedure was conducted in two stages. First, a

---

[1] VHB Publication Rating version 3, https://www.vhbonline.org/fileadmin/vhb/Services/vhb-rating/WI/VHB_Rating_2024_Area_rating_WI.pdf

technical screening was applied to exclude papers that were inaccessible due to paywall restrictions, classified as RIP, or lacked a full-text version suitable for analysis. Second, a full-text screening was conducted to ensure that only publications meeting certain DSR-specific criteria were retained: Papers were excluded at this stage if they did not report on an actual DSR project, failed to describe or construct an artefact, focused exclusively on methodological or conceptual considerations, lacked an artefact-related evaluation, or presented an experimental design without clear DSR framing.

The resulting set of publications forms the empirical foundation for the derivation of artefact-related design patterns. The analysis focuses on identifying abstract artefact types that serve as intermediaries between problem characteristics and solution artefact construction. The literature review funnel is illustrated by Fig. 5.

3.2   Coding of Functional Characteristics and Classification of Artefacts

To identify (i) meaningful clusters of functional requirements and (ii) correct artefact type assignments from the DSR studies covered in the dataset, we applied a structured coding approach. The relevant publications which remained after the screening process were coded along two complementary dimensions: (1) the *construction perspective* (type of the respective DSR outcome) and (2) the *functional perspective* (problem characteristics).

The *construction perspective* is based on the classification proposed by Vaishnavi et al. (2019), which includes eight types of artefacts: *constructs, models, frameworks, architectures, design principles, methods, instantiations, and design*

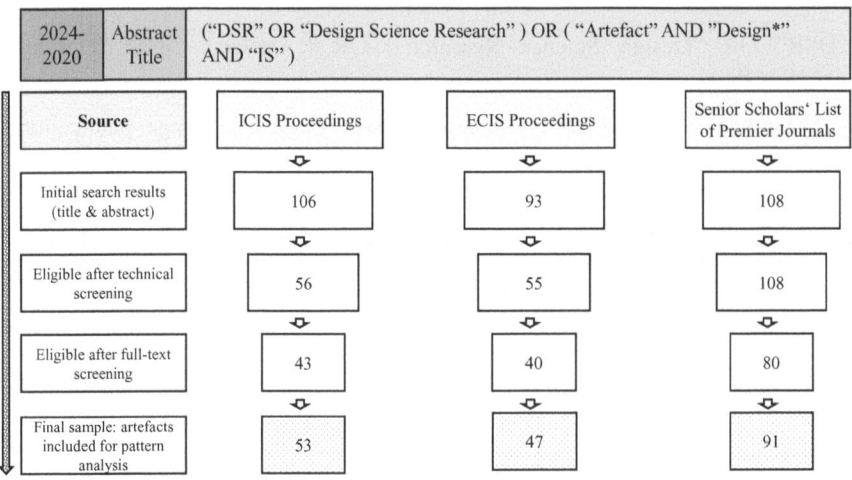

Fig. 5 Literature analysis funnel

theories. One researcher identified one or more artefacts described in each paper. This proposal served as the basis for independent coding by two researchers along both dimensions. The objective was to identify and code the artefact with the highest level of abstraction to the appropriate category within the respective coding dimension. Supporting artefacts (e.g., methods or metrics that serve primarily to enable or complement the development of other design components) were deliberately excluded from the core analysis. These artefacts typically function as intermediate outputs that support the construction of a more central, higher-level artefact, rather than constituting independent design contributions. The goal was to select and code the artefact that directly links the problem and the proposed solution logic. All cases of coding disagreement were discussed between the coders until consensus was reached. If consensus could not be achieved, the case was referred to the workshops with the whole author team for final resolution.

The *functional perspective* builds on the categories discussed in Sect. 2.1. We applied a five-point coding scale aligned with three predefined functional dimensions: abstraction level (primary artefacts vs. secondary artefacts), knowledge type (solution-oriented artefacts vs. process-oriented artefacts), and contextualization (high situatedness vs. low situatedness). In cases where the two coders diverged by more than two scale points, the case was discussed jointly. If no consensus could be reached, the case was first reviewed independently by a senior scholar and subsequently discussed in a joint workshop with the full author team. In cases of minor disagreement ($\leq$ two scale points difference), the average of both coders' values within the respective dimension was used, resulting in decimal-coded values that reflect nuanced interpretation.

Throughout the five-week coding phase, the two primary coders engaged in regular exchange. In total, five dedicated coding workshops were held. The first workshop served to calibrate and refine the coding scheme. The second and third workshops focused on the publications from ICIS and ECIS, respectively. The fourth and fifth workshops covered the Basket publications. In addition, short-term clarifications were handled informally as needed during the process. For 10 cases (representing around 5% of the analyzed publications), no agreement could be reached between the two coders. These cases were reviewed by a third senior scholar to provide an independent and neutral perspective. Based on the assessment of the senior scholar, the respective cases were discussed in a joint author team workshop and integrated into the final coding through collective agreement.

Two additional workshops were held with the full author team. In the first additional workshop, the coding scheme and initial results were discussed and slightly refined. The second additional workshop focused on reviewing the final coding outcomes and discussing all unresolved or particularly complex cases.

3.3   Clustering Procedure for Structuring the Functionality Perspective

The aim of the clustering procedure is to derive meaningful clusters of functional requirements based on the categorization of DSR studies regarding their documented functional requirements. Clustering was selected as an explorative, data-driven method to uncover latent structures and groupings. In contrast to a priori classifications, this unsupervised approach allows for the emergence of empirical regularities that may reveal previously unrecognized. By identifying groups of functional requirements that exhibit similar configurations along the functional dimensions, the clustering lays the groundwork for a structured analysis of design pattern classes and their potential explanatory value.

The clustering was based on the full dataset comprising the 191 artefacts, each of which having been systematically coded as described above. In line with the exploratory nature of the analysis and to preserve interpretability, no additional normalization or scaling was applied prior to clustering. As each dimension was measured on a comparable scale and informed by a shared conceptual foundation, the unweighted combination was deemed appropriate for identifying patterns of functional similarity. This three-dimensional feature space served as the input for the clustering procedure, providing a coherent representation of the respective functional requirements.

We applied k-means clustering as an unsupervised machine learning technique. The algorithm partitions the dataset into k clusters by minimizing within-cluster variance, thereby grouping artefacts with similar configurations across the three functional dimensions. The number of clusters was set to $k = 7$, based on a balance between expected functional diversity and interpretability of results. To determine a suitable number of clusters, we initially applied formal optimization techniques, including the Elbow method and Silhouette analysis, both of which pointed to a three-cluster solution. A three-cluster partitioning however proved analytically unhelpful because it resulted in a cluster of very specific problems, a cluster of very abstract problems, and an ambiguous cluster with all other studies. While statistically supported, this low-resolution clustering did not offer the level of functional differentiation needed to identify meaningful design patterns. We therefore chose a seven-cluster partitioning which allowed for a more nuanced grouping of requirements which supported better interpretable associations. The clustering was implemented in R using the k-means() function from the base stats package. In our case, no fixed seed was applied, and default settings were used (meaning the results reflect a single run of the algorithm without multiple initializations). Each resulting cluster represents a distinct combination of functional requirements, i.e., similar artefact profiles of the respective studies across abstraction level, knowledge type, and situatedness. To identify a representative DSR study (and requirements and artefact) for each cluster, we first calculated the arithmetic mean of all artefacts within the respective cluster along the relevant coding dimensions. The five artefacts closest to this centroid (based on Euclidean distance) were then shortlisted, and the most representative one was selected through manual assessment. This combination of quantitative and qualitative selection ensured both consistency and contextual appropriateness.

Given the exploratory nature of our analysis, we did not apply formal validation metrics such as silhouette scores, Davies–Bouldin index, or cluster stability measures. Instead, we assessed the plausibility and interpretability of the resulting clusters through manual inspection and alignment with the underlying categories. Each cluster was examined for internal coherence and functional distinction, based on the distribution of requirements across abstraction level, knowledge type, and situatedness. While we acknowledge that the absence of formal validation limits the statistical rigor of the results, the identified clusters were sufficiently distinctive and could be meaningfully interpreted, so that we consider them suitable to serve as a basis for the subsequent derivation of design pattern candidates.

3.4 Pattern Identification

To systematically identify indicative design pattern candidates between the seven clusters of functional requirements and the eight artefact construction types, we analyzed empirically grounded associations. They reflect which classes of functionality are typically addressed through which forms of artefact design and vice versa. In this context, we differentiate between PC pattern candidates and PA pattern candidates and thereby also consider (notable) absences of expected associations as absence pattern. These patterns constitute empirically observable configurations that may also indicate conceptual white spots, contextual incompatibilities, or yet-underexplored design strategies.

To support the identification of these patterns, we visualized the directed associations using a Sankey diagram, implemented in R with the "ggalluvial" package. This step aimed not at statistical generalization, but at facilitating a visually guided exploration. To enhance interpretability and reduce noise from insignificant links, we applied a minimum frequency threshold: only associations with more than two occurrences were considered. Connections below this threshold are excluded from further analysis. As a result of this restriction, the artefact type *construct* was excluded from the pattern analysis, as it appeared in only three cases, each with a connection strength of one. This adjustment led to the final Sankey diagram which is shown in Fig. 6. The visualization serves as a heuristic tool to highlight stronger and weaker relational paths, thereby highlighting indicative PC and PA pattern candidates and that may inform subsequent reflection and design-oriented theorizing.

4 Results

This section reports the results of our analysis, structured according to the two research questions of this study. We first present the seven clusters of functional requirements, thus empirically structuring the space of functionalities. Building on associations between functional and construction perspective, we then outline the design pattern candidates, starting with the PC design pattern candidates and subsequently introducing the PA design pattern candidates.

4.1 Clusters of Functional Requirements

Our cluster analysis reveals seven types of functional requirements based on the functional design perspective of the analyzed DSR studies. Each cluster of functional requirements is characterized by specific functional properties and associated design challenges. Table 2 presents the cluster characteristics together with an exemplary study that has been identified by being close to the theoretical cluster center.

The "*Conceptual Differentiation Problem*" cluster is characterized by a somewhat high level of abstraction, a mix of extensional and intensional knowledge, and

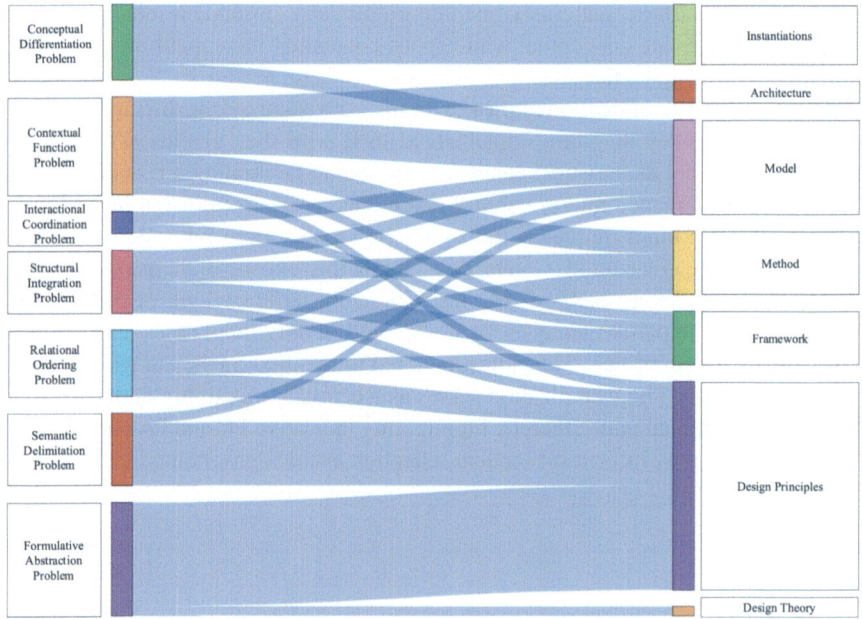

Fig. 6 Overview of associations between problem characteristics clusters and solution artefact types

Table 2 Seven types of functional requirements

Name of cluster	Cluster profile	Problem class description	Exemplary Studies
Conceptual differentiation problem	*Abstraction*: Somewhat high *Knowledge type*: Mixed *Situatedness*: Medium	A problem class in which relevant phenomena are not clearly distinguished from one another, preventing systematic classification, comparison, or mapping	"Beyond Paper and Plastic: A Meta-Model for Credential Use and Governance" (Richter et al., 2023)
Contextual function problem	*Abstraction*: Low *Knowledge type*: Extensional *Situatedness*: Situated	A problem class in which specific situations lack recognizable purpose, role expectations, or operative direction in its specific context	"Getting Personal: A Deep Learning Artifact for Text-Based Measurement of Personality" (Yang et al., 2023)
Interactional coordination problem	*Abstraction*: High *Knowledge type*: Intensional *Situatedness*: Somewhat situated	A problem class in which the conditions, patterns, or logic of interaction between socio-technical elements remain undefined or ambiguous	"A temporal graph framework for intelligence extraction in social media networks" (Chung & Lai, 2023)
Structural integration problem	*Abstraction*: High *Knowledge type*: Intensional *Situatedness*: General	A problem class in which the internal organization of elements is inconsistent, fragmented, or undeveloped, despite contextual embedding	"Lawfulness by design - development and evaluation of lawful design patterns to consider legal requirements" (Dickhaut et al., 2023)
Relational ordering problem	*Abstraction*: Medium *Knowledge type*: Somewhat intensional *Situatedness*: Situated	A problem class in which relevant elements cannot be organized, positioned, or differentiated due to the absence of shared relational logic	"Handling the Efficiency–Personalization Trade-Off in Service Robotics: A Machine-Learning Approach" (Tofangchi et al., 2021)
Semantic delimitation problem	*Abstraction*: Medium *Knowledge type*: Intensional *Situatedness*: Medium	A problem class in which key terms, elements, or boundaries are interpreted inconsistently, preventing shared understanding	"Designing a Method to Nudge Analytics with Artificially Generated Data" (Kowalczyk et al., 2023)
Formulative abstraction problem	*Abstraction*: High *Knowledge type*: Intensional *Situatedness*: Medium	A problem class in which the problem itself is described at a level of abstraction that inhibits orientation, delimitation, or actionable reasoning	"A Picture is Worth a Collaboration: Accumulating Design Knowledge for Computer-Vision-based Hybrid Intelligence Systems" (Zschech et al., 2021)

medium situatedness. It refers to a problem class in which relevant phenomena are not clearly distinguished from one another, preventing systematic classification, comparison, or mapping. The study *"Beyond Paper and Plastic: A Meta-Model for Credential Use and Governance"* (Richter et al., 2023) illustrates this through its engagement with a fragmented and inconsistently articulated landscape of credential types, uses, and governance contexts, where conceptual overlaps hinder structured analysis and discussion. Similarly, *"Peer-to-Peer Loan Fraud Detection: Constructing Features From Transaction Data"* (Xu et al., 2022) addresses a setting in which fraudulent behaviors are not readily separable from legitimate ones due to information asymmetry and the lack of established conceptual boundaries, complicating attempts to identify and categorize fraud-specific patterns.

The *"Contextual Function Problem"* cluster is defined by low abstraction, extensional knowledge, and high situatedness, and encompasses problem classes where specific situations lack recognizable purpose, role expectations, or operative direction within their contextual frame. Research in this area deals with settings that are novel, fragmented, or ambiguous in terms of their functional structure, making it difficult for users or systems to interpret and act meaningfully. In this light, the study *"Getting Personal: A Deep Learning Artifact for Text-Based Measurement of Personality"* (Yang et al., 2023) highlights the challenge of inferring personality traits from natural text, where the absence of established interpretive anchors makes it difficult to derive functionally relevant psychometric indicators from everyday written language. Similarly, *"My Real Avatar Has a Doctor Appointment in the Wepital: A System for Persistent, Efficient, and Ubiquitous Medical Care"* (Zahedi et al., 2022) addresses the unclear role of digital patient representations within medical environments, where expectations, responsibilities, and procedures are underdefined, leading to uncertainty in the coordination and continuity of care across physical and virtual spaces.

The *"Interactional Coordination Problem"* cluster is defined by high abstraction, intensional knowledge, and somewhat situated context. It captures a problem class in which the conditions, patterns, or logic of interaction between socio-technical elements remain undefined or ambiguous. The study *"Changebots —Designing Chatbots to Support Blood Donor Behaviour Change"* (Müller & Reuter-Oppermann, 2023) addresses a setting in which the interaction between digital agents and diverse blood donor profiles lacks clear coordination rules, with behavioral dynamics, user roles, and engagement strategies varying across individual, organizational, and technological boundaries. Likewise, *"A Temporal Graph Framework for Intelligence Extraction in Social Media Networks"* (Chung & Lai, 2023) highlights the challenge of modeling interactions within complex, evolving socio-technical systems like GitHub communities, where patterns of engagement between human actors and knowledge artefacts shift over time, complicating the identification and orchestration of meaningful relational structures.

The *"Structural Integration Problem"* cluster is marked by high abstraction, intensional knowledge, and a generally decontextualized nature. It encompasses problem classes where internal structures are inconsistently organized, fragmented, or insufficiently developed, even when contextually embedded. In this vein, the study *"Lawfulness by Design—Development and Evaluation of Lawful Design Patterns to Consider Legal Requirements"* (Dickhaut et al., 2023) addresses the challenge of fragmented legal understanding within systems development, where vague, technology-neutral regulations leave developers uncertain about how to align system elements with normative requirements, creating internal misalignments between technical logic and legal compliance. Likewise, *"Critical Evaluation in Pursuit of Socially Responsible Design Science in Information Systems"* (Monson, 2020) confronts the difficulty of maintaining coherent evaluative structures when integrating normative value positions into DSR, highlighting tensions between functional rigor and ethical considerations that complicate the internal logic of socially responsible system design.

The *"Relational Ordering Problem"* cluster is defined by a medium level of abstraction, somewhat intensional knowledge, and high situatedness. It refers to problem classes in which relevant elements cannot be effectively organized, positioned, or distinguished due to the absence of shared relational logic. The study *"Handling the Efficiency–Personalization Trade-Off in Service Robotics: A Machine-Learning Approach"*(Tofangchi et al., 2021) exemplifies this problem through its focus on autonomous vehicle operations, where the lack of a consistent structure for balancing system-wide efficiency with individual user preferences complicates the relational ordering of driving behavior, configurations, and user interaction patterns. Similarly, *"Human Identification for Activities of Daily Living: A Deep Transfer Learning Approach"* (Zhu et al., 2020) addresses a setting in which human activities within multi-resident environments defy stable attribution, as the relational boundaries between individuals and their sensor-based behavioral traces are blurred, making it difficult to consistently distinguish who performs what action based on limited and ambiguous sensor data.

The *"Semantic Delimitation Problem"* cluster is characterized by a medium level of abstraction, intensional knowledge, and medium situatedness. It refers to problem classes in which key terms, elements, or boundaries are interpreted inconsistently, preventing shared understanding among actors or within a system. The study *"Designing a Method to Nudge Analytics with Artificially Generated Data"* (Kowalczyk et al., 2023) addresses such inconsistencies in the conceptualization and use of synthetic data in analytics, where varying interpretations of utility, generation techniques, and application contexts hinder consistent methodological reasoning and communication. Likewise, *"Enabling Agile Environments— Software Tools Revisited with an Agile Mindset"* (Mordi & Schoop, 2022) confronts ambiguities in the understanding of agile principles and their alignment with digital tool use, where divergent meanings of "agile mindset" and varying appropriations of supporting tools complicate a cohesive view of technology-enabled agile transformation.

The *"Formulative Abstraction Problem"* cluster is defined by high abstraction, intensional knowledge, and medium situatedness, capturing problem classes in which the problem itself is framed so abstractly that it inhibits clear orientation, delimitation, or actionable reasoning. In such settings, key aims, concepts, or user needs often remain underdefined, making it difficult to structure or operationalize design tasks. The study *"Beyond Dashboards? Designing Data Stories for Effective Use in Business Intelligence and Analytics"* (Gunklach et al., 2023) exemplifies this challenge through its engagement with the vague notion of "effective use" in business intelligence, where the lack of conceptual clarity around what constitutes meaningful interaction or understanding for different user groups complicates the development of communicative data representations. Similarly, *"A Picture is Worth a Collaboration: Accumulating Design Knowledge for Computer-Vision-Based Hybrid Intelligence Systems"* (Zschech et al., 2021) addresses a domain in which the conceptual basis of hybrid intelligence is not yet stabilized, making it difficult to coherently frame the socio-technical design of human–AI collaboration in computer vision systems, particularly when aiming to abstract generalized design knowledge from diverse and practice-driven cases.

4.2   Design Pattern Candidates

As discussed in Sect. 2.3, design pattern candidates are understood as significant associations that can be observed between the seven clusters of functional requirements and the eight artefact solution types. They represent for which class of functional requirements usually which artefact types are designed (vice versa). As pointed out, we differentiate PC pattern candidates and PA pattern candidates and also discuss "absence patterns," i.e., notable absence of associations between functionality clusters and artefact types. Figure 6 illustrates the identified associations graphically.

Problem-Construction Design Pattern Candidates

We discovered a total of 16 significant associations between problem clusters and solution artefact types, encompassing both positive ("is associated with…") and negative ("is not associated which…") relationships. While positive relationships indicate that a construction type is likely to address certain functional requirements, negative relationships indicate that a construction type is unlikely to address such requirements.

These associations were synthesized into a set of PC pattern candidates, presented in Table 3. Each candidate consists of a functional requirement cluster, its associated (positive or negative) relationships to construction types, and a concise rationale explaining why certain solution artefact types are more or less suitable in providing the respective functionalities.

In several cases, a single problem cluster is linked to multiple construction types, reflecting the multifaceted nature of real-world design challenges. The explanations illustrate how different types of solution artefacts interact with the problem characteristics—whether by enabling abstraction, clarifying semantics, or guiding interaction or integration.

Table 3 Problem-construction design pattern candidates

Functional requirements cluster	Relationships	Potential explanation
Conceptual differentiation problem	+: Conceptual differentiation problem is associated with models and frameworks −: Conceptual differentiation problem is not associated with methods −: Conceptual differentiation problem is not associated with design principles −: Conceptual differentiation problem is not associated with instantiations	+: Models and frameworks can define key elements and their relations in a way that enables conceptual separation −: Methods focus on procedures rather than conceptual clarity, and thus do not resolve definitional ambiguity −: Design principles and instantiations presuppose conceptual clarity and are not suitable for generating it
Contextual function problem	+ Contextual function problem is associated with instantiations + Contextual function problem is associated with models	+: Instantiations demonstrate how something works in a real situation, which helps clarify functional purpose within a context +: Models can also define operational elements and their relations in a way that supports the functional understanding of a context
Interactional coordination problem	+ Interactional coordination problem is associated with design principles −: Interactional coordination problem is not associated with design theory	+: Design principles can formalize behavioral or structural patterns that guide interaction between components or actors −: Design theories operate at a higher level of abstraction
Structural integration problem	+ Structural integration problem is associated with design principles & methods −: Structural integration problem is not associated with design theory −: Structural integration problem is not associated with instantiation	+: Both principles and methods can impose coherence by aligning elements through structured procedures or guiding heuristics −: Design theories describe abstract knowledge but are not typically used to align internal structures of a specific system −: Instantiations show functioning artefacts but do not impose structural integration across system elements
Relational ordering problem	+ Relational ordering problem is associated with models, methods, and architectures −: Relational ordering problem is not associated with instantiations	+: These artefact types define or enact positioning of elements, models via representation, methods via procedural sequencing, architectures via system layout −: Instantiations realize decisions but do not support the comparative or positional logic across alternatives
Semantic delimitation problem	+ Semantic delimitation problem is associated with methods and frameworks -: Semantic delimitation problem is not associated with instantiation and design theory	+: Methods operationalize meaning through use, and frameworks provide structural boundaries that help delimit conceptual space −: Instantiations rely on stable meanings rather than defining them; design theories formalize knowledge but do not resolve semantic ambiguity in application

(continued)

Table 3 (continued)

Functional requirements cluster	Relationships	Potential explanation
Formulative abstraction problem	+ Formulative abstraction problem is associated with design patterns and design theory	+: These artefact types can operate at high levels of abstraction and are suited to giving shape, structure, or orientation to abstract problem formulations

Problem-Analysis Design Pattern Candidates

We identified a total of 14 relevant associations between solution artefact types and functionality clusters, encompassing both positive relationships ("is associated with…") and negative relationships ("is not associated with…"). In several cases, solution artefact types are associated with multiple classes of functional requirements. Positive associations suggest that certain artefact types appear to be particularly well suited to addressing the functional demands of specific problem clusters. In contrast, negative associations indicate that a given artefact type is generally considered less suitable for addressing certain classes of functional requirements due to mismatches in abstraction level, conceptual clarity, or procedural focus.

The proposed PA pattern candidates are presented in Table 4. Each entry describes a construction artefact type, its observed associations (positive and negative) with functional requirements, and a concise explanation that outlines the reasoning behind each relationship. These pattern candidates provide conceptual guidance for researchers who have a preferred artefact type and seek to better understand to which extent that solution type is well capable or incapable of addressing the functional requirements of their design problem.

The table offers a reverse perspective compared to Table 3: Rather than starting from functional requirements, it begins with construction artefact types and explores their analytical fit with the problem space. As such, it complements the earlier view and further supports reflection on the alignment between design intent and artefact suitability.

5   Discussion and Conclusions

This study proposes empirically grounded design pattern candidates that represent associations between classes of functional requirements and their respective construction artefact types. Drawing on an analysis of 191 DSR studies published in leading IS outlets over the five-year period from 2020 to 2024, we analyze how they associate functional requirements with solution artefacts. On that foundation, the proposed pattern candidates provide an indication which artefact types are more or less suitable for certain classes of functional requirements. When "read" in the opposite direction, the proposed pattern candidates provide an indication which

Table 4 Problem-analysis design pattern candidates

Construction Artefact Type	Relationships	Potential explanation
Instantiations	+ Instantiation is only associated with contextual function problem	+: Instantiations demonstrate applied use in a specific context, making them suitable for clarifying functional purpose in situ; they are not designed to resolve abstract or conceptual problems
Architecture	+ Architecture is only associated with relational ordering problem	+: Architectures define the spatial or functional arrangement of components, which directly addresses the need to position elements in structured relation to one another
Model	+ Model is associated with relational ordering problem −: Model is not associated with Formulative abstraction problem, but otherwise with any other type of problem (to a certain extent)	+: Models formalize elements and their relationships, making them ideal for representing comparative or positional logic within a conceptual or system space −: Models require at least a minimally defined domain or structural basis. They cannot operate when the problem formulation is too abstract or indeterminate to identify components, agents, or boundaries
Method	+ Method is associated with relational ordering problem, semantic delimitation problem, structural integration problem −: Method is not associated with contextual function problem, conceptual differentiation problem, interactional coordination problem, and Formulative abstraction problem	+: Methods define procedural or organizational logic, which can clarify relational sequences, reduce semantic ambiguity through operationalization, and enforce structural coherence −: Methods require an already specified problem context, terminology, and functional logic; they cannot define context, meaning, or abstract formulations themselves
Framework	+ Framework is associated with semantic delimitation problem −: Framework is not associated with contextual function problem -: Framework is not associated with Formulative abstraction problem −: Framework is not associated with interactional coordination problem and conceptual differentiation problem	+: Frameworks define structural boundaries and organizing dimensions that help reduce interpretive ambiguity across concepts or domains −: Frameworks operate at a mid-to-high abstraction level and cannot specify local function, guide concrete interaction, or establish fundamental conceptual distinctions

(continued)

Table 4 (continued)

Construction Artefact Type	Relationships	Potential explanation
Design principles	+ Design principles are associated with Formulative abstraction problem, structural integration problem, and interactional coordination problem −: Design principles are not associated with contextual function problem −: Design principles are not associated with conceptual differentiation problem	+: Design principles provide high-level guidance that can address abstract formulation, align structural coherence, or impose behavioral logic on interaction −: Principles presuppose a design logic and conceptual clarity; they are not suitable for clarifying local function or disambiguating foundational concepts
Design theory	+ design theory is only associated with Formulative abstraction problem	+: Design theories operate at a high level of abstraction and are suited to structuring, explaining, or shaping complex problem formulations that lack delimitation

application contexts are more or less fitting with certain artefact types. This study builds on and extends the Lösser and Winter's (2025) study by analyzing a much larger empirical basis of DSR studies, elaborating the clustering of functional requirements, distinguishing between different types of design pattern candidates, and exploring interpretations for these pattern candidates. The discussion and conclusions are organized into four parts. First, we reflect on the characterization of clusters of functional requirements in the problem space and discuss their empirical grounding and theoretical relevance. Second, we examine the role and value of design patterns in the design process. Third, we critically assess the limitations of the study, including conceptual and methodological challenges. Finally, we outline implications for future design-oriented research, highlighting opportunities for refinement, extension, and practical application.

5.1 Characterizing Clusters of Functional Requirements in the Problem Space

We propose a novel empirical approach that enables a structured, evidence-based clustering of functional requirements into functionality-oriented types. This clustering builds on a three-dimensional categorization of the functional perspective of DSR artefacts (abstraction level, knowledge type, and contextualization) and results in seven distinct clusters. In doing so, the approach provides a clear distinction from existing conceptualizations. Unlike prior abstract or normative categorizations, our method derives insights from a large dataset of relevant DSR studies, thereby grounding the classification in empirical evidence and contributing to ongoing discussions on the relationship between problem and solution spaces in DSR. The resulting empirical clarity not only facilitates navigation within the problem–solution nexus but also enhances theoretical understanding by uncovering latent structures and interrelations between functional requirements. We found the naming of the clusters to be highly relevant, not merely a technical or stylistic concern, but central to both theoretical precision and practical application. Clear, meaningful, and intuitive names significantly improve the interpretability and communicative value of the clusters. They foster their applicability in academic discourse and practice. Thoughtful naming supports a deeper understanding of the underlying logic of each cluster, increases accessibility across audiences, and helps translate empirical insights into actionable knowledge. In this way, naming serves as a key mechanism for bridging empirical observation and conceptual clarity.

5.2   Role and Value of Patterns in the Design Process

The pattern candidates identified in this study offer considerable value beyond the application of traditional design knowledge, like design principles or design theories. Our pattern candidates provide initial, empirically based orientation in the design process without prescribing explicit solutions. Meaningful associations support the exploration of both observed and potential relationships (including those that are not explicitly represented in the data). As reflected in the pattern candidates, it is also valuable to explicitly disclose non-observed associations (e.g., the absence of a connection from a more abstract cluster in the functional perspective downward to a more instantiated solution in the construction perspective), as such omissions may indicate implicit assumptions or structural gaps in the current understanding of design processes. The pattern candidates are expected to be particularly useful in the early phases of the DSR process (e.g., during problem formulation and conceptual exploration). At this stage, they offer initial guidance at the interface between problem framing and artefact design—making them especially valuable for novice researchers. At the same time, they expand the perceived design space and provide conceptual stimuli to also inform experienced researchers.

5.3   Limitations of this Study

To contextualize the findings and delineate the scope of interpretation, several methodological and analytical limitations must be considered.

First, our analysis is restricted to what is explicitly reported in published DSR papers. As a result, we are only able to examine artefacts in their finalized, documented form. This excludes the underlying development trajectories, including intermediate outputs, iterative refinements, and supporting artefacts that may have substantially shaped the design process, thereby neglecting meaningful distinctions between subtypes of artefacts (e.g., conceptual models, computational models, or frameworks), which can differ significantly in form, function, and abstraction level. The methodological status of such intermediate artefacts remains unclear. Elements such as requirement models or evaluation setups were excluded from our coding unless they were explicitly positioned as independent design contributions. However, the distinction between intermediate and final artefacts is often ambiguous. This is particularly evident in the case of constructs, which frequently function as conceptual building blocks but are rarely presented as autonomous outcomes. As typical intermediate artefacts, constructs were therefore excluded and do not appear in our dataset. The question of when an artefact qualifies as a standalone result remains conceptually unresolved and calls for further theoretical clarification. An additional noteworthy observation relates to the tendency of many studies to present highly abstract artefacts (particularly in the form of design principles) as their primary contribution, even when the core problem-solving logic of the research is grounded in more concrete artefacts (like methods, procedural models, or solution-oriented frameworks). This practice raises critical questions about the representational choices made by researchers and suggests a potential mismatch between the underlying design rationale and the level of abstraction employed in the artefact presented.

Second, the distinction between instantiations and evaluation artefacts is difficult to operationalize. Some instantiations function as independent design outcomes, whereas others appear to serve solely as validation mechanisms for more abstract artefacts. Their functional value often lies in their role as demonstrators rather than in the artefact itself. This ambiguity affects the reliability of both functional and construction-oriented classification, especially in cases where publications provide limited detail.

Third, inconsistent terminology across the DSR literature introduces further limitations. Terms such as framework, method, or design principle are frequently used without clear definition or are applied to artefacts that differ substantially in abstraction, purpose, and generality. This lack of terminological precision impairs the consistency and comparability of artefact classification across studies and has also been emphasized by Weigand and Johannesson (2023) who call for a more precise and systematic use of artefact-related terminology.

Fourth, although the coding procedure was designed to minimize bias through independent coding, coordination steps, and review by a senior scholar, interpretive judgment was required. This was especially the case in the functional perspective (with separation between representing a solution and prescribing a procedure). We are aware that the three coding dimensions are not fully independent from one another, as certain artefact types tend to align with specific functional characteristics. Nevertheless, we treated them as analytically distinct in order to capture complementary aspects of artefact classification. While other function-construction constellations are theoretically conceivable, they did not appear in our dataset. The coding outcomes therefore reflect the patterns observed in practice, but do not exclude the possibility of alternative configurations.

Fifth, our selection of publication outlets was intentionally limited to top-tier IS venues, specifically the AIS Basket of 11 journals and the proceedings of ICIS and ECIS. While this ensured consistency with established standards of the IS discipline, it also resulted in the exclusion of other highly DSR-relevant outlets such as DESRIST and BISE. These venues often publish conceptually rich or foundational contributions, including taxonomies or conceptual models, which may have been underrepresented in our sample. In contrast, papers from ICIS and ECIS tended to focus on narrowly scoped contributions, often centered around the articulation of design principles and their evaluation through instantiations. Furthermore, publications that did not explicitly position themselves as DSR projects were excluded through our search strategy, which may have contributed to the limited presence of certain artefact types in the dataset (e.g., taxonomies).

5.4 Implications for Future Research

Building on the findings and limitations of this study, several directions for future research emerge. First, there is a need for a more systematic conceptual differentiation between different types of artefacts (see also Chapter "Typology of IS Artefacts: Providing an Organizing Foundation for Design Science Research Outcomes" of this book). This includes clearer distinctions between core and supporting artefacts, as well as between process-oriented and outcome-oriented artefacts. While this study focused on the most abstract artefact per publication, future work could develop more robust criteria to define when an artefact qualifies as an independent design contribution. This would also help to clarify the status of constructs, requirement models, and instantiations developed primarily for evaluation purposes.

Second, the artefact pattern perspective introduced in this study could be extended through more advanced analytical techniques. For example, hierarchical clustering may reveal deeper structural regularities and enable a multilayered understanding of how artefacts relate to different problem types. Such approaches could uncover hidden dimensions within the design space and support a more fine-grained classification of artefact-function constellations.

Third, the proposed distinction between PC pattern candidates and PA pattern candidates opens up a new conceptual lens for theorizing about design artefacts. Future research could formalize these pattern types through structured representations or typological models. This would allow for systematic comparison and reuse of design knowledge across projects while also supporting reflective design practices. In particular, the identification of recurring candidates and the mapping of their properties could offer a valuable starting point for developing context-sensitive design guidance without prescribing normative solutions.

Finally, future research could explore the relationship and potential dependencies between functional and construction-oriented coding dimensions. While our results indicate observable alignment patterns, a more systematic investigation of their interdependencies may yield important insights into how artefact types relate to their intended use and level of abstraction. This could contribute to a better theoretical understanding of artefact logic in DSR and inform future classification schemes.

References

Alexander, C. (1979). *The timeless way of building*. Oxford University Press.

Alexander, C., Ishikawa, S., Silverstein, M., Jacobson, M., Fiksdahl-King, I., & Angel, S. (1977). *A pattern language*. Oxford University Press.

Chandra Kruse, L., Seidel, S., & Gregor, S. (2015). Prescriptive knowledge in IS research: Conceptualizing design principles in terms of materiality, action, and boundary conditions. In *48th Hawaii international conference on system sciences (HICSS 2015)* (pp. 4039–4048) Kauai, Hawaii, USA.

Chung, W., & Lai, V. S. (2023). A temporal graph framework for intelligence extraction in social media networks. *Information & Management, 60*, 202306.

Dickhaut, E., Janson, A., Söllner, M., & Leimeister, J. M. (2023). Lawfulness by design—Development and evaluation of lawful design patterns to consider legal requirements. *European Journal of Information Systems, 33*, 1–28.

Drechsler, A., & Dörr, P. (2014). What kinds of artifacts are we designing? An analysis of artifact types and artifact relevance in IS journal publications. In M. C. Tremblay, D. VanderMeer, M. Rothenberger, A. Gupta, & V. Yoon (Eds.), *Advancing the impact of design science: Moving from theory to practice (Proc. DESRIST 2014)*. Springer.

Drechsler, A., & Hevner, A. R. (2018). Utilizing, producing, and contributing design knowledge in DSR projects. In S. Chatterjee, K. Dutta, & R. P. Sundarraj (Eds.), *Designing for a digital and globalized world*. Springer.

Engel, C., Leicht, N., & Ebel, P.. (2019). The imprint of design science in information systems research: An empirical analysis of the AIS Senior scholar's basket. In *International conference on information systems, ICIS*. Munich, Germany.

Gamma, E., Helm, R., Johnson, R., & Vlissides, J. (1995). *Design patterns: Elements of reusable object-oriented software*. Addison-Wesley.

Gregor, S., & Jones, D. (2007). The anatomy of a design theory. *Journal of the Association for Information Systems, 8*, 312–335.

Gregor, S., & Hevner, A. R. (2013). Positioning and presenting design science research for maximum impact. *MIS Quarterly, 37*, 337–355.

Gunklach, J., Jacob, K., & Michalczyk, S.. (2023). Beyond dashboards? Designing data stories for effective use in business intelligence and analytics. In *31st European conference on information systems (ECIS2023)*. Kristiansand, Norway.

Hevner, A. R., March, S. T., Park, J., & Ram, S. (2004). Design science in information systems research. *MIS Quarterly, 28*, 75–105.

Iivari, J. (2007). A paradigmatic analysis of information systems as a design science. *Scandinavian Journal of Information Systems, 19*, 39–64.

Kowalczyk, P., Röder, M., Rottmann, J., & Thiesse, F. (2023). Designing a method to nudge analytics with artificially generated data. In *44th International conference on information systems (ICIS 2023)*. Hyderabad, India.

Lösser, B., & Winter, R.. (2025). Towards design patterns—Finding suitable artefact type candidates for a design problem. In *HICSS-58*, 5365–74. Waikoloa Village, HI.

March, S. T., & Smith, G. F. (1995). Design and Natural Science Research on Information Technology. *Decision Support Systems, 15*, 251–266.

Monson, M.. (2020). Critical evaluation in pursuit of socially responsible design science in information systems. In *28th European conference on information systems (ECIS, 2020)*. An Online AIS Conference.

Mordi, A., & Schoop, M. (2022). Enabling agile environments - Software tools revisited with an agile mindset. In *30th European conference on information systems (ECIS 2022)*. Romania, Timişoara.

Müller, H. M., & Reuter-Oppermann, M. (2023). Changebots - Designing Chatbots to support blood donor behaviour change. In *44th International conference on information systems (ICIS 2023)*. Hyderabad, India.

Nunamaker, J. F., Jr., Chen, M., & Purdin, T. D. M. (1991). Systems Development in Information Systems Research. *Journal of Management Information Systems, 7*, 89–106.

Offermann, P., Blom, S., Schönherr, M., & Bub, U. (2010). Artifact Types in Information Systems Design Science—A literature review. In J. Robert Winter, L. Zhao, & S. Aier (Eds.), *5th International conference on design science research in information systems and technology (DESRIST 2010).* Springer.

Pahl, G., Beitz, W., Feldhusen, J., & Grote, K.H. (2007). *Engineering design: A systematic approach.* Springer.

Peffers, K., Tuunanen, T., Rothenberger, M. A., & Chatterjee, S. (2007). A design science research methodology for information systems research. *Journal of Management Information Systems, 24*, 45–77.

Richter, D., Praas, C. R., & Anke, J. (2023). Beyond paper and plastic: A meta-model for credential use and governance. In *31st European conference on information systems (ECIS 2023).* Norway, Kristiansand.

Samuel, B. M., Khatri, V., & Ramesh, V. (2018). Exploring the effects of extensional versus intensional representations on domain understanding. *MIS Quarterly, 42*, 1187–1209.

Tofangchi, S., Hanelt, A., Marz, D., & Kolbe, L. M. (2021). Handling the efficiency–personalization trade-off in service robotics: A machine-learning approach. *Journal of Management Information Systems, 38*, 246–276.

Tuunanen, T., Winter, R., & Vom Brocke, J. (2024). Dealing with complexity in design science research - a methodology using design echelons. *MIS Quarterly, 48*, 427–458.

Vaishnavi, V. K., Kuechler Jr., W., & Petter, S. (2019). *Design science research in information systems.* Accessed May 28, 2021, from http://www.desrist.org/desrist/content/design-science-research-in-information-systems.pdf.

Venable, J. R. (2006). The role of theory and theorising in design science research. In S. Chatterjee & A. Hevner (Eds.), *International conference on design science research in information systems and technology* (pp. 1–18) Claremont, CA, USA.

vom Brocke, J., & Maedche, A. (2019). The DSR grid: Six Core dimensions for effective capturing of DSR projects. *Electronic Markets, 29*, 379–385.

vom Brocke, J., Winter, R., Hevner, A., & Maedche, A. (2020). Special issue editorial—Accumulation and evolution of design knowledge in design science research: A journey through time and space. *Journal of the Association for Information Systems, 21*, 520–544.

Weigand, H., & Johannesson, P. (2023). How to identify your design science research artifact. In *2023 IEEE 25th Conference on business informatics (CBI)*, 1–10.

Weigand, H., Johannesson, P., & Andersson, B. (2021). An artifact ontology for design science research. *Data & Knowledge Engineering, 133*, 101878.

Winter, R. (2008). Design science research in Europe. *European Journal of Information Systems, 17*, 470–475.

Winter, R., Gericke, A., & Bucher, T. (2009). Method versus model—Two sides of the same coin? In A. Albani, J. Barijs, & J. L. G. Dietz (Eds.), *Advances in Enterprise engineering III.* Springer.

Xu, J., Chen, D., Chau, M., Li, L., & Zheng, H. (2022). Peer-to-peer loan fraud detection: Constructing features from transaction data. *MIS Quarterly, 45*, 1777–1792.

Yang, K., Lau, R. Y. K., & Abbasi, A. (2023). Getting personal: A deep learning artifact for text-based measurement of personality. *Information Systems Research, 34*, 194–222.

Zahedi, F. M., Zhao, H., Sanvanson, P., Walia, N., Jain, H., & Shaker, R. (2022). My real avatar has a doctor appointment in the Wepital: A system for persistent, efficient, and ubiquitous medical care. *Information & Management, 59*.

Zhu, H., Samtani, S., Chen, H., & Nunamaker, J. F. (2020). Human identification for activities of daily living: A deep transfer learning approach. *Journal of Management Information Systems, 37*, 457–483.

Zschech, P., Walk, J., Heinrich, K., Vössing, M., & Kühl, N. (2021). A picture is worth a collaboration: Accumulating design knowledge for computer-vision-based hybrid intelligence systems. In *29th European conference on information systems (ECIS 2021).* Virtual AIS Conference.

The manufacturer's authorised representative in the EU is Springer
Nature Customer Service Centre GmbH, Europaplatz 3, 69115 Heidelberg,
Germany. If you have any concerns regarding our products, please
contact ProductSafety@springernature.com

Printed and bound by CPI Group (UK) Ltd, Croydon, CR0 4YY
29/04/2026
02099455-0018